Illusive Identity

The Blurring of Working-Class Consciousness in Modern Western Culture

Edited by
Thomas J. Edward Walker

LEXINGTON BOOKS
Lanham • Boulder • New York • Oxford

LEXINGTON BOOKS

Published in the United States of America
by Lexington Books
4720 Boston Way, Lanham, Maryland 20706

12 Hid's Copse Road
Cumnor Hill, Oxford OX2 9JJ, England

British Library Cataloguing in Publication Information Available

ISBN 0-7391-0347-4 (cloth : alk. paper)
ISBN 0-7391-0348-2 (pbk. : alk. paper)
Library of Congress Control Number: 2002101688

Printed in the United States of America

♾™ The paper used in this publication meets the minimum requirements of American
National Standard for Information Sciences—Permanence of Paper for Printed Library
Materials, ANSI/NISO Z39.48–1992.

For the worker's vanguard

Contents

Acknowledgments

The editor wishes to express his appreciation for the expertise, enthusiasm, and dedication of Libby Harrington and Cynthia Gwynne Yaudes, authors, scholars, and radicals in the making. Without their tireless efforts this book would never have been completed.

Introduction

According to British historian Douglas Tallack, part of the dynamics of twentieth-century modernism is the rejection of nineteenth-century sensibilities.[1] In examining the process of the evolution of a working-class consciousness in modern Western culture, it is important to consider the impact of this rejection upon traditional working-class identities. Furthermore, it must be acknowledged that this impact did not occur as a result of any single phenomenon. Modernism's influence on Western working-class consciousness was as much a protracted phenomenon as it was an immediate response to the exigencies of industrial power.

A focus on how a community-based consciousness evolves, particularly one that is at odds with the intruding nature of modernization, is historically important to the construction of working-class identities in the West in the nineteenth century. Identifying cultural directions influenced through the evolution of past traditions and inheritances, which are in turn confronted by the changing political nuances of industrial relations, makes it easier for scholars to present a stronger interpretation of the evolution of Western class consciousness. Community structure and organization, for instance, assisted skilled workers to lend their support to nonskilled workers in the formation of working-class collectives throughout much of the nineteenth century. Consequently, what it meant to be a worker during this time can be identified within the cultural context of the emerging industrial communities of the west.

Current scholarship has shown that cultural traditions along with the limited autonomy of the labor community in the West during the nineteenth century came together to influence the idea of a class-based society. Industrial power and government authority to protect it had not as yet been formally realized. Workers knew who they were as a class. Rather than think of themselves as individual workers or members of a certain trade, many organized into collectives which produced a class-based social identity. As Kim Voss shows in her investigation of the Knights of Labor in the United States:

> a labor movement was initially built long before the factory proletariat came to dominate the population of wage earners. . . . [C]raftsmen began to think and act like *workers* rather than members of this or that trade. It is important to think of the early development of the labor movement as the first movement of class formation rather than as any final making of the working class.[2]

But as the nineteenth century moved to its conclusion, working-class identity came more and more under the influence of the industrial class. Social institutions began to take their lead from powerful industrialists, assisted in the process by government policy formation. The ability to define life's meanings through traditional community structures gave way to other influences such as the newly visible social transformations and economic development, spurred on by industrial progress. By the turn of the twentieth century, worker identity became increasingly measured by standards set for the socialization processes of formal and modern bureaucratic institutions, technology, and urbanization. Educational institutions, structures of capital formation, governmental policy, and commercial communication networks all lent their anatomies of power to the manipulation of traditional community structures to address the needs of an industrial-based society. In such an environment, the transformation of a class-based consciousness was effected.

The relationship between formal institutions and the creation of social identities grew to include a new cultural phenomenon as well: consumerism. The industrial need to break with preindustrial notions of social organization and individual identities was at the forefront of this modern cultural identity. New forms of mass entertainment with industrial and "progressive" notions for satisfying emotional needs in this transformation setting assisted in the emergence of a new consumer culture. Industrial elites and their support groups, which included the emergence of a new stratum of professional-managers, extended the nuances of community-based nineteenth-century class distinctions. According to historians Richard Wightman Fox and Jackson Lears:

> The search for the origins of consumer culture should begin by concentrating on the activities of urban elites during the last two decades of the nineteenth century. . . . The significance of three developments in the late nineteenth century United States: the maturation of the national marketplace, including the establishment of national advertising; the emergence of a new stratum of professionals and managers, rooted in a web of complex new organizations (corporations, government, universities, professional associations, media foundations, and others); the rise of a new gospel of therapeutic release preached by a host of writers, publishers,

ministers, social scientists, doctors and advertisers themselves . . . undertook to
harmonize the relations between labor and capital.[3]

Scholarly assumptions concerning the relationship between transformation of
social consciousness and centrally controlled formal institutions in the West have
periodically surfaced in the twentieth century. Literature addressing the consumption of products and images produced by a corporate media (television, radio, and
other mass marketed forms of culture) is of particular significance. Debates over
the Marxian notion that people create their own meaning in conditions not necessarily of their choosing have been as historically particular as they have been unique,
but the conclusions have remained generally the same. In the words of social critics Ian Angus and Sut Jhally:

> The identification and organization of individuals as social beings through the
> mediation of images and the seeking of pleasure through the experience of the
> consumption of these images has been an evolving issue in the manipulation of
> [contemporary] cultural politics for political ends.[4]

As popular responses to corporately produced products and images increasingly blur represented notions of class, traditional working-class identities are replaced by more modern market-oriented means of satisfaction. Advertising plays a
large role in this process. The manipulation of social identities by the advertising
media in the twentieth century has helped to reshape nineteenth-century institutional and individual social identity paradigms. New individual and collective identities are constructed in the process. As advertising encourages workers to consume more products, their social group identities come to be defined less by class
and more by the consumptive group that the advertisement had created, molded,
and targeted.

Changing parameters of working-class identities are a transatlantic phenomenon. What happened in the United States at the turn of the twentieth century also
happened in Europe. In Great Britain, for instance, the rise of commercially produced ideas of culture began to influence an incipient cultural synthesis between
traditional notions of working-class identity and the mass consumption of commercial products. Combined with the forces of managerial ideology and state-
legislated legal formations, media-produced cultural identities and lifestyles increasingly blurred traditional notions of class. Social movements of the past became interspersed with mass cultural identities. With new class formulations
altering past community-based and industrially defined working-class identities,
hard-won labor empowerments were replaced by emerging consumer "empowerments" (consumer rights versus worker's rights). In the process there arose a new
consciousness vilifying class-based cultural traditions, origins, and inheritances.
At the same time, this new consciousness gave praise to new virtues of modern
traditions surrounding the phenomenon of mass production and mass consumption.

Ideas of modern culture being at odds with traditional culture provide insight into the capability of workers, as a class, to secure for themselves an equal role in determining political, economic, and social policies in Western society. In chapter 1, Daniel J. Doyle looks at popular responses to advertising "suggestions" in the cocoa industry in turn-of-the-century Great Britain. His analysis points to the consequences for working-class consciousness resulting from the profound transformation of tradition-based working-class identities to newer, more modern, culture-based and consumer-defined class identities, encouraged by worker responses to mass-produced culture and imagery. If one is to understand social class transformulations of the period, an historical analysis of the influence of commercial applications to traditional worker social identities must be made. As Stuart Hall suggests:

> One of the main differences standing in the way of a proper periodization of popular culture is the profound transformation in the culture of the popular classes which occurs between the 1880s and the 1920s. . . . Many of the real difficulties (theoretical as well as empirical) will only be confronted when we begin to examine closely popular culture in a period which begins to resemble our own.[5]

Such patterns of consumption also apply to the construction of state-inspired social identities. In Nazi Germany during the 1930s, official propaganda aimed at the transformation of class-based identities took center stage during the building of National Socialism. Government programs, marketing, and technological strategies manipulated cultural inheritances to effect the dismantling of traditionally homogenous industrial proletariat structures. Early twentieth-century ideas of skilled workers organizing an industrial proletariat in Germany were challenged by official messages that encouraged conformity to a more nationalistic work ethic. The consumption by workers of the ideology of National Socialism (encased in a therapeutic framework of cultural purpose) identified workers as the same as all other members of German society. Sacrifice and obedience to the "Fatherland" became the fundamental current of social identity. While authoritarian government power encouraged working-class acceptance of such notions, the propaganda was crafted in such a manner that it never became a burden for any "true German." Jacques Ellul offers insight into how such official propaganda can be accepted as popular culture:

> Propaganda must not only attach itself to what already exists in the individual, but also express the fundamental currents of the society it seeks to influence. Propaganda must be familiar with collective sociological presuppositions, spontaneous myths, and broad ideologies. By this we do not mean political currents or temporary opinions that will change in a few months, but the fundamental psychosociological bases on which a whole society rests, the presupposition and myths not just of individuals or of particular groups, but those shared by all individuals in a society, including men of opposite political inclinations and class loyalties.[6]

Assisted by the political nuances emerging from an official revisionist national history and the social consumption of commercially-produced images representing a "higher," more "moral" group-based identity, German workers now had an "ongoing purpose" for their labor. Individual questioning of this new identity was muted by rising standards for personal behavior officially recognized through government sanction. Ritual reinforced the entire process. Displacing class-based gratification (reflected in the working class having a say in the political decision-making process) were individual rewards for workers (medals, certificates, and public praise) who toiled ceremoniously for the state. The acceptance by workers of such sanctions was at once a support mechanism for officially designated social identities, and, at the same time, a legitimization for authoritarian control of the state.

Chapter 2 by Douglas Lea examines how Nazi policy and propaganda encouraged an alteration of traditional German working-class culture. He makes clear how the influence of this new official culture, implemented through the use of official and commercial verbal and visual symbolism for the sole purpose of encouraging working-class support for the National Socialist State, replaced traditional frameworks for class-based identity.

Consumer culture is more than a value system. It is a way of life. Power and power relationships are at its core. It has a network of support mechanisms that condition a rejection of multi-faceted interpretations of history. Only those traditions which are necessary to the maintenance of the status quo are introduced into the culture of consumption. Politically dominant institutions introduce cultural images which encourage consumers to dream, speculate, associate with, and absorb current meanings of social identity. This type of mass culture plays an important role in the modern process in which individuals seek and create meaning about their everyday existence. Ways of dealing with life's special moments and antagonisms often follow commercially organized cultural guidelines. But such a process promotes a sensory depthlessness on the part of the recipient. Without thinking, modern individuals mouth the words they hear on television, the radio, or in film. Standardization becomes the operative word in consumer culture. Past experience, present uncertainties, and speculation about the future all narrow as the individual becomes measured by narrowly interpreted standards. Everyone consumes "standard information." Technology, for instance, is either state-of-the-art or outdated. Any ideas regarding the impact of advanced technology on the working class are rarely considered. Class dichotomies have no place to emerge. In the process, the worker becomes politically docile, alienated from the political decision-making center. The voice of the worker emerges through commercial networks in a one-way transmission. There is no debate. The network sets the agenda which is often narrowly defined. Television "town meetings," radio talk shows, Op-page editorials, and film biographies are, by their very creation, a one-way communication. The element of power clearly rests in the hands of the narrator, the communications personality, the publisher, or the officially-sanctioned hero. To be the narrator is to be the expert authority, the one who is seen addressing the issues, the one who tells it like it is, the professional, or simply, the one who is important enough to be seen and heard. As Edward Said suggests, "the cult of expertise and professionalism . . . has so restricted our scope of vision that a positive (as opposed to an implicit or passive) doctrine of non-interference has set in."[7]

Chapter 3 addresses the manipulation of the modern Italian working class. Pietro Lorenzini illustrates the relationship between the modern commercial communications industry and the shaping of working-class consciousness in a manner which distorted the organic nature of working-class culture in Italy between 1950 and 1985. Lorenzini shows how the persistence of such distortion influenced the creation of new social identities around which new signifiers of social status emerged. Based upon images which challenged traditional community autonomy and delivered through social frameworks prescribed by religious personalities, and public notions of entertainment and morality, the idea that personal identity was no longer represented along class lines became a new political ideology. In the process of examining the class displacement of modern Italian workers through the stimulation of unconscious class-blurring images accepted as cultural tradition, Lorenzini incorporates the struggles of Italian workers with the new cultural politics of the commercial media system and its rising power to shape of new public representations of working-class culture.

Any book on the transformation of social identity encouraged by the proliferation of media would not be complete without an analysis of the music of political persuasion and social significance. In chapter 4, "From Guthrie through Dylan to Springsteen: Losing the Working Touch," David Sims explores the lyrics of three of America's most notable and popular singers/songwriters and the possible gradual erosion of popular music as an authentic and intellectual transmitter of working-class assumptions, values, beliefs, and aspirations. Sims' thesis adds to the literature surrounding the construction of social identity and the mobilization of class-based forces through music. While the persistence of music's limitations in inspiring a class consciousness may be a transitional phenomenon, if only due to the rise of cultural consumerism, such a limitation must be fully recognized as being potentially devastating to class-based consciousness and political formation. R. Serge Denisoff has commented on how the influence of music upon class resentments and distinctions has not been powerful enough on its own to mobilize social movements in the past:

> If the power and quality of a song were social determinants of political power, then the Black man would have overcome decades ago; the Industrial Workers of the World, not the CIO, would have unionized factory workers. . . . Without further belaboring this point, it should by now be blatantly clear that the [brainwashing] thesis is not a pervasive one.[8]

Reasons for this are many and have been debated by scholars throughout the twentieth century. However, an important aim of Sims' article is to show just how the commodification of music helps to invent new normative behaviors which challenge existing notions of a class-based society.

The consumption of music like other goods, despite its organizational messages, can actually dissolve its political meaning. This paradoxical conclusion is aided and abetted by political power relationships, and the social recognition that the market is the nucleus of society. Sims examines the interaction of these frameworks of power vis-à-vis the phenomenon of how commercial media production networks entice the listening public to purchase musical offerings. During this process, listeners often acquiesce their intellectual activities, challenging any political message that is being sent to them through the music itself. Once this happens, the music becomes standardized; it loses its social and political discriminative capability. In the end, group consciousness is subverted and replaced by an individually manipulative experience that serves to isolate the individual to the position of social consumer rather than political activist. All lyrical suggestions about the construction of group-based social identities are rendered moot in the process. As Sims suggests, rather than mold and direct enthusiasm for the activation of group consciousness and class identity, the listener receives the music, and assumes that its reception requires no effort beyond that which is consumer-oriented. The desire to possess the "standard" replaces the call to action.

In similar fashion, the call to action was often muted within one of the most actively critical voices in the United States in the 1920s: the "little magazine." Artistic, literary and radical journals such as *Seven Arts, The Little Review,* and *Survey* were "little" in that they typically attracted only a few thousand subscribers. The precarious financial situation of many of them also made for infrequent publication and short periods of existence. Nevertheless, among groups of cultural critics, labor organizers and socialist activists, these magazines were read and cited quite widely. They functioned as an intellectual forum for developing and debating ideologies and organizational tactics, and therefore serve as valuable sources for exploring efforts to define and create working-class consciousness.

In chapter 5, Cynthia Gwynne Yaudes investigates this theme by examining *Labor Age* (a monthly "little magazine" published between 1921 and 1933) vis-à-vis the popular press of the period. Driven by the "socialist cause," *Labor Age* promised to fill a "well-defined need" for discussion of labor organization and assured readers that it would report and interpret the "up-to-date happenings from the battle-line of the struggle." In covering many of the same issues and events, the popular press drew upon other influences besides the evocation of a classless society; profound communal, social and personal identities shaped the way in which readers understood the media's message. Yaudes outlines the tension that builds between the ideological orientation of *Labor Age* and the cultural orientation of the popular press, and analyzes the fissures such tension caused in *Labor Age*'s efforts to inspire a viable American working class toward a socialist reality.

The infrastructure of mass culture includes the component of official culture (cultural standards organized by the interaction of the procedural and substantive policy-making processes of government). In the final chapter I examine how official press releases, interacting with commercial media networks, generated new interpretations of context which galvanized popular resentment against the activities of the International Workers Order. Claiming that the organization was not a labor organization like other American labor groups, official culture penetrated existing social context in subtle ways which, when identified by the consumer, justified the United States government's right to dismantle the IWO. Such intertextual manipulation by powerful agencies of government and commerce serves to promote the transfer of meaning from one cultural context to the next in a manner which alters cultural traditions. Seeing the effects of such cultural alterations adds new dimensions and alternatives to traditional textual interplay. In the case of the United States versus the IWO, the result was the effecting of a social control mechanism that restricted any satisfactory understanding of the political events taking place.

The shift from a production-oriented to a consumer-based culture described herein helped to transform existing constitutions and constructions of social identities, in particular class-based identities. By examining the cultural and political nuances of specific times and organizational representations this book hopes to give rise to three issues of central importance: the identification of social identities through the consumption of transformational grammars and the mediation of images by dominant agencies newly charged with cultural communications; the notion of cultural displacement of working-class identity and its influence on self-image; and the acceptance of an evolving cultural hegemony which is at odds with cultural ideals of the recent past.

Thomas J. Edward Walker
Williamsport, Pennsylvania

Notes

1. Douglas Tallack, *Twentieth Century America: Intellectual and Cultural Context* (New York: Longman, 1991).

2. Kim Voss, *American Exceptionalism: The Knights of Labor and Class Formation in the Nineteenth Century* (Ithaca, N.Y.: Cornell University Press, 1993), 5.

3. Richard Wightman Fox and T. J. Jackson Lears, eds., *The Culture of Consumption: Critical Essays in American History, 1880–1980* (New York: Pantheon Books, 1983), xi.

4. Ian Angus and Sut Jhally, eds., *Cultural Politics in Contemporary America* (New York: Routledge, 1989), 2.

5. Stuart Hall, "Notes on Deconstructing the Popular," in *People's History and Social History*, ed. Raphael Samuel (Boston: Routledge and Kegan Paul, 1981), 229.

6. Jacques Ellul, *Propaganda: The Formation of Men's Attitudes* (New York: Vintage, 1965), 38–39.

7. Edward Said, "Opponents, Audiences, Constituencies and Community," in *Postmodern Culture*, ed. Hal Foster (Port Townsend, Wash: Bay Press, 1983), 145–146.

8. R. Serge Denisoff, *Sing a Song of Social Significance* (Bowling Green, Ohio: Bowling Green State University Press, 1983), viii.

1

Cocoa and Class in British Popular Press Advertising: A Process of Cultural Agency

Daniel J. Doyle

The nineteenth century in Britain witnessed, as elsewhere in the industrial world, the formation of a "consumer." Changes in personal and social identity were essential subliminal factors associated with the creation of the consumer mentality. Newspapers and advertising were crucial to this social transformation. The context was broad, including elements of mass production, literacy, communication, and economic organization, among other factors. The consequences were likewise diverse. Worker identiti es, linked with trade and class, were co-opted to create and eventually homogenize a new consumer mass identity in which individual aspirations replaced political and group aims.[1]

At the beginning of the twentieth century, the rise of the popular press in Britain (symbolically initiated with the publication of the *Daily Mail* in 1896), and the emergence of modern display press advertising created the markets necessary to sustain the developing mass production system. A study of various products featured in the new format ads reveals significant social indicators. Cocoa offers a special insight, owing to its social connotations. From its introduction in Europe in the sixteenth century until the nineteenth century, chocolate was associated with the rich.[2] Innovations in production techniques and marketing transformed cocoa and other products of the principal chocolate manufacturers.

The new capitalist objective of increased profits, derived from economies of scale, resulted in a replacement of small-scale production with commodity culture

dependent on marketing.[3] This fundamental shift in the economy was directly linked
to changes in manufacturing technology, organizational shifts in production, expansion of the scale of distribution, and an emergence of new strategies for marketing. Viewed as a whole, these components demonstrate the evolving cultural
hegemony of capitalism.[4] Social identity and cultural values were reshaped by
such major changes.

The concept of social class was central to these commercial and cultural images and the interests they served. Class, in a social-structural sense, was often
connected with "class" as a notion of quality. Signs of class were telegraphed in
advertisement illustrations through a variety of means. More subtle distinctions in
portraiture through shading, posture, relative size, and positioning, along with other
aspects of individual presentation, combined with statements representing social
interactions to convey attitudes toward class.

The study of class has emphasized the role of the working class in the determination of their own consciousness. The "active" self-definition is central to E. P.
Thompson's scholarship and the analysis by Gareth Stedman Jones and Peter
Stearns.[5] The issues involved in the concepts of popular culture and mass culture
necessitate the investigation of methods of agency, and are not limited to the working class. Inherent in the concept of mass culture is the attempt to form a coalition
that transcends class lines. As Raymond Williams states, the economic sector of a
society could not be separated from the moral and intellectual components. "Society and individual experience were alike being transformed, and this driving agency
[economic organizations], which there were no adequate traditional procedures to
understand and interpret, had, in depth, to be taken into consciousness."[6] The importance of such an effort is crucial to understanding the ramifications for the
nature of the mass culture, and focus on a specific product such as cocoa elucidates
the broad dimensions of change.

Eric Hobsbawm views the notion of class as fluid.[7] This is particularly appropriate for a period of organizational shifts in the economy associated with the
move toward large-scale production. A principal alteration of class for workers
moved from identities connected with trade to a single working-class identity.
According to Hobsbawm media played an important role in this process during the
period 1870 to 1914.[8] The role of advertising is particularly vital in evaluating the
influence of the press.

The rise of the British popular press at the end of the nineteenth century was
an important vehicle for the distribution of ads. Although circulation figures achieved
were minor numbers in comparison to the mid-twentieth century, the new press
created a quantum jump in readership from what had existed previously in the
daily press[9] and represented a stark contrast with the anti-lower class readership
represented by the not-too-distant "Taxes on Knowledge."[10] Changes in technology, literacy, and attitudes toward the availability of a press for "the people" combined with industrial aims by the end of the nineteenth century to stimulate the
simultaneous development of press and press advertisements.[11]

The composition of the "new readership" is central to the discussion of the impact created by the popular press. Previous attitudes towards the press in Britain reflected a conscious effort to restrain the nonelite from access to knowledge. As an attribute of class definition, the relationship of printed material was pivotal.

Following the removal of the special taxes, economics and desire constituted the primary obstacles to developing a wider readership. Most papers were still too costly for the general populace. For example, the *Times* (3 d.) appealed largely to the upper strata. The cheaper popular press that was to emerge was also designed for and received by a new and different audience. The first of the new papers were primarily weeklies, including Sunday papers such as *News of the World*. These papers ranged in content including sports, advertisements, and general material largely of entertainment value. Readership was diverse depending on content of the publication. The middle and lower-middle classes were the likely readers of these newer publications.[12]

The major test and principal opportunity for influencing the "new readership" of a daily press was the creation of new features, shortened text per story, and lower reading level. Cost ($\frac{1}{2}$ d.) also became an important factor. The *Daily Mail*, first published on May 4, 1896, initiated many of these approaches in inaugurating the cheap daily. Up to that point the cheapest dailies were 1 d. In addition to news, the *Daily Mail* included sports, social gossip, women's section (a "Daily Magazine" which was heavily illustrated), and a "newspaper novel" (*feuilleton*). Story length and column size were adapted to the needs of a train-riding clientele. Northcliffe demonstrated an awareness of readability suited to a wide audience and instructed staff writers to write "so plainly that he (the writer) could be understood by the lowest intelligence."[13]

The broad readership of the *Daily Mail* included the middle class, lower-middle and working classes. The cost alone indicates that workers were fewer in number and tended to come from the ranks of "labour aristocracy." Northcliffe viewed the graduate of Board Schools as a major audience. The white-collar worker (lower middle class) was the primary target. The *Daily Mail* masthead proclaimed that the paper was for the "Busy Man." Advertisers often referred to the surrogates as "Brain Workers" or persons whose work was mental. Geoffrey Crossick sees the reader of the popular press as essentially lower-middle class.[14]

These expanding media provided manufacturers with new opportunities to reach potential customers. An added attraction was that the new audience was more likely to be open to new techniques and to be accepting new products. Advertisers, especially those developing new techniques, created multidimensional messages reflecting objects, ideology, values, and society. These commercial statements responded in a direct manner to the primary aim of selling a particular product; however, layered within the advertiser's creation—often in an encoded process—were implications of broader cultural significance regarding values and social structure. Illustrators and copywriters borrowed from existing conventions of literature and art. Viewed in a collective sense over time these images of a "pictured" reality were charged with the potential of shaping and altering the individual and collective conscious.

The boundaries of social groupings along occupational and broader structural lines in society and as pictured in the press changed in the early twentieth century. Some of the leading advertisers and the commercial enterprises they served abandoned narrow occupational identifications in favor of broader associations of class. Others sought to extend market categories in social terms to create a homogenized audience which did not yet exist—in effect proclaiming the existence of a mass society. Commercial expediency, social change, and the nature of the new press influenced these approaches, as they developed.

The period 1851–1914 witnessed a total transformation of the advertising medium in the broadest marketing sense. An increasingly visual form of product marketing began with the Crystal Palace exhibition of 1851 and accelerated through the 1880s due to technological innovations in printing.[15] Raymond Williams contends that the "new" period associated with the printing technologies and emergence of a popular press also resulted from "certain characteristics of the new 'monopoly' (corporate) capitalism."[16] Advertising became a factor in achieving market control. These fundamental economic needs precipitated a redirecting of advertising agencies and newspaper responses. The new roles of commercial art and writing expanded to function as "official art of modern capitalist society."[17] Williams sees advertising as having assumed new responsibilities beyond those of selling goods and services. The new ads act as definers of social and personal values. This process became more important as the nature and size of the audience for advertising changed from individuals or social groups to the masses.[18]

Advertising serves as what Eugen Weber calls an "agent" in the process of cultural interaction.[19] Those who affect culture—in this instance the middle classes —attempt to transmit values to the lower classes. Even the size of the audience and the scope of its identity are targets of manipulation. The roots of this expanded role of advertising as identified by Williams rest in the period of reformulation, during which the methods of effective use of illustration and text copy were developed. An examination of exemplary formats provides access to the methodology of commercial cultural agency.

Jacques Ellul's analysis of propaganda includes the function of propaganda as a process of integration, wherein cultural conformity is the desired end.[20] This particular view is relevant to establishing the significance of advertising in relation to social and economic change. Advertising as propaganda "thus aims at making the individual participate in his society in every way. It is a long-term propaganda, a self-reproducing propaganda that seeks to obtain stable behavior, to adapt the individual to his everyday life, to reshape his thoughts and behavior in terms of the permanent social setting . . . for the individual can no longer be left to himself."[21] Cocoa advertising typifies the multidimensional function of propaganda as cultural integration. Cocoa advertising promotes a product and seeks action (purchase, use, and continued purchase), while it simultaneously supports the prevailing economic system, affirms the associated values used to promote the product (health, nationalism, work ethic), encourages acceptance of technological change, and facilitates the fundamental shift from producer to consumer.

Press advertising in a range of commodities, such as cocoa, merits examination as illustrative of broader trends. Efforts to build identities or relationships in one marketing area can be and were tied to other areas. If a segment of ads built a larger identity while using a set of established or encoded conventions by other ads, then the impact of the two systems were energized beyond their surface messages. The combined effect produced the potential for a Malthusian geometric progression as to the potential for influencing the culture.

The process accelerated when advertising emerged from its dormant stage. Until the 1880s advertising was largely restricted in its format. Single column space, limited diversity of typographic styles and size, and minimal use of illustrations were the rule. Publishers were a major factor in maintaining this traditional approach. At first gradually, and then with increasing speed by the turn of the century, the display[22] ad format broke its bonds. Advertisements progressed in size, quality, diversity of technique, and attention to audience. Typographic changes which had started the trend continued. The amount and focus of the text also altered. The "new" ad was usually greater than single column width. Contracted text yielded to the expanded use of illustrations.[23]

The importance of the increased attention to illustrated ads draws emphasis from the ideas of E. H. Gombrich and John Berger. They assert that art functions as the symbol for the viewers' perception of the world. Art creates and uses conventions, stereotypes, and self-reflective symbols that form the context of the viewers' background for understanding or relating to reality. Art, therefore, is a medium primed for the role of cultural agency. According to Berger, publicity proceeds from a basic proposal—the transformation of the viewer through purchase of the object seen.[24]

Symbols or signs form the background for advertising's energized potential toward cultural manipulation. The use of symbols in commercial aspects of a mercantile culture has a definite history that predates public literacy. Until the eighteenth century retailers were primarily identified by symbols that were understood by all. With the rise of literacy the use of names and titles replaced the symbolic pictographs employed by tradesmen's cards, for instance.[25]

The presence of symbols in advertisements was evident to the ad designer of the turn of the century. Karl Kloufe, writing in *The Poster* (1899), commented in "Symbolism in Advertising" on the role of signs. After alluding to the negative association with the "Symbolist" art movement as a "decadent association of the deadliest affront" to the commercial advertiser, he recalled the historic use of symbols in the marketing of goods. Kloufe described the poster (and thus illustration) as a continuation of the commercial tradition and emphasized the approach of the advertiser who "still strives to proclaim his wares in a roundabout fashion, by suggesting a train of thought that will bring the loiterer by a series of brain exercises to the article advertised." The author concluded that symbolic associations were necessary but should be obvious.[26]

The wider concept of symbolism suggests that a variety of messages are conveyed to the viewer—some apparent, others hidden. The symbols relay a host of relationships and meanings, some of which are less obvious. Judith Williamson, in *Decoding Advertisements*, states that many of the signs and associations in advertising are drawn from sources outside the print medium. Thus, the interpreter of ads must be sensitized to the variety of responses, associations, and meanings possible within an ad, and versed in the general nature of advertisements. To Williamson the function of the signs is to serve as a "referent" to ideology and social conventions.[27] Berger and Williamson postulate a capitalistic ideological motivation as the base of reference.[28]

Varda Langholz Leymore stresses the role of symbols in advertising as a "transformation process." The reader becomes involved in the process of understanding the message. To Leymore, the image of the user presented in the ad is fundamental to the comprehension of the transformation process. This "surrogate" consumer depicted in the ad is essential to the act of "mediation, not just in the commercial sense, but also and most importantly in the perceptual plane."[29] The cultural agent (producer and advertiser) bridges the abstract and concrete. Values, beliefs, and attitudes are part of the mediation process.

Richards contends that capitalism extends its control of society through manipulation of the visual language.[30] A visual language, dependent to some degree on existing high culture forms, serves as the expanding vocabulary of the advertisements.[31] Symbols of class are included in this nonverbal text.[32] The ability to deliver the new image-laden ad is facilitated by the technological developments of the late nineteenth-century printing revolution. This connection of emerging image-dependent marketing associated with consumer products demonstrates the subtlety of Ellul's notion of integration. For Ellul "propaganda is an indispensable condition for the development of technical progress and the establishment of a technological civilization."[33]

Images in any form often serve as social class identifiers in both conscious and subconscious ways.[34] Whether advertising images are accepted as "art" is only one aspect of that social dimension. The broader issue of image as social transmitter of class associations and attendant values is central to an understanding of the function of the role of the newly emergent advertising in the broader cultural changes in late nineteenth- and early twentieth-century industrial societies.

Images of class are frequent themes in advertising. Ads in the period 1896 to 1913 ranged from specific occupational appeals to class- and mass-based approaches. Presentation of goods and the concomitant images of class value systems in a progressively broader representation of social structure represented a new marketing opportunity. A generalized audience facilitated sales for a mass-production economy.

Because of existing class-based identities, cocoa advertising presents an opportunity to examine the process of building a larger, unified audience. The simultaneous developments of group definition in cocoa ads with layered messages in the clothing and cigarette publicity are part of this cross-commodity review that is necessary in the analysis of the cultural significance of advertising. The collective impact was fundamental to the role of agency.

"Cocoa," as a commodity, resulted from a technological process developed in 1828 by a Dutch chemist, Van Houten, who discovered a way to reduce the fat content of the cocoa bean by two-thirds.[35] By the 1870s, Van Houten brand had agencies in London, Leeds, Liverpool, Edinburgh, Glasgow, and Dublin as part of a national distribution strategy.[36] The remaining product became known as "cocoa." This process reduced the need to adulterate cocoa with alkali material such as starches to moderate the fatty taste.[37] The overall social context for cocoa bean products followed three phases of social class associations. From its introduction into Europe in the sixteenth century until the late eighteenth century, the price of the product defined chocolate as a luxury for the upper classes. During the first three quarters of the nineteenth century, chocolate expanded its market to include the middle class. In a capitalist economy, the demands of mass production began to necessitate an expanded consumer market. Cocoa products began to fulfill the demand in the last quarter of the nineteenth century. The cost of cocoa remained relatively stable and would to some degree remain a factor in its social class association, unlike the declining prices of tea and coffee in the late nineteenth century.[38]

Cocoa manufacturers were major advertisers, and cocoa was among the early group of products promoted through the new display ad in the popular press. Some cocoa products made frequent reference to social identifications. These class identities made cocoa a particularly good source for class analysis and the building of larger markets. Specific connections with Keir Hardie's *Labour Leader*[39] and the involvement of the Rowntree name with issues of social improvement and the study of poverty further extend the importance of analyzing cocoa ads.

Seebohm Rowntree, son of the head of the Rowntree firm at that time, published in 1913 a sociological study of poverty in York. He separated the working class largely by income into two groups, although a review of occupations indicates a delineation also based on skilled versus unskilled. His third grouping was "Servant Keeping." Cocoa appears in an accounting of daily menus for specified subjects studied only in this third group.[40]

Three firms—Frey, Cadbury and Rowntree—were leaders in British production by the early twentieth century.[41] Four firms were the leaders in press advertising—Epps, Dr. Tibble's Vi-Cocoa, Cadbury, and Rowntree. Van Houten, which was noted for its posters, infrequently used press advertising, and did not use any poster themes in the press. The cocoa manufacturers illustrate Raymond Williams' contention that advertising was stimulated by industrial needs for new markets. Cadbury, Britain's cocoa manufacturing leader by 1894, and Rowntree emphasized advertising as part of their firms' development.[42]

Epps did not employ any of the techniques common to other manufacturers

such as illustration, graphic design, or
testimonials[43] (Figure 1). Of the remaining three, Vi-Cocoa was the most frequent advertiser in the first years of the
twentieth century. "A Proved Success/
It Is Now in the Homes of Hundreds of
Thousands of the People" proclaimed
a full-page Vi-Cocoa ad in the Daily
Mail on January 11, 1897. This asso-

Figure 1.1

ciation with "the People" was established by the use of testimonials—in this case
a Railway Guard and Nurses. Vi-Cocoa borrowed this use of letters of testimony
from the format of patent medicine advertisers. In the case of Tibble's Vi-Cocoa, a
survey of the occupations depicted reveals the targeted audiences and the potential
links between occupation and alleged qualities of the product.

Cocoa ads were evident in the *Labour Leader* by summer, 1898.[44] At first these
ads were placed in the single column of display typographic ads on the front page.
Ads for this period by Cadbury and Vi-Cocoa did little more than indicate in large
typeface the companies' names and supply a brief statement. These ads were similar in format to the Epps ad. By September 24, 1898, Tibble's was soliciting testi-

Figure 1.2

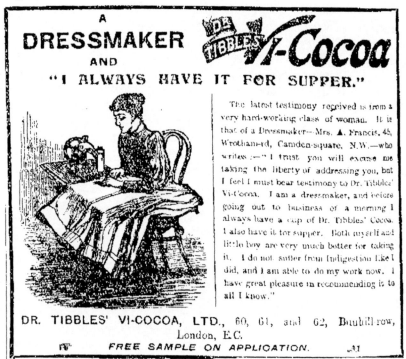

monials. Cadbury demonstrated an approach to narrow, targeted audience in the *Labour Leader*[45] with a claim that they had "a good record, and one we Socialists can admire."

Vi-Cocoa used testimonials in a campaign of occupational identification. The early 1900s saw many examples of testimonials in the pages of the *Daily Mail*, *Daily Express,* and *Labour Leader*. One of the first appearances in the *Daily Mail* featured a "Dressmaker"[46] (Figure 2). The description of the occupation is featured in the ad headline and in the representational nature of the illustration. The actual person involved is only identified in the small print of the copy. Further expressions such as "Another Nurse," "Yet Another Nurse," or "Another Seaman" suggest the minor significance of the person.[47] At times the pitch to fellow workers is evident from the ad subtitle such as "Domestic Servant—recommends Vi-Cocoa to her Fellow Servants." The issue of the personality of the "testimonial writer" is rare with the exception of "Author of *White Slaves of England*"[48] (Figure 3).

The importance of the theme of personality and its association with prestige is demonstrated by a few ads (Figures 3 and 4). The two individuals who emerge in these early ads are both of higher status. This sense of distinction is supported by the illustration. The author and "Hardware Merchant"[49] (Figure 4) are the only figures presented as portraits without background. The character of the individual is

Figure 1.3

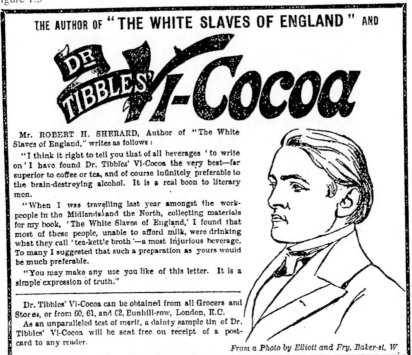

THE AUTHOR OF "THE WHITE SLAVES OF ENGLAND" AND

DR TIBBLES' Vi-Cocoa

Mr. ROBERT H. SHERARD, Author of "The White Slaves of England," writes as follows :

"I think it right to tell you that of all beverages ' to write on ' I have found Dr. Tibbles' Vi-Cocoa the very best—far superior to coffee or tea, and of course infinitely preferable to the brain-destroying alcohol. It is a real boon to literary men.

"When I was travelling last year amongst the work-people in the Midlands and the North, collecting materials for my book, 'The White Slaves of England,' I found that most of these people, unable to afford milk, were drinking what they call ' tea-kettle broth '—a most injurious beverage. To many I suggested that such a preparation as yours would be much preferable.

"You may make any use you like of this letter. It is a simple expression of truth."

Dr. Tibbles' Vi-Cocoa can be obtained from all Grocers and Stores, or from 60, 61, and 62, Bunhill-row, London, E.C.

As an unparalleled test of merit, a dainty sample tin of Dr. Tibbles' Vi-Cocoa will be sent free on receipt of a post-card to any reader.

From a Photo by Elliott and Fry, Baker-st, W.

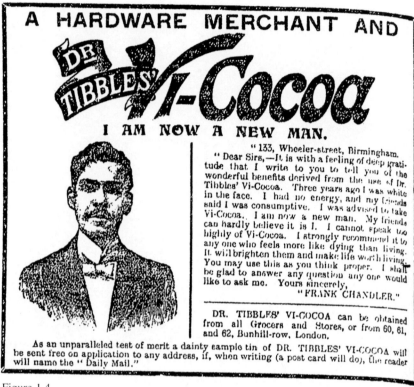

Figure 1.4

thus more important than the stereotyped occupational role established by environmental context. The illustrations are different but the visual message is similar. The author is drawn "from a photo"—in itself an exclusive signal as this is the only case in the series of mention of a photograph by Vi-Cocoa. The sense that the testimony is real is enhanced by the reference to photography.[50] Although the line drawing is simple in technique the clothing, hair style, and jaw suggest rank. The Hardware Merchant is presented in direct position. The effect of the drawing is to suggest a photographic product through shading, which also communicates a sense of personality.

Contrast these drawings with those from the same period that represent the common style: Railway Porter, Worker in the Forge, and Laundry Worker[51] (Figures 5, 6, and 7). In these and later cases, the drawing depicts stereotyped figures identified by setting. They function with the same formulaic structure as the old shop signs. Individuality is of no consequence. In these unskilled, working-class occupations, the face is often turned or so darkened that characteristics are not evident. The message is clear: personal qualities are not of merit. The occupations

A RAILWAY PORTER AND

DR TIBBLES' Vi-Cocoa

"FOR NIGHT DUTY IT IS INVALUABLE."

Mr. F. FITZGERALD, 136, Broad-lane, South Tottenham, writes :—

"Last winter after reading several of the testimonials from users of Dr. Tibbles' Vi-Cocoa, I determined to give it a trial, and have used it ever since. I could not now do without it. Being a railway porter, and having to get up at 3.30 a.m., I found that a cup of Vi-Cocoa before going out in the morning was very beneficial ; and for night duty it is invaluable, being most cheering and invigorating. I cannot speak too highly of its merits.

"You are at liberty to publish this statement if you like."

Stores, or from Dr. TIBBLES' VI-COCOA, Limited, 60, 61, and 62, Bunhill-row, London, E.C.

Dr. TIBBLES' VI-COCOA, 6d., 9d., and 1s. 6d., can be obtained from all Chemists, Grocers, and

DAINTY SAMPLE FREE TO ANY ADDRESS.

Figure 1.5

A WORKER IN A FORGE—AND

DR TIBBLES' Vi-Cocoa

"GIVES HIM NEW LIFE."

Mrs. BROUGHTON writes :—

"My husband has received great benefit from Dr. Tibbles' Vi-Cocoa, for which I feel very thankful. He works in a forge, and when he feels overdone with heat and fatigue he takes a drink of Vi-Cocoa, and it seems to refresh and give him new life. He uses a packet a week, and he feels quite a new man. I shall have much pleasure in recommending it to my friends, and you are at liberty to use this statement if you like."

Dr. Tibbles' Vi-Cocoa can be obtained from all Grocers, Chemists, and Stores, or from 60, 61, and 62, Bunhill-row, London, E.C.

DAINTY SAMPLE FREE ON APPLICATION.

Figure 1.6

A LAUNDRY WORKER AND

Dr Tibbles' Vi-Cocoa

Not tired and languid after using VI-COCOA.

Mrs. CAINE, 48, Jackson Street, Woolwich Common.

I trust you will excuse my taking such a liberty in writing to you, but I feel as if I must write and tell you that I find Vi-Cocoa most nourishing and refreshing. My husband is now serving in South Africa, but before sailing, I gave him a tin of Vi-Cocoa. He has since written home for another tin of the same, which I sent him, and I am very pleased to say he received it before he went away. I have often come home from the Laundry tired and languid, but after having a cup of Vi-Cocoa have felt a great deal better. I have great pleasure in recommending Vi-Cocoa to all I know. I shall be sending another tin out to my husband next mail.

"Undoubted purity and strength."—*Medical Journal*. "In the front rank of really valuable foods."—*Lancet*.

Favoured by the Homes and Hospitals of Great Britain. Dainty Sample Tin free to any address.

Address: DR. TIBBLES' VI-COCOA, LTD., 60, Bunhill Row, LONDON, E.C.

Dainty Sample Free.

Figure 1.7

selected often serve to represent the efficacy of the product. Strength and endurance in hard labor are the key. The symbolic aspect is most evident in an ad with the label of Engine Driver[52] (Figure 8). The locomotive is shown without any person.

Eye contact, evident in the Hardware Merchant, is generally lacking in the common-style ads. Exceptions are found in larger formats (three columns) where young women and men of higher status look at the reader. Domestic Servant (female) and Accountant look up or directly out from the page; whereas Straw Blocker, Grocer's Assistant, Shoeing Smith, and Painter do not.[53] Women and people of rank are attractive or worthy of recognition; others are less so, or must keep their eyes on their work! Erving Goffman contends that females more than males are portrayed in ads with head and eye aversion as a sign of deference or lack of power in what he calls a "Ritualization of Subordination." When males are portrayed in this manner, lower class status is usually the attribute conveyed.[54]

A wide range of occupations are presented in the three papers. Although there is a slight emphasis toward lower-middle class occupations (various shop assistants) in the *Daily Mail* and *Daily Express*, the difference may result from the

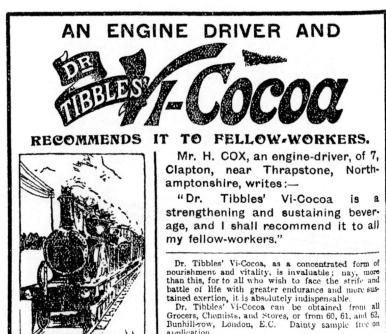

AN ENGINE DRIVER AND DR TIBBLES' Vi-Cocoa

RECOMMENDS IT TO FELLOW-WORKERS.

Mr. H. COX, an engine-driver, of 7, Clapton, near Thrapstone, Northamptonshire, writes:—

"Dr. Tibbles' Vi-Cocoa is a strengthening and sustaining beverage, and I shall recommend it to all my fellow-workers."

Dr. Tibbles' Vi-Cocoa, as a concentrated form of nourishment and vitality, is invaluable; nay, more than this, for to all who wish to face the strife and battle of life with greater endurance and more sustained exertion, it is absolutely indispensable.

Dr. Tibbles' Vi-Cocoa can be obtained from all Grocers, Chemists, and Stores, or from 60, 61, and 62, Bunhill-row, London, E.C. Dainty sample free on application.

Figure 1.8

greater frequency of ads in the dailies. Some figures appear in the *Labour Leader* as well as the dailies.[55]

Nurses, railway workers, and the military are the most common occupations portrayed in the ads in all three papers. Nurses suggest health; railway workers vigilance. Military themes relate to the rigors of life—especially at sea—and only occasionally to the Boer War. These and other military testimonials do reflect a class element in that sergeant is the highest rank ever listed. The presence of railway workers may represent an appeal to a growing segment of the working class whose employment is directly linked to increasing reliance on technology.[56]

The distinctions in class symbolism demonstrated through juxtaposition of characters reveals conscious attitudes about class. In addition to single, status-specific advertising cocoa firms used small and large group settings. One of the first to use group settings was Rowntree[57] (Figure 9), with the frequently used headline, "A delicious and economical Cocoa." The illustration depicts a member of the aristocracy and a lower-class man joining cups of cocoa in the air. The main body of the text continued—"appreciated alike by peer and peasant; in the palace and in the cottage."

The conventions of clothing and implements are employed.[58] The ad implies that Rowntree is used by all social groups—"all sorts and conditions of men, women, and children, under all circumstances." Universality suits a mass market target; yet the figures and the text indicate that the upper and lower classes are actually separate classes. Similar to the extreme distinctions in clothing, the symbolic touching of the cups of cocoa results in no actual physical contact between the representative classes being made. Even the package, positioned in the middle, serves as a barrier.

Vi-Cocoa presented "Two New Friends"[59] (Figure 10) in a half-page illustrated ad featuring a Blacksmith and a Nurse as stereotypes of strength and nourishment. The nurse's facial characteristics are almost identical to an illustration of a nurse[60] who is "One of Hundreds."

Jackson Lears's analysis of advertising in the United States emphasized a theme of therapeutic quality found in the messages of medicine, religion, and adver-

A delicious and economical Cocoa,

appreciated alike by peer and peasant; in the palace and in the cottage. A gratifying, satisfying Cocoa—made from the best parts of the best Cocoa beans. Pleasing the palate, strengthening the system. Rowntree's Elect Cocoa is an excellent and economical food-drink for all sorts and conditions of men, women, and children, under all circumstances and in all seasons.

Rowntree's

ELECT Cocoa

NEXT TIME—TRY ROWNTREE'S.

Figure 1.9

tising. Thus the use of nurses fits this strategy.[61] Cocoa products were long associated with medicinal qualities, probably as a result of the "rich" or fatty taste. Although the advertisements did not suggest substitution of cocoa for other beverages, consumption figures indicate that the average use of alcohol and coffee declined in the late nineteenth century. Cocoa ads changed their qualitative association from medicine to wholesomeness in this period.[62] Medicinal appeals for prod-

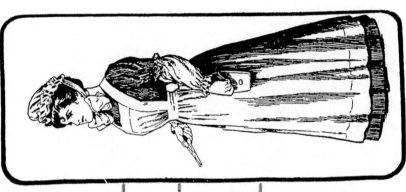

Figure 1.10

Figure 1.11

Figure 1.12

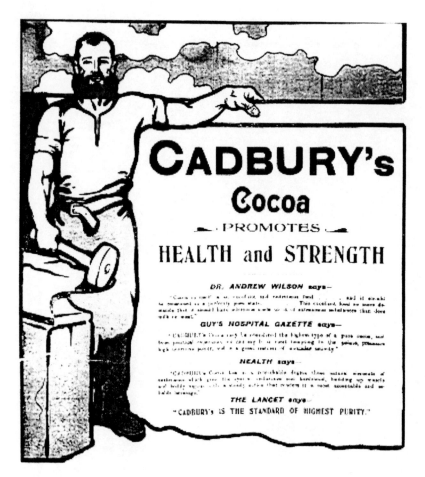

Figure 1.13

Figure 1.14

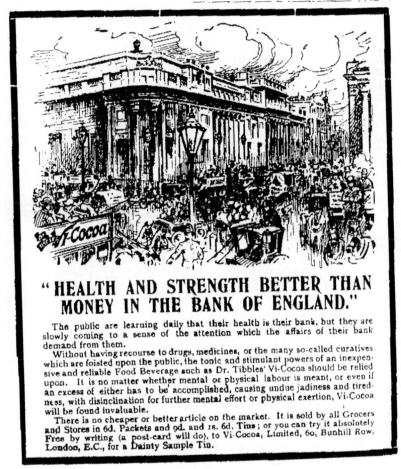

Figure 1.15

ucts also drew association with competing ads for patent medicines, which were the first common form of newspaper advertising, and which also were among the first ads to use illustrations.[63] However, at this period few of these products were among the leaders in the new display ad strategy. Vi-Cocoa clearly was in the patent medicine tradition, as the full name was "Dr. Tibble's Vi-Cocoa."

The theme of generalized representation of a larger audience appeared in two half-page ads in the *Daily Mail*[64]—"A Prosperous New Year to Friends Everywhere" (Figure 11) and "British Workers Everywhere Recommend"[65] (Figure 12). A substantial progression in imagery is evident in these ads. In the first (Figure 11), forty persons are wholly or partially drawn—it is a large gathering. Occupation and status distinctions are made especially in foreground figures: nurses, servants, military, rural workers, and four top hats are present. The distance in the Rowntree's

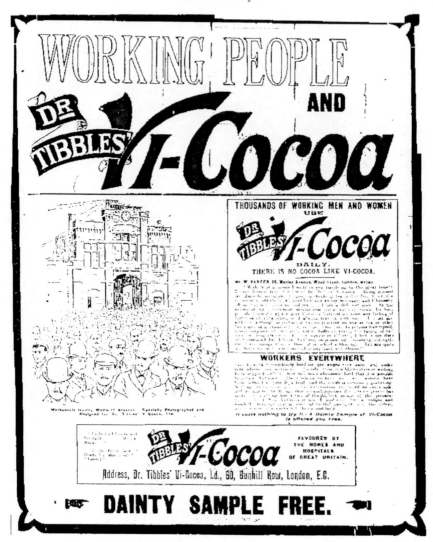

Figure 1.16

ad is gone; proximity results in intimacy. The testimonials are from a Bus Conductor, Architectural Modeller, Brushmaker, Nurse, Seaman, Wine Porter, and Goods Guard (railway). The illustrations represent a broad spectrum, while the messages are narrower.

The 1903 ad (Figure 12) for "British Workers" has thirty-two people in two rows at the top and bottom of the ad. Almost all are seen full figure with groupings of two to four established in poses that suggest conversation. Aprons are plentiful, sleeves are rolled, caps and other distinguishing head gear are present. These are not real people; however, an effort has been made to enliven the drawing, to create a sense of gathering through different gestures, postures, head positions, and placement of the hands. People are massed together into a theme of group identity. The testimonials relate not only to occupation, but include references to a national approach—a Lancashire Weaver and Fireman on the Midland Railway.

A romanticized sense of worker emerged in Cadbury ads, further demonstrating co-option[66] (Figure 13). The worker at forge is in contrast to the earlier Vi-Cocoa ad (Figure 10). The Cadbury "worker" "promotes Health and Strength" in its imagery—at ease with himself and his role—and headline.

The notion of a broad, at times classless, public is evident in an illustration-free Rowntree ad in 1904[67] (Figure 14) that states, "For the People" as its headline. The ultimate endorsement is provided by the symbol and claim of "By Royal Warrant" and the separate, larger statement "Makers to the King." Vi-Cocoa continued to use the occupational theme in 1904 but shifted the background of the correspondent. "Market Gardener"[68] portrays a foreman shown watching women bent over at work. Specialized trades such as Carpenter, Crane Driver, and Electric Car Driver (trolley) are also used.[69]

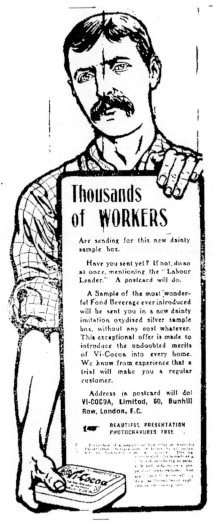

Figure
1.17

While the specific occupations still provide testimonials, broader groupings gain increased use. "The public are learning daily that their health is their bank"[70] (Figure 15). A clearer emphasis on workers is evident in "Working People . . . Thousands of Working Men and Women" who are depicted (men only) emerging from a factory in a scene that blends into a sea of caps and bowlers (signifying classes merging or dissolving together)[71] (Figure 16). The subheading states, "Workers Everywhere." The unity of workers is further shown in "Thousands of Workers—Are sending for this new dainty sample box"[72] (Figure 17). A worker (sleeves rolled, soft collar, casually brushed hair)

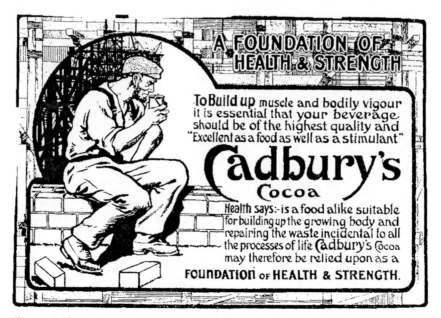

Figure 1.18

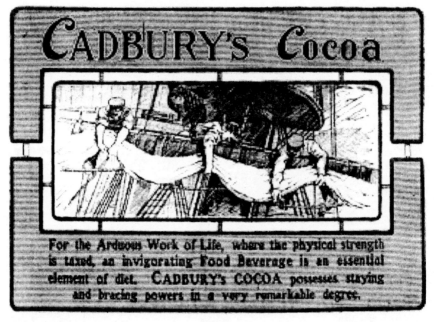

Figure 1.19

Figure 1.20

holds the box and, in effect, the text of the ad. The theme continued with Vi-Cocoa as "The Food Beverage of the People."[73] The reader in this instance is the housewife responsible for providing "health, happiness and success." Here a monetary value is seen linked to the earlier ad of health as a "bank," now that these values are "convertible terms."

The prevalence of caps in this ad is significant as a clear signifier of working class. Hobsbawm has observed that caps emerge as a marker for working class during the period 1870 to 1914, both in drawn images and photographs. The cap was not evident as a class identifier in 1870 but had become so by 1914.[74] A review of cocoa ads to this point suggests that the cap was more prevalent in group ads, where a mix of social groups is intended, than in single figure ads.

Cadbury ads continued promoting health and strength through the idealized worker. Illustrations are artfully framed, further removing the picture from reality[75] (Figures 18 and 19). Cadbury also used nationalism as a theme—similar to cigarette ads in 1900-1901 with "England, my England!"[76] The worker is cause for patriotism because Cadbury employs "thousands of British workpeople." The "C" of Cadbury enveloping the British Isles furthers the idea of identification with Britain; thus a national product. Rowntree states that "The People have given their 'vote' and 'support' to Rowntree's."[77] Political behavior can be sublimated in a social and economic message. The call to the growing wave of popularity, in a classless sense, is seen in a Rowntree ad— "Remarkable Popularity" is illustrated by a bar graph depicting the dramatic sales growth of Rowntree's Elect Cocoa from 1890 to 1906.[78] Numbers are important to advertisers and to those measuring profit.

The worker, as visual symbol, continued to dominate Vi-Cocoa ads. "Our Working Friends" and "All Workers Drink" proclaims a 1906 text[79] (Figure 20). The copy explains that "almost all classes of the working population" support cocoa. The specific occupational ads were no longer necessary. The image of worker and strength was now central. The hammer grew from resting on shoulder[80] (Figure 21) to a force that literally grew from the cup.[81] (Figure 22) The worker and cocoa were unified as one in a merged symbol of strength. "This worker," replaced by the tool/technology, is no longer a person or a class; product now embodies the qualities of a person. The worker has also been replaced by the tool/technology.

Additional notions emerged in still later ads. Cadbury led with a "Genuine high-class beverage" while later stating it was made under ideal conditions of labor in an English factory.[82] New benefits, a layering so evident in other product advertising (such as clothing), were added by Vi-Cocoa in 1908 with the text—"The Man Who Always Wins . . . Plumpness, happiness, and health."[83] The reference to body size characterized lower classes as thin compared to upper class plumpness. Another tactic in an 1908 ad header included "The Man Who found IT."[84] He testifies to the healthiness of the product. The testimonial had returned without any occupational identification. A full text ad in 1909 uses the banner "Hold Your Place"[85] to connect Vi-Cocoa with monetary success in a world of competition. In this case, the emphasis is on brain fatigue benefits without reference to physical labor. Mental work had been linked with physical labor in the cocoa "Bank of England" ad presented earlier (Figure 15).

Figure 1.21

Figure 1.22

"Workers," as a group, and "Public" themes continued in 1909 with the claim "Everyday crowds of busy pilgrims in Search of Daily Bread set about to traverse the country called Life."[86] "Modern Life" is captured in the header "Nervous Breakdown,"[87] where the "high pressure at which mental life is maintained contributes to [breakdowns'] prevalence." "All from the Public" without reference to occupation is a testimonial in 1911.[88]

Cocoa ads progressed from specific to general. Trades melded with others to form the "worker." Worker, as symbol of health and strength, eventually became the symbol of benefits beyond these basic values. Blue and white collar merged to form the "public." Concerns no longer focus on occupations or even on group identity as in the later ads. Personal concerns of getting ahead suggest a shift to individualist thinking. A person joined a mass (Hobsbawm's single class), while at the same time becoming isolated by focusing on self. This new image portrayed in the ads is in stark contrast to Keir Hardie's view of the worker as an independent person, as in his term the "Collier Man."[89]

Cultural agency directed by economic motives presented information in a variety of commercial categories. The conventionally encoded statements paralleled the tendency to define audience in larger numbers. Occupation became class and progressed to "public." Aspirations for social mobility exploited or promoted a vicarious mobility produced by consumer goods which could substitute for actual changes in occupation or income.

"Reader beware" should have emblazoned the masthead of the new newspapers that targeted an expanding readership to embrace the lower-middle and working classes. Whether the publications were profit-centered ventures such as the *Daily Mail* and *Daily Express* or leftist- or socialist-leaning papers such as the *Daily Herald* and *Labour Leader*, ads such as those generated by cocoa manufacturers enticed readers with images and associations that were layered in ways that had the potential to strip the readers of their identities. Images of class were transformed from group identity with political potential to symbolic signs used to sell a commodity. Trade and class associations gave way to a new mass identity of a "public" persona numbering in the millions, yet isolated as individuals.

Consumption of cocoa either in drink or advertising image included the ingestion of a new mentality: Cocoa became a libation with potentially brain-numbing powers.

Notes

1. Eric Hobsbawm, "The Forward March of Labour Halted?" in *The Forward March of Labour Halted?* ed. Martin Jacques and Francis Mulhern (London: NLB, 1981).

2. Waverley Root, *Food* (New York: Simon and Schuster, 1980), 72.

3. Thomas Richards, *The Commodity Culture of Victorian England: Advertising and Spectacle, 1851–1914* (Stanford, Calif: Stanford University Press, 1990), 2.

4. Richard Wightman Fox and T. J. Jackson Lears, eds., *The Culture of Consumption: Critical Essays in American History, 1880–1980* (New York: Pantheon Books, 1983), 4.

5. Gareth Stedman Jones, *Languages of Class: Studies in English Working Class History, 1832–1982* (New York: Cambridge University Press, 1983); Peter N. Stearns, "Efforts at Continuity in Working-Class Culture," *Journal of Modern History* 52 (December 1980): 626–655; and E. P. Thompson, *The Making of the English Working Class* (New York: Pantheon Books, 1963).

6. Raymond Williams, *Culture and Society* (New York: Harper and Row, 1958), 280.

7. Eric Hobsbawm, *Workers: Worlds of Labor* (New York: Pantheon Books, 1984), 194.

8. Hobsbawm, *Workers*, 197.

9. The size and rapid increase in readership of the *Daily Mail* (London) may be contrasted with the circulation figures for the elite-focused *Times* (London) and the *Daily Express* (London)–a new, modern-style paper aimed at the middle class. Estimated circulation figures:

1907:	*Times*	45,000
	Daily Mail	500,000
1914:	*Daily Mail*	1,000,000
	Daily Express	250,000

10. The advertising tax was repealed in 1853 and the general stamp tax on newspapers in 1855. These taxes were criticized as attempts to restrict access to information by the lower classes. For specifics on the debate over the taxes see: Joel Wiener, *The War of the Unstamped: The Movement to Repeal the British Newspapers Tax*, (Ithaca, N.Y.: Cornell University Press, 1969).

11. Alan J. Lee, *The Origins of the Popular Press, 1855–1914* (Totowa, N.J.: Rowman & Littlefield, 1978) and Joel Weiner, ed., *Papers for the Millions: The New Journalism in Britain, 1850s to 1914* (New York: Greenwood Press, 1988).

12. Lee, *Origins of the Popular Press*. For forerunners of the popular press, see Patricia Hollis, *The Pauper Press* (London: Oxford University Press, 1970).

13. Harold Herd, *The Making of Modern Journalism* (London: G. Allen & Unwin Ltd., 1927), 59.

14. Geoffrey Crossick, ed., *The Lower Middle Class in Britain, 1870–1914* (New York: Croon Helm Ltd., 1977), 34 and 95–96.

15. Thomas Richards, *The Commodity Culture of Victorian England: Advertising and Spectacle, 1851–1914* (Stanford, Calif.: Stanford University Press, 1990).

16. Raymond Williams, *Problems in Materialism and Culture* (London: NLB, 1980), 177.

17. Williams, *Problems in Materialism*, 177.

18. Williams, *Problems in Materialism*, 177–78, 184 and 187ff.

19. Eugen Weber, *Peasants into Frenchmen* (Stanford, Calif.: Stanford University Press, 1976).

20. Jacques Ellul, *Propaganda: The Formation of Men's Attitudes* (New York: Vintage Books, 1965), 74.

21. Ellul, *Propaganda*, 74.

22. Display is characterized by deviations from standard newsprint in typeface size or style, use of white space, and increasing emphasis on illustrations rather than text.

23. Frank Presbrey, *The History and Development of Advertising* (Garden City, N.Y.: Doubleday, 1929); Henry Sampson, *A History of Advertising from the Earliest of Times* (London: Chatto and Windus, 1874) and Blanche B. Elliot, *A History of English Advertising* (London: Business Publications Limited, 1962).

24. E. H. Gombrich, *Art and Illusion* (New York: Pantheon Books, 1961), 7–9, 29, 47, 87, 129–31, and 138; and John Berger, *Ways of Seeing* (New York: Viking Press, 1972), 139.

25. Robert Collison, *The Story of Street Literature: Forerunner of the Popular Press* (London: Longman, 1973), 12–13.

26. Karl Klaufe, "Symbolism in Advertising," *The Poster* (January 1899): 9.

27. Judith Williamson, *Decoding Advertisements* (London: Boyars, 1978), 11–12 and 17ff.

28. John Berger, *Ways of Seeing* (New York: Viking Press, 1972), 86ff; and Williamson, *Decoding Advertisements*, 12.

29. Varda Langholz Leymore, *Hidden Myth* (New York: Heinemann, 1975), 34–37.

30. Richards, *The Commodity Culture of Victorian England*, 3.

31. Berger, *Ways of Seeing*.

32. Patrick Joyce, *Visions of the People: Industrial England and the Question of Class 1848–1914* (Cambridge, U.K.: Cambridge University Press, 1991), chapter 6.

33. Ellul, *Propaganda*, x.

34. Susan G. Josephson, *From Idolaltry to Advertising: Visual Art and Contemporary Culture* (Armonk, N.Y.: M. E. Sharpe, 1996), 3ff.

35. Marcia and Frederic Morton, *Chocolate: An Illustrated History* (New York: Crown Publishers, Inc., 1986), 47.

36. J. Othick, "The Cocoa and Chocolate Industry in the Nineteenth Century," in *The Making of the Modern British Diet*, ed. Derek J. Oddy and Derek S. Miller (Totowa, N.J.: Rowman and Littlefield, 1976), 83.

37. Morton, *Chocolate*, 47.

38. Othick, "The Cocoa and Chocolate Industry in the Nineteenth Century," 19 and 82.

39. Keir Hardie was one of the first members of the working class elected to Parliament—in 1892. As a Scottish socialist he served as the founding chair of the Independent Labour Party, a forerunner of the Labour Party. He began the *Labour Leader* in 1893 and continued with active involvement with that weekly until 1904. Fred Reid, *Keir Hardie: The Making of a Socialist* (London: Croon Helm, 1978); and Iain McLean, *Keir Hardie* (New York: St. Martin's Press, 1975).

40. B. Seebohm Rowntree, *Poverty: A Study of Town Life* (London: Thomas Nelson & Sons, 1913), 263ff, 285, and 297–99.

41. Othick, "The Cocoa and Chocolate Industry in the Nineteenth Century," 77–90.

42. Asa Briggs, *Social Thought and Social Action: A Study of the Work of Seebohm Rowntree, 1871–1954* (London: Longman, 1961); Anne Vernon, *A Quaker Business Man: The Life of Joseph Rowntree, 1836–1925* (London: Allen & Unwin, 1958); and Iolo A. Williams, *The Firm of Cadbury* (London: Constable and Co. Ltd., 1931).

43. *Daily Mail* (London), 2 February 1900.

44. *Labour Leader* (London), 2 July 1898.

45. *Labour Leader*, 17 June 1899.

46. *Daily Mail*, 8 January 1900.

47. *Daily Express*, 29 August 1900, 21 May 1901, and 28 November 1901.

48. *Daily Mail*, 6 January 1900.

49. *Daily Mail*, 20 January 1900.

50. John Tagg, *The Burden of Representation* (Minneapolis: University of Minnesota Press, 1993), chapter 1.

51. *Daily Mail*, 5 January 1900 and 5 February 1900; and *Labour Leader* 15 December 1900.

52. *Daily Mail*, 12 January 1900.

53. *Daily Express*, 26 September 1900, 16 March 1901, 29 May 1901, and 24 September 1901; and *Labour Leader*, 18 May 1901 and 7 February 1903.

54. Erving Goffman, *Gender Advertisements* (Cambridge, Mass.: Harvard University Press, 1979), 40ff.

55. *Daily Mail* and *Daily Express*: Gentleman's hairdresser, tailor, shop assistant, clothier assistant, grocer's assistant, accountant, compositor. *Labour Leader* figures common with dailies were: miner, postman, wire fencer, porter.

56. Railroad workers had increased from fewer than 100,000 in 1870 to 400,000 by 1911. Hobsbawm, *Workers,* 187.

57. *Labour Leader,* 26 January 1901.

58. Joyce, *Visions of the People,* 168–69.

59. *Daily Mail,* 15 January 1902.

60. *Daily Express,* 23 December 1901.

61. T. J. Jackson Lears, "From Salvation to Self-Realization: Advertising and the Therapeutic Roots of the Consumer Culture, 1880–1930," in *The Culture of Consumption: Critical Essays in American History, 1880–1980,* ed. Richard Wightman Fox and T. J. Jackson Lears (New York: Pantheon Books, 1983), 1–38.

62. Othick, "The Cocoa and Chocolate Industry in the Nineteenth Century," 81, 85, and 87.

63. David Vincent, *Literacy and Popular Culture: England 1870–1914* (New York: Cambridge University Press, 1989), 166ff.

64. *Daily Mail,* 2 January 1904.

65. *Daily Mail,* 22 January 1903.

66. *Labour Leader,* 16 January 1904.

67. *Labour Leader,* 18 November 1904.

68. *Labour Leader,* 30 January 1904.

69. *Labour Leader,* 19 March 1904, 9 April 1904, and 26 May 1905.

70. *Labour Leader,* 28 October 1904.

71. *Labour Leader,* 28 April 1905.

72. *Labour Leader,* 13 October 1905.

73. *Labour Leader,* 27 October 1905.

74. Hobsbawm, *Workers,* 194 and 199. Joyce's selection of photographs to distinguish between "Faces of Poverty," "Faces of Respectability," and an image of "roughness" relies on clothing more than facial features. Joyce, *Visions of the People,* 152–54.

75. *Labour Leader,* 10 November 1905 and 8 December 1905.

76. *Labour Leader,* 9 December 1905.

77. *Labour Leader,* 9 February 1906.

78. *Labour Leader,* 5 October 1906.

79. *Labour Leader,* 2 March 1906.

80. *Labour Leader,* 16 March 1906.

81. *Labour Leader,* 30 March 1906.

82. *Labour Leader,* 9 November 1906.

83. *Labour Leader,* 12 June 1908.

84. *Labour Leader,* 4 September 1908.

85. *Labour Leader,* 12 February 1909.

86. *Labour Leader,* 9 July 1909.

87. *Labour Leader,* 1 July 1910.

88. *Labour Leader,* 27 January 1911.

89. Joyce, *Visions of the People,* 77 and 82.

2
Nazi Labor to 1939: From Working-Class Consciousness to the "People's Community"

Douglas A. Lea

From its inception, one of the main goals of the National Socialist German Worker's Party was to win over those workers. The workers constituted not only the largest class in Germany, but also a group prone to antiauthoritarian politics. Hitler believed that national unity was a prerequisite for German expansion, and he was determined to win the workers away from Marxist Socialism and for nationalism. Before 1933, despite Nazi efforts in their "urban plan" to attract labor, the majority of the working classes had remained loyal to the moderate Social Democratic Party (SPD). More radical workers tended to support the German Communist Party rather than the Nazis. The attempt to establish an alternative Nazi trade union, the National Socialist Factory Cell Organization (NSBO), had little success in gaining adherents among the vast majority of workers. While up to twenty percent of the membership of the Nazi Party were workers, these tended to be employees of small firms or the government, not part of the organized labor movement.[1] After seizing power, therefore, a basic aim of the Nazis was to eliminate independent, and potentially hostile, labor organizations and to gain the workers' support for the new National Socialist order.

Establishing institutional control over labor was only part of this policy. The Nazis sought also to instill in the workers an acceptance of the new regime. Former class identities and distinctions were to be subsumed by the new "People's Community" idea and workers and employers were to be seen as equal members of the

"Factory Community," contributing to the national revival of Germany. The support of labor for the new order was to be achieved not only by providing work and benefits, but by stressing the egalitarian and communal aspects of the new state. Thus, as a Nazi party official declared, the "demands for liberty, equality, and fraternity, with which the German worker was betrayed by liberal-Marxist demagogues (will) become reality thanks to National Socialism."[2] Supplementing these "socialist" notions, the government promoted a labor ideology portraying work at all levels as a noble and honorable activity, and a true service to the "People's Community." Nazi propaganda made great use of verbal and visual symbolism to advance these ideas. Along with this, the activities of the Reich's Labor Service and the German Labor Front, with its two related organizations, the Beauty of Labor and Strength through Joy, sought through financial and nonfinancial inducements to encourage working-class support for the National Socialist state.

Shortly after Hitler was appointed Chancellor in January 1933, the Nazis began to put into effect the policy of *Gleichschaltung,* or coordination, in which all social and political institutions in Germany were to come under the control of the new state. A significant part of this policy was the "coordination" of labor. Radical workers lost representation with the destruction of the German Communist Party after the Reichstag fire in February. The next step was to neutralize the moderate Social Democratic Party, the staunchest opponent left against the Nazis. Since the SPD's remaining strength was in the free trade unions, it was a logical move for the Nazis to dissolve the unions. At the same time, German business leaders were becoming concerned with the radicalism of the NSBO which was striving now more than ever to win the support of the workers. NSBO leaders saw Hitler's appointment in January as the beginning of a revolutionary reordering of German society, with the their organization leading the way to improved rights and conditions for workers in the new National Socialist state. Nazi leaders were increasingly concerned that the activities of the NSBO would alienate German business. But they could not ignore the interests of the workers.[3]

On May 2, Nazi detachments occupied and closed all free trade union offices, confiscated their funds and arrested their leaders. Four days later, the German Labor Front (DAF) was founded, headed by Dr. Robert Ley. Its purpose was to provide for workers a substitute for the closed trade unions. For German business, the DAF was to be the first step in neutralizing the NSBO. By the end of 1933, the NSBO was purged of its radical members and placed under the complete organizational control of the Labor Front. Along with the closing of the unions, the right of collective bargaining was abolished on May 19, and government officials were to settle labor disputes and determine labor contracts thereafter. The SPD was then banned officially on June 22. Throughout May and June, workers' clubs and cooperatives were either closed or "coordinated" under Nazi control. Units of the SA, SS, Gestapo, and regular police conducted systematic raids in working class residential districts, confiscating communist and socialist literature, antifascist leaflets, printing presses, club files and funds, personal weapons, and anything which could potentially aid subversive labor activity. These raids, together with numerous threats, beatings, and arbitrary arrests, created an atmosphere of terror and insecurity in working-class strongholds, weakening labor solidarity and making underground resistance extremely difficult.[4]

To calm fears over the new regime's repressive actions, the DAF organized mass meetings of workers in which they were assured that their rights and interests would be preserved. A propaganda campaign was launched on the eve of the union closings when, in a wonderful example of National Socialist irony, the government sponsored May Day festivities, transforming the traditionally Socialist holiday into an official day of national celebration. After the destruction of the trade unions, Dr. Ley issued a proclamation in which he emphasized the need to integrate the workers into the new order:

> Today we are opening the second chapter of the National Socialist revolution. True, we have power, but we do not yet have the whole nation, we do not have you workers 100 per cent; and it is you whom we want. We will not let you alone until you give us your entire and genuine support. You too shall be freed from the last Marxist manacles, so that you may find your way to your people. For we know that without the German worker there is no German nation. . . . Workers, I swear to you we shall not only preserve everything which exists, we shall build up even further the protection of the worker's rights, so that he can enter the new National Socialist State as a completely worthwhile and respected member of the nation.[5]

Like that of so many organizations in Nazi Germany, the role and function of the Labor Front were not well-defined. Although it replaced the trade unions, and membership in it was virtually compulsory for most workers, it was to have no significant role in labor relations or the formation of economic and social policy. Dr. Ley never fully accepted these limitations, attempting often to expand the formal powers of the Labor Front, but the official Reich Ministries of Labor and Economics, and individual economic advisors like Wilhelm Keppler, were successful in counseling Hitler against this, arguing that the DAF was not competent to handle such authority. Business leaders were concerned also that the Labor Front, backed by the power of the new state, might be an even stronger representative of the workers than the old trade unions. Keeping its powers limited was one way of reassuring German business. But the Nazis also took action to broaden the DAF's membership by incorporating both workers and enterprise owners into the organization. It was now to represent equally all working people regardless of class and skill level, and both employers and employees. As such, its role was largely propagandistic and it was to be a symbol of the "People's Community," helping to educate all working Germans "to support the National Socialist State and to indoctrinate them in the National Socialist mentality."[6]

The Labor Front was a direct branch of the Nazi Party with corresponding national and regional organizations. It was structured also according to separate branches of industry, commerce, and trade. The DAF was one of the largest institutions in Germany, with 20 million dues-paying members, giving it an annual income three times larger than that of the Nazi Party itself. It came to possess a large business empire which included banks, housing associations, insurance companies, and the Volkswagen automobile factory. Despite the Front's limited formal powers, its 45,000 officials, with Dr. Ley's prompting, saw themselves as the Party's representatives and used their position to apply a not insignificant amount of pressure on employers and employees whom they regarded as uncooperative or subversive.[7] The chief influence of the Labor Front, however, came from the activities of its two subsidiary organizations, the Beauty of Labor and Strength through Joy, which attempted to promote worker support for the Third Reich (these organizations will be discussed later).

On January 20, 1934 the Law for the Ordering of National Labor was introduced. It became the basic law governing work and labor relations in the Nazi state. Party functionaries and DAF officials had no direct hand in formulating the Law. It was drawn up by officials of the Ministry of Labor and Ministry of Economics and provided significantly stronger powers to the government and employers in controlling labor relations. The Law transferred ultimate authority over labor relations to state officials, the Reich Trustees of Labor. There were twelve of these, each covering a separate region, and they were subordinate to Franz Seldte, the Reich Minister of Labor. Under the control of these Trustees emerged a new system of labor relations based on the concept of the "Factory Community," formed by the "plant leader" (employer) and his "plant followers" (employees). This "Factory Community" represented a new "quasi-feudal relationship" between leaders and followers based on mutual obligations, and replaced the old system of labor relations based on legally binding contracts collectively negotiated between employers' organizations and trade unions.[8]

In theory, the "Factory Community" was to end conflict between employer and employee by creating an atmosphere of mutual trust and cooperation based on common goals and values in aid of the new National Socialist order. In practice, it strengthened employers' powers over workers immensely. As "plant leaders," individual employers were given wider authority over the workers in their factory to implement government directives and fulfill the state's economic and rearmament goals. The Works Councils which had represented unionized workers' interests in the former Weimar Republic were replaced with new "Councils of Trust," whose members were chosen by employees from a list compiled by the employer. The powers of these Councils were limited almost exclusively to consultative functions, and they met under the chairmanship of the "plant leader." The only substantive power possessed by the Councils was that of direct appeal to the region's Reich Trustee of Labor against employer abuses. Such appeals were rare, however, given the obvious difficulty of overcoming opposition to such appeals by the employer/chairman. From 1936, these already weak Councils were made virtually obsolete by the government's continual "postponement" of new elections to them. The regime was alarmed by the increasing tendency of workers to use the elections to express dissatisfaction with the Councils through absenteeism and block "No" votes for the approved list of candidates.[9]

The only other source of representation for workers were the so-called Courts of Honor, which replaced the former Labor Courts of Weimar. These courts were based on the Nazi concept of a "social honor" code which was to be followed in the "Factory Community" by both employers and employees. The Courts of Honor dealt with breaches of the "social honor" code, such as misuse of a plant leader's power, overt exploitation of labor, injuring the honor a plant member, disturbing the peace of the plant, inciting followers against the plant leader, and so on.[10] In practice, these courts, which were under the supervision of the Reich Trustee of Labor, dealt with only the most obvious cases of abuse of power by employers (like physical mistreatment of employees, for instance). Out of a labor force of over twenty million only a little over five hundred cases were heard between 1934 and 1936, and of these only just over three hundred ended with a definite penalty.[11]

Denied real trade union representation and the right to true legal redress, German workers were brought under the institutional control of the National Socialist state and were even more under the power of the employers. Without any institution or organization to articulate and represent their interests collectively, workers in Nazi Germany had to act individually to attempt to win any improvements in their wages and working conditions. They continued to represent a class in sociological terms, but workers were encouraged or forced to act and increasingly to see themselves in individualistic or other non-class collective terms, such as members of a particular branch of industry or individual "Factory Community."[12]

This predicament was reinforced by other developments. Faced with the need to increase workers' productivity without raising wages (which would have cut into money for rearmament), the state encouraged the movement from industry-wide wage agreements to those for individual "Factory Communities." Along with this, the move from hourly wages to piece-work rates based on individual performance was promoted. Both trends placed wage decisions more in the hands of employers and encouraged a breakdown in workers' solidarity both across industry and within each factory, as individual workers sought to improve their position relative to that of their workmates. A report of the German Social Democratic Party in Exile (SOPADE) from November 1935 indicates the early success the Nazis had in undermining the traditional collective solidarity among workers. SOPADE saw the economic crisis of the depression working to the advantage of the new regime because it "induced the worker to place a low value on negotiated wage agreements—the most precious achievement of collective action—and to seek work at any price." The Nazis had:

> reduced the worker to the point that he often goes to the boss on his own to try to avert a deterioration in wages, especially over piece rates, and gets a concession out of the boss on the condition that he tells his workmates nothing about it. One often has the impression, particularly with young workers, that the idea no

longer even occurs to them that their demands might carry more weight if backed by collective action—even if only on the smallest scale.[13]

Rewards based on individual achievement served to keep overall labor costs low while increasing worker productivity. This policy was strengthened by the "self-inspector" and "self-calculator" schemes developed in many industries. Self-inspectors were particularly reliable workers who were given the honor of being exempted from supervisory inspection. Self-calculators were particularly fast workers who were given the right to fix their own piece-rates. While giving these individuals some independence and the ability to earn more money, the scheme was promoted at the expense of other workers, since management tended to adjust overall piece-rates to the productivity of the self-calculators.[14] These schemes were meant also to cut the costs involved in employing foremen and supervisors. The workers' sense of solidarity was undermined also by the tendency to replace wage increases with substitutes like holiday bonuses, increased sick pay, and other benefits based on length and quality of service. These measures increased the workers' sense of dependence on the "Factory Community" and encouraged them to view such benefits as gifts from the "plant leader" as a reward for loyalty, rather than as gains won through collective worker action and negotiation.[15] Many workers were prepared to give up class solidarity in exchange for these rewards.

By the time economic conditions favored the reemergence of collective action, workers were in no position to pursue it. By 1936–37, the regime's public works and rearmament programs created so many jobs that demand for labor (particularly skilled labor) exceeded supply by half a million.[16] Many workers took advantage of their improved position in the labor market to gain better wages, conditions and mobility. Recorded cases of go-slows and absenteeism increased. The number of workers giving notice rose also and labor turnover increased particularly in the armaments industries. Nazi authorities attempted to inhibit these developments through administrative restrictions on mobility and threats of penalties. But these measures were rarely effective due to the armaments firms' rapacious demand for labor. Despite these favorable conditions, workers could not pursue their interests collectively since trade union representation was nonexistent. Instead, what gains were achieved came as a result of individual or small group bargaining. That improvements in the material position of skilled workers were won during the rearmament boom period is clear. But the very success of the workers' "individualist guerrilla warfare" had the effect of reducing further the possibilities of collective action and class solidarity.[17]

Moreover, the Nazi fusion of social and racial policy, in the form of "social racism," had a profound impact on labor. In the interest of "race hygiene" and the promotion of a healthy Aryan race, the Nazis pursued the separation of races and the elimination of genetically inferior individuals from the German gene pool. Workers whose good behavior and job performance showed the Nazis that they possessed "biological value" could expect improved housing and working conditions, and were encouraged to have children to expand these traits in the collective racial body. But the Nazis intended also to eliminate the biologically inferior from the workforce since their presence threatened the Aryan race's ability to dominate the international struggle for survival against the world's other races. This stress on "social racism" put tremendous pressure on workers to conform to the required standards of productivity and labor discipline. Breaches of these standards, from poor performance to absenteeism, were now read as symptoms of biological deficiency requiring punishment and possibly reeducation in a labor camp. Failure to change one's ways could result in being branded a "community alien" or "antisocial element" and require segregation from the healthy body of the racial community. Workers were well aware of the possibility of such action being taken against them by the Gestapo. It is fair to argue that the persecution of German workers through "social racism" was virtually as great a danger as persecution for political opposition to the new order.[18]

The institutional controls and coercive policies of the Nazi state help explain to some extent the acquiescence of the majority of workers to the new regime. But a number of more positive inducements were offered by the Nazis. Hitler believed that it was not enough to control and neutralize labor to serve Nazi goals. The loyalty and support of the workers had to be sought and their integration into the new order became a high priority. Of course, the primary means for winning the support of labor was providing jobs. With at least one-third of the workforce unemployed when the Nazis came to power, creating secure employment was a powerful means to gaining greater acceptance from labor. The full employment of the late 1930s was perhaps the most important factor in attracting worker acceptance of the Nazis. As one contemporary Social Democrat pointed out, "They had four, five, even six years of unemployment behind them—they would have hired on to Satan himself."[19]

Despite secure jobs, however, most workers were far from financial prosperity. Overall, real incomes declined throughout the 1930s due to the government's attempt to pay for rearmament through wage freezes and higher taxes, along with higher prices for increasingly scarce food and clothing due to the national autarky program, despite the declining quality of these commodities. Compulsory membership dues to the Party, the Labor Front, and social insurance schemes also took a bite out of a worker's wages. To survive, longer hours were necessary and increasingly required by the state to fill production quotas. Some workers were able to raise their standard of living by acquiring skills and working in the key industries like armaments, building construction, and mechanical instruments. But most laborers faced material hardship despite their steady employment.

The Nazi regime could not raise wages significantly and hope to pay for rearmament, so the Labor Front was early on given the task of developing alternative inducements to placate the workers. Dr. Ley suggested a series of reforms to begin the process of creating a sense among the workers that they were indeed part of a

new, egalitarian "Factory Community." Ley was convinced that all forms of symbolic interaction between members of the community should express this new
egalitarianism. In his earliest public appearances as leader of the DAF, he made it
a point to walk up to individual workers, talk to them personally, and give them his
hand as a "simple hand-shake of two men," a demonstration of respect between
equals. The hierarchical distance between him, as leader, and the workers was to
be seen as having been overcome.[20] Many symbolic distinctions between blue-
and white-collar employees were to be removed. Attempts were made to end the
different customary forms of address for employees; *"Sie"* for white-collar workers and the less respectful *"Du"* for blue-collar workers. To end the practice of
only blue-collar workers punching a time clock, Ley introduced a mandatory morning rally, or *Betriebsappell*, for all employees as a joint plant ceremony to start the
work day. Neither of these reforms were popular or took hold, but they were less
absurd than some of Ley's other suggestions. His "plant family scheme," in which
a plant leader plus one white-collar and one blue-collar plant follower shared a
week together at a DAF holiday home, and his idea for plant-organized beer and
sausage evenings in which everyone addressed each other as *"Du,"* were very unpopular and probably caused more discomfort and embarrassment for the participants than anything else. Moreover, distinctions persisted between white- and blue-
collar workers over such important issues as job security, seniority status, and
pension and insurance benefits.[21]

More successful were two new organizations introduced by Dr. Ley in November 1933: the Beauty of Labor and Strength through Joy. The Beauty of Labor
encouraged employers and employees in the "Factory Community" to create a
more pleasing work environment. Clean washing and changing facilities, canteens
with hot meals, good lighting, ventilation, music, and greenery were to be introduced into the factory setting. Sports facilities, like soccer fields and pools, were
built also. The cost of all of this was borne by both the employers and the state,
with employees providing most of the labor for free. Improvements in working
conditions were certainly made through these Beauty of Labor activities.

Strength through Joy (KdF) sought to organize the leisure time of the labor
force to build support for the new regime. It was funded initially from confiscated
trade union assets, and later supported by dues paid to the Labor Front. Membership was not compulsory, but it was strongly encouraged, particularly through the
financial lure of inexpensive activities offered only to members. KdF was a classic
example of a totalitarian state's determination to influence all aspects of the lives
of its citizens, including their spare time when they are neither working nor sleep-
ing. Dr. Ley wrote, "There are no more private citizens. The time when anybody
could do or not do what he pleased is past."[22] Patterned after Mussolini's
"Dopolavoro" organization in Fascist Italy, Strength through Joy arranged cultural
activities, adult evening classes, sporting and gymnastics events, guided outdoor
hikes and bicycle tours, and, perhaps most important, inexpensive vacations and

package tours within Germany as well as abroad (made increasingly possible since the government extended the number of annual paid vacation days from three to between six and twelve, depending on the sector of the economy, by 1939).[23]

The motives behind Strength through Joy activities were much deeper than a simple desire on the part of the Nazis to entertain and keep occupied the German worker. Sports were seen as a means for producing both physical health and a healthy mental attitude. A KdF sports office was organized in 1934, under Anatol von Hubbenet, to convince workers of the benefits of exercise and make sports available to the broad masses. Instruction and facilities for swimming, skiing and gymnastics for younger people, and golf and bicycling for older people, were provided at relatively moderate cost to KdF members. Strength through Joy emphasized also sports in the factories, believing that they would improve worker alertness and prevent industrial accidents. KdF promoted the use of the factory sports facilities provided by the Beauty of Labor and encouraged plant directors to require workers to engage in some form of exercise at least a few hours every week. Physical proficiency tests were to be required also at regular intervals to educate workers to view excellence on the job as a product of both mental and physical efficiency.[24] The National Socialist order regarded personal fitness not as an individual concern but a duty to the collective, a notion embodied in the slogan, "Your health does not belong to you!" Inter-factory sports competitions were organized as well to instill a greater sense of loyalty to the individual "plant community."[25]

Along with sports, providing other fulfilling leisure pursuits was seen as promoting relaxation and producing a reinvigorated and efficient laborer in the workplace. Gerhard Starcke, the press officer of the Labor Front, stated, "We do not send our workers on vacation on our own ships or build them massive bathing facilities at the sea for fun, either for ourselves or for the individual who has the chance to make use of them. We do it only because we are interested in preserving the working capacity (*Arbeitskraft*) of the individual and in order to send him back to work strengthened and refreshed."[26]

The organization's activities contained also a heavy emphasis on egalitarianism and membership in the national "People's Community." Now ordinary citizens could participate in luxury pursuits formerly reserved for the wealthy like vacations abroad on Strength through Joy-owned cruise ships. A "KdF Fleet" of some twelve vessels, including the two new 25,000-ton ships *Wilhelm Gustloff* and *Robert Ley*, carried members to such destinations as the Norwegian fjords, Copenhagen, the Canary Islands, the Azores, Portugal, Gibraltar, Tripoli, Italy, and Greece. Significantly, all passengers as well as the crew were to share equal accommodation and all ship facilities, as befitted any activity sponsored by the new National Socialist state. The *Wilhelm Gustloff* and *Robert Ley* were designed specifically as "classless" ships, with standard cabins, large halls, a banquet room, theater, sports hall, and conservatory shared by all KdF members without differentiation.[27] Dr. Ley took every opportunity to emphasize the benefits of these cruises and the new esteem with which German workers were now held in Nazi society.

"The worker sees that we are serious about raising his social position. He sees that it is not the so-called 'educated classes' whom we send out as representatives of the new Germany, but himself, the German worker, whom we show to the world."[28]

Travel excursions within Germany were sponsored also by the KdF and were seen as a way to overcome the traditional particularism, or localism, of Germans and give them a better sense of their national identity and their membership in the "People's Community." Farmers were brought to cities to sightsee and visit workers in factories, while urban citizens were encouraged to visit the rural regions. Economic benefits for rural hotelkeepers and the state railways motivated the Nazis to promote KdF travel activities as well.[29] A typical example of a weekend trip sponsored by the KdF was an excursion from the town of Muenster to rural Nettelstedt in July 1934. A special "KdF train" was chartered and the trip was heavily publicized in the Muenster press, stressing the "strength" one could obtain for the coming working week if one spent Sunday in this relaxing fashion. The day's activities included hiking, a theatrical play, and an arranged fellowship luncheon meeting with the local inhabitants. The inclusive price of the trip was a moderate 3.20 marks for KdF members, which made this and other similar excursions very affordable to the average German worker.[30]

Workers were even provided with the possibility of owning their own automobile when the first Volkswagen factory was set up near Fallersleben under Strength through Joy auspices in May 1938. An inexpensive "people's car" was to be made available to the masses to remove the automobile's former "class character" as an elite status symbol. Hitler participated personally in the ground-breaking ceremonies at the factory and the new automobile was called the "KdF Wagen" in honor of the organization's role in providing this new transportation opportunity for the masses. A savings scheme, in which some 360,000 people paid weekly contributions to the DAF, was developed by KdF planners to make the car easier to purchase. Production began in early 1939, but sales to civilians never took place due to the outbreak of World War II in September. The "people's car" was instead modified and used as an all-purpose military vehicle during the war.[31]

Cultural and educational activities, formerly dominated by the upper classes, were also now opened to the masses. The KdF "leisure office" arranged inexpensive concerts, plays, operas, cabaret nights, folk festivals, films, art exhibitions, and museum tours. As members of the new "People's Community," it was important for all citizens to have access to the products of "superior" German culture. The National Socialists argued that workers in the past had been denied exposure to artistic entertainments not only for economic reasons, but due to the previous atmosphere of social exclusiveness surrounding cultural activities.[32] The new social order would end the alienation of workers toward drama and music that presumably existed in Germany. Dr. Ley stated in a speech celebrating Strength through Joy's third anniversary in 1936 that the organization's programs had begun to "arouse and mobilize the intellectual and ethical capabilities inherent in the German workman by enabling him to realize the beauty and grandeur of life in nature, art and the company of those of his fellows who share his own views. In doing so, we have broken with a social convention that had been valid for decades and have removed the antagonism between work and culture."[33] KdF also organized large amateur factory theatrical clubs and choral groups (from the project called "The German Worker Sings Again") to provide workers with an important sense of participation in the new egalitarian culture of the "People's Community." Popular programs providing lessons in public singing were organized as well, and new song books meant to revive interest in traditional German folk music were made available. Art exhibitions were set up in factories and often included original pieces for sale to workers, directly or through an installment plan, at inexpensive prices.[34]

Another emphasis of Strength through Joy programs was adult education. The KdF "popular education" office promoted adult education to again show German workers that they now had greater opportunities for intellectual improvement and career advancement in the "People's Community." The program also created another venue in which the state could indoctrinate the masses in National Socialist principles. The promotion of adult education was also another example of the Nazis attempting to gain totalitarian control over the free time of German citizens. Gerhard Starcke said that the program was designed to "give every person the opportunity to further his education and to organize his leisure time according to his inclinations."[35] Part of this program was the expansion of available library services for the public by KdF. Open access to German Labor Front libraries for KdF members, the construction of new libraries in factories and worker residential districts, and the creation of mobile libraries were all part of this program. To ensure that these libraries served the purpose of indoctrination, their books were chosen in cooperation with "ideological officials" from the Reich Literature Chamber. The KdF's adult education program was promoted more directly by the establishment of three hundred education facilities where workers could enroll easily for courses either at minimal or no cost. These facilities offered academic and technical courses in foreign languages, mathematics, typing and shorthand, graphic arts, applied sciences, and vocational arts. Along with these more traditional educational and career-oriented offerings were courses promoting aspects of Nazi ideology. Examples of such courses are "The Nation's Health," "Racial Biology," and "Race and Heredity," all of which expounded the racial and eugenics theories of the new regime. The desire to indoctrinate Germans is seen even more clearly in some of the titles of the adult education lecture series held in factories: "History of National Socialism," "The Leader's Principles," "National Socialism and Economics," "National Socialism and the Race Problem," and "The Jews and the History of the Peoples of the World."[36]

The success of Strength through Joy activities was mixed. At a KdF convention in Hamburg in 1938, Dr. Ley declared officially, "There are no longer classes in Germany. In the years to come, the worker will lose the last traces of inferiority feelings he may have inherited from the past."[37] But, according to the evidence, the workers tended to be unimpressed with the "People's Community" propaganda. They were, however, very pleased to take advantage of the benefits on offer and were prepared to credit the Nazis with providing these opportunities. Particularly popular were the travel and vacation programs, despite the fact that most could not afford the more expensive cruises on the Baltic and Mediterranean seas. In 1938, 7 million Germans took advantage of the relatively inexpensive shorter excursions, while only 130,000 took overseas cruises.[38] The Volkswagen program was very enthusiastically received, despite the fact that production for home consumers was suspended when the war broke out, and no one received their promised automobile.

Whatever their shortcomings, the activities of the German Labor Front's two organizations, the Beauty of Labor and Strength through Joy, gave Hitler's deputy, Rudolf Hess, some reason to boast about the new advantages gained by German workers:

> It is of much importance that we should assess the social position of the German worker, not on the basis of "an increase in wages or no increase in wages," but from a consideration of what position the workers, the employees or the small tradesmen now hold within the national community. And in this case we need only go through Germany with eyes open to discover that the ordinary citizen can do things in Hitler's Germany which in other countries are open only to a privileged class but never to the workers . . . [39]

If Hess somewhat overstated his argument, the reports of the German Social Democratic Party in Exile, obviously hostile to the Nazi regime, provide a credible analysis of the DAF's real successes. A report from July 1935 assessed the intentions behind Labor Front and other labor policies:

> "Labor" organization is trying to create vast canteens, so that workers can no longer discuss things with their colleagues during breaks. Where it is at all possible, groups of workers are split into the smallest viable units. This means that attempts by workers to discuss even the most elementary matters among themselves take on the character of illegal activities. Outside the factories, the Nazi association "Strength through Joy" attempts to organize their free time, so that they do not get any "stupid ideas". The Labor Front is not only an embarrassing solution, but also a large-scale attempt to prevent the worker from associating with others, whether it be privately or in purely social circles or clubs, without being subject to control. [40]

By the late 1930s, SOPADE was forced to admit that Nazi policies were having some success with German workers. "The experience of recent years has unfortunately demonstrated that the petit-bourgeois inclinations of part of the working class are unfortunately greater than we had earlier recognized."[41] Other reports were more specific. "Strength through Joy is very popular. The events appeal to the yearning of the little man who wants an opportunity to get out and about himself and to take part in the pleasures of the 'top people'." Commenting on the Volkswagen program, a SOPADE report suggested that the enthusiasm which many Germans had for it amounted to a "KdF-Car psychosis" which helped divert attention from domestic problems and material shortages. "This car psychosis, which has been cleverly induced by the Propaganda Ministry, keeps the masses from becoming preoccupied with a depressing situation. Hitler has acquired domestic political credit with the car savers until the delivery of the car. For, it is well-known that, while they are saving up for a particular commodity, people are prepared to make quite a lot of sacrifices."[42]

The Labor Front continued to promote the psychological submersion of the workers first in the "Factory Community" and then in the national "People's Community" as a way to gain their support through non-material means for the Nazi state. A crucial aspect of this was the attempt to persuade workers to regard work not only as a means to provide for themselves materially, but also as a noble activity and an important service to the "People's Community." "Work ennobles" was a characteristic phrase for this policy. Work at all levels and skills was seen as the highest duty in life and perhaps the main reason for one's existence. No distinctions were to be made between manual labor and other forms of work—all were equally noble and a true service to the state. Hitler stated that manual labor "neither pollutes, nor dishonors," and he hoped "to lead everyone at least once in his life to manual labor" to destroy any prejudice against that form of work.[43]

Another organization created to promote Nazi economic and social policies was the Reich's Labor Service. It was in this Service that German males would get that experience with manual labor Hitler wanted for them. The Labor Service was for the Nazis the chief institutional manifestation of their version of "socialism." Formerly a public works organization of the Weimar Republic, the new Labor Service was to be used also to provide employment, as well as a cheap labor source for government projects (particularly land reclamation, crucial to Nazi hopes for agricultural self-sufficiency). All German males between eighteen and twenty-five were required to serve six months in the organization. Another function of the Labor Service was to provide pre-military training. Service members underwent two-and-a-half hours of parade drill every day. Service members also received daily political indoctrination emphasizing the nobility of work, especially manual labor, and their position as important members and promoters of the "People's Community." Since males of all classes had to serve, this was meant to break down traditional social distinctions, and create greater allegiance to a common national identity. [44]

In a speech on May Day 1934, Hitler outlined the motives behind the Labor Service and the Nazi ideological stance on labor:

> We want to destroy the arrogance with which unfortunately so many intellectuals feel that they must look down upon labor, and on the other hand we wish to strengthen their self-confidence through their consciousness that they too can perform manual labor. But beyond this we wish to contribute to the mutual understanding of the different classes in order to reinforce the tie which binds together the community of the people . . . We all know that it is not words or outward professions that lead to the establishment of this community; that needs an inner unlearning, a new education of the people.[45]

Hitler saw the Labor Service as one of the many new organizations of the Nazi state which served as "national and social smelting-furnaces in which gradually a new German man will be formed." He concluded:

> Men have praised and admired artists, architects, and engineers; they have spoken of German science, German handicrafts, German business life, but the working man they have for the most part forgotten . . . The National Socialist State will put an end to this unhappy development . . . Today, on May Day, we meet to celebrate the fame of the army of those millions who, as unknown and nameless Soldiers of Work, in the sweat of their faces, in town and country, in the fields, in the factory and the workshop, cooperate to produce those goods which rightly raise our people into the ranks of the civilized nations of the world and enable it to hold that place of honor.[46]

Recent research has focused on the National Socialist's attempt to appeal also to skilled workers by stressing "German quality work" and the "honor of labor"—two enduring "cultural icons" in German society from the Wilhelmine and Weimar periods. Using rich verbal and visual symbolism in their mass meetings and marches and media propaganda, the Nazis played on the traditional pride manual workers took in efficiency, orderliness, dexterity, toughness, self-discipline, and hard work. The Nazis used the written and spoken word to convey these ideas, but they also employed visual images in film, photographs, and posters, depicting the orderly workplace and laboring bodies interacting with their machines and tools. As David Crew explains, "The Nazi language of labor expressed meanings many German workers attached to their work that the Marxist language of class did not."[47]

Marxist theory stresses the alienation of manual labor under capitalism, and the need to overcome it through a socialist revolution. National Socialism promoted the "honor" of all types of labor within the framework of the existing capitalist system. Hitler stated that, "Spirit, brain and fist, worker, farmer, citizen," all belonged as equally respected members of the "People's Community."[48] In place of socialism, the Nazis promised joy in all work and respect for quality work and efficiency. They promised also a reorganization of society according to a new "hierarchy of merit" in which accomplishment in the workplace, not social background or type of work pursued, was the key to the achievement of high status in the new National Socialist order. If the Nazi regime did not entirely submerge class identities and distinctions with its community rhetoric, it did offer German workers new opportunities and new forms of recognition for their talents and achievements.[49] This is part of the explanation for the acquiescence, if not the full-fledged support, of German labor for the Nazi regime.

The Nazis also promoted productive work as a patriotic duty benefiting Germany in its struggle against other states and peoples. Work was depicted as a "battle of labor" and workers the "soldiers of labor," crucial to the defense of the Fatherland. Manual labor was not just work by hand, but by "fist," and competition promoted among individual workers, work-teams, and even between factories was meant to symbolize the broader "struggle" between Germany and its enemies.[50]

The regime's labor policy was not wholly unique. Its use of material incentives, joined by wage and benefits differentiation, Taylorist discipline, and a stress on the principle of efficiency in the work place, was reflective of the general emphasis on scientific management and rationalization in all industrialized countries since the beginning of the twentieth century. But the Nazis incorporated these ideas into their own concept of a German "efficiency community." Rationalization was at the core of National Socialist labor policy "as its goal and legitimation and, at the same time, as a means of containing the working class." [51]

Of course, the extent to which German Labor supported, or simply acquiesced to, the Nazi regime is probably an impossible question to answer completely. Workers, like all other individuals in Germany, were influenced in their attitudes toward the new government by many different variables: age, geographical location, occupation, political stance, personality and personal experience, all played a role in shaping workers' perceptions. Some workers, especially those in industries connected to the rearmament boom, were materially better off under the Nazis, while those in such fields as consumer production and agriculture were in a worse position. These differences in material position make it difficult to generalize about the workers as a class. Moreover, older workers probably felt very perceptibly the loss of labor rights and freedoms they had possessed before the Nazis came to power. Many of these workers had fought for such rights as collective bargaining, free trade unions, and freedom of movement and vocational choice. But younger workers, whose first experience of working life was unemployment, may well have missed these rights far less, now that they were gainfully employed and had genuine opportunities for advancement. [52]

But one must not forget that labor dissatisfaction did exist and real resistance did occur. Many German workers were discontented with their lack of rights in the workplace, the pressure from the increased hours and regimentation of labor, the incompetence of the appointed Nazi workers' representatives, and the high cost of subscriptions and social welfare contributions which were felt to be financing not only rearmament but also corrupt officials. Open criticism and large-scale resistance was difficult and rare since this would lead inevitably to coercive intervention by the regime. Nonconformist behavior by individuals was much more effective as a form of resistance. Increasing rates of sickness and absenteeism became increasing concerns of employers and suggest the presence of low morale and discontent among many workers. The work of historians such as Tim Mason, Detlev Peukert, and F. L. Carsten has shown also that small-scale strikes, spontaneous work-stoppages, slow-downs, and organized group insubordination did occur which suggests the continuance of class-conscious behavior and collective action by some workers despite Nazi coordination and repression. Catholic workers, as another example, attempted to rebel against the regime's suppression of their church and such policies as the Nazi T–4 euthanasia program.

At the same time, some labor support for the Nazi state could be related to non-class identities and considerations. Workers, like other Germans, could be nationalistic and take pride in the regime's foreign policy successes in the 1930s.

The return of the Saarland to Germany in 1935, the remilitarization of the Rhineland in 1936, and the annexations of Austria and the Sudetenland by 1939—all accomplished without war—could create support for the Nazis from workers. Like other segments of German society, many workers were also racists who supported the regime's racial beliefs and policies. Workers, like other Germans, could be brought also to support the regime due to a personal attachment they felt toward Hitler himself. Many, who may have been ambivalent toward the more radical and extreme ideas and policies of the Nazi party and state, could find in the person of Hitler an individual to whom they could give their allegiance. The "cult of personality" attached to Hitler, constructed by him and Nazi propagandists, portrayed the "Leader" as heroic, charismatic, infallible and messianic. He was depicted also as above the fray of politics and a moderating influence on his more extreme underlings in the Nazi movement. The personal figure of Hitler was, therefore, often exempt from the day-to-day criticisms of the regime because of the high regard so many Germans had for him. Workers were prone to the appeals of this "Hitler Myth" like all other segments of German society.[53]

Recent interpretations have challenged the validity of assumptions held concerning the motivation of German workers. Tilla Siegel states, "To ask whether the behaviour of people indicates their approval or their rejection of the Nazi regime presupposes that people did indeed consciously act according to their attitude towards the regime, that their view of the regime governed their behaviour."[54] She argues that fear of Nazi repression forced many of those German workers who disliked the regime to dissociate themselves from it. Many workers coped with their oppression by not thinking coherently about their attitudes toward the Nazis, and dealing with inner conflicts over their passivity by maintaining attitudes dissociated from the regime. Thus, many workers who stayed at their jobs, produced for the Nazis, and conformed, did not look on this as supporting the regime, but as a way to avoid repression, earn a living, respect law and order, and/or take pride in a job well done.

In the final analysis, although one may never be able to answer fully the question of how much the workers acquiesced to, or supported, the Nazi regime, the combination of state controls and repression, the material attractions of secure work, and the emotional and psychological appeal of the "People's Community" helped to turn German labor into, as Richard Grunberger has termed it, a largely "undifferentiated segment of Nazi society" and, therefore, not a significant threat to the Nazis' existence. [55]

Notes

1. Michael Burleigh and Wolfgang Wippermann, *The Racial State: Germany 1933–1945* (Cambridge, U.K.: Cambridge University Press, 1991), 283.

2. David Schoenbaum, *Hitler's Social Revolution: Class and Status in Nazi Germany 1933–1939* (New York: W.W. Norton and Co., 1980), 77.

3. J. Noakes and G. Pridham, eds., *Nazism 1919–1945: A History in Documents and Eyewitness Accounts,* Vol. I (New York: Schocken Books, 1983), 336.

4. Detlev Peukert, *Inside Nazi Germany: Conformity, Opposition, and Racism in Everyday Life* (New Haven, Conn.: Yale University Press, 1987), 103–4.

5. Noakes and Pridham, *Nazism 1919–1945,* 332.

6. Noakes and Pridham, *Nazism 1919–1945,* 338.

7. Noakes and Pridham, *Nazism 1919–1945,* 347–48.

8. Noakes and Pridham, *Nazism 1919–1945,* 339–43.

9. Noakes and Pridham, *Nazism 1919–1945,* 342–43; and Peukert, *Inside Nazi Germany,* 107 and 110.

10. Richard Grunberger, *A Social History of the Third Reich* (London: Penguin Books, 1971), 250.

11. Noakes and Pridham, *Nazism 1919–1945,* 343.

12. David Crew, ed., *Nazism and German Society 1933–1945* (New York: Routledge, 1994), 6.

13. Peukert, *Inside Nazi Germany,* 114.

14. Grunberger, *A Social History,* 256.

15. Noakes and Pridham, *Nazism 1919–1945,* 371–72.

16. Grunberger, *A Social History,* 241.

17. Peukert, *Inside Nazi Germany,* 112–13.

18. Crew, *Nazism and German Society,* 6–8.

19. Crew, *Nazism and German Society,* 4.

20. Alf Luedtke, "The 'Honor of Labor': Industrial Workers and the Power of Symbols under National Socialism," in *Nazism and German Society 1933–1945,* ed. David Crew (New York: Routledge, 1994), 70–71.

21. Grunberger, *A Social History,* 253.

22. Schoenbaum, *Hitler's Social Revolution,* 107.

23. Noakes and Pridham, *Nazism 1919–1945,* 352.

24. Michael Merritt, "Strength through Joy: Regimented Leisure in Nazi Germany," in *Nazism and the Common Man: Essays in German History (1929–1939),* ed. Otis C. Mitchell (Minneapolis, Minn.: Burgess Publishing Co., 1972), 69–70.

25. Burleigh and Wippermann, *The Racial State,* 289–290.

26. Schoenbaum, *Hitler's Social Revolution,* 106–107.

27. Merritt, "Strength through Joy," 67.

28. Schoenbaum, *Hitler's Social Revolution,* 105.

29. Schoenbaum, *Hitler's Social Revolution,* 104.

30. Merritt, "Strength through Joy," 66.

31. Merritt, "Strength through Joy," 74.

32. Merritt, "Strength through Joy," 70.

33. Merritt, "Strength through Joy," 72.

34. Merritt, "Strength through Joy," 71.

35. Merritt, "Strength through Joy," 72.

36. Merritt, "Strength through Joy," 72–73.

37. Schoenbaum, *Hitler's Social Revolution,* 106.

38. Jackson Spielvogel, *Hitler and Nazi Germany: A History* (Englewood Cliffs, N.J.: Prentice Hall, 1988), 97.

39. Spielvogel, *Hitler and Nazi Germany,* 97.

40. Burleigh and Wippermann, *The Racial State,* 290–91.

41. Burleigh and Wippermann, *The Racial State,* 294.

42. Noakes and Pridham, *Nazism 1919–1945,* 353.

43. Luedtke, "The 'Honor of Labor,'" 74.

44. Spielvogel, *Hitler and Nazi Germany,* 98.

45. Noakes and Pridham, *Nazism 1919–1945,* 354.

46. Noakes and Pridham, *Nazism 1919–1945,* 354–55.

47. Crew, *Nazism and German Society,* 9 and 67.

48. Luedtke, "The 'Honor of Labor,'" 74.

49. Crew, *Nazism and German Society,* 68.

50. Luedtke, "The 'Honor of Labor,'" 75.

51. Tilla Siegel, "The Attitude of German Workers," in *Fascist Italy and Nazi Germany: Comparisons and Contrasts.* Ed. Richard Bessel (Cambridge, U.K.: Cambridge University Press, 1996), 67. *See also* Tilla Siegel and Thomas von Freyberg, *Industrielle Rationaliserung uster dem Nationalsozialismus* (Frankfurt/Main. 1991).

52. Schoenbaum, *Hitler's Social Revolution,* 110.

53. Ian Kershaw, *The "Hitler Myth": Image and Reality in the Third Reich* (Oxford, U.K.: Oxford University Press, 1987), 253–69 and Peukert, *Inside Nazi Germany,* 109.

54. Siegel, "The Attitude of German Workers," 71.

55. Grunberger, *A Social History,* 240.

3
Italian Workers and Paradiso: The Don Camillo Stories of Giovanni Guareschi in Their Historical Setting

Pietro Lorenzini

Giovanni Guareschi's fictional characters, Don Camillo and Giuseppe Bottazzi (nicknamed Peppone), are among the most recognizable comedic protagonists to emerge out of Italian popular literature during the Cold War. Don Camillo,[1] the Catholic priest, and his rival Peppone, the communist mayor, were popularized throughout Italy first in print and later in cinema. While Guareschi's Don Camillo stories initially achieved fame in postwar Italy and continued to be popular through the 1960s, the fictional characters he wrote about transcended geographic boundaries and became much loved in Europe, the Americas and parts of Asia. Moreover, the translation of the Don Camillo tales from Italian into numerous other languages, as well as the foreign language dubbing of Don Camillo films, also helped ensure that the tales of Don Camillo would become enormously successful agents of cultural hegemony throughout much of the Cold War era.

From the first printing of Giovanni Guareschi's Don Camillo stories, the rivalry between Don Camillo, the provincial cleric, and the small-town mayor, Giuseppe Bottazzi, reflected the titanic struggle between the United States and the Soviet Union and their respective allies.[2] Once the Don Camillo stories became box office hits, they proved to be especially valuable agents of political propaganda, Italian style. Projected onto the silver screen, Don Camillo and Peppone clearly personified the struggle for the hearts and minds of the common folk in post–World War II Italy. Infused with well-crafted comedy and the burlesque actions of the stubborn priest and pompous "Red" politician, the Don Camillo tales depicted the Cold War as the latest version of that familiar and eternal struggle between divinely inspired virtue and human frailty.[3]

The Don Camillo stories are particularly attractive to those interested in the cultural interplay between history, literature, film, and politics because Guareschi's engaging publications and the films they inspired reflected Cold War anti-Communist sentiments dominant in Italy and Western Europe as well as in the United States and its ideological allies around the globe. As the creator of new popular culture icons, Guareschi was able to capture the attention of a wide audience which was otherwise immersed in the all-too-real struggles between the superpowers and their allies. Italian anti-Communists, in particular, embraced Guareschi's peasant priest as they recognized the importance of the Don Camillo character in the cultural wars between left and right. Throughout the Italian peninsula, these tales and the laughter they sparked proved to be powerful weapons in the West's Cold War arsenal.[4] And yet, curiously, the popularity of Guareschi's Don Camillo tales also transcended the chasm which divided the Cold War world into two opposing political camps. In fact, while the Don Camillo stories were widely popular within conservative circles, they also found some support among those who favored political and economic change. This paradox can be explained partly by considering the impact which the Cold War had on the varied sectors of society. As a result of the stark and frightening realities of the Cold War, the Don Camillo stories became immensely popular among disparate social, economic, and ideological groups because Guareschi used the tensions of Cold War Italian politics as a way of underscoring both the dilemma and humor of everyday life. The comedic and farcical actions of the cleric, Don Camillo, and the "Red" mayor, Peppone, acted to underscore the absurdity of conflict on the personal level. In addition, the human face which Guareschi gave to the country priest and to the provincial Communist mayor, who often became engaged in ideologically inspired rowdy fistfights, spoke to the ridiculous nature of the Cold War by hinting that both the national and international struggles between left and right were similar acts of buffoonery. This chapter, therefore, will attempt to offer an assessment concerning how a pro-Western political hegemony was promoted in Cold War Italy through the genre of popular fiction as expressed in the adventures of Don Camillo and Peppone, but it will also seek to explain how Guareschi's stories also found favor in less conservative circles and thus transcended, to some degree, political ideology and conflict.[5]

In the preface to Giovanni Guareschi's fourth and perhaps most successful novel, *Don Camillo's Dilemma*,[6] the author explained that he had created the lovable priest and simple Communist mayor and had placed them in a typical, yet fictitious, "Red Village" in the Po River valley in the late winter of 1946. The Po river runs through parts of Lombardy, Parma, Reggio Emilia, and the Veneto, regions where the political and social struggle between the left and right was highly charged. Guareschi, a Milanese journalist from the agriculturally rich province of

Parma, gave birth to these northern Italian protagonists while working for the popular magazine *Oggi* and the promonarchist publication *Candido*. The former was an important nationwide magazine similar to *Life* and the latter, a weekly periodical edited and largely written by Guareschi, enjoyed a much more restricted popularity. Although Guareschi had written his first Don Camillo short story for *Oggi*, he chose to print the piece in *Candido* because the latter magazine's submission deadline was at hand. Guareschi's inability to write a short piece in time to meet the *Oggi* deadline proved auspicious. While both magazines were successful in their own right, the author believed that his country priest and "Red" politician flourished because their adventures proved popular to the more receptive readers of *Candido*.[7]

Genuinely surprised by the popularity of the short stories published in *Candido*, Guareschi wrote first one and then five more books centered on the exploits of Don Camillo. Translation of the Don Camillo works from Italian to French, English, German, Lithuanian, Polish, Swedish, and Spanish ensured success in Europe, the United States and in Latin America. By 1954, for example, Guareschi's first Don Camillo book, originally titled *Mondo piccolo: Don Camillo*, had sold over 800,000 copies in France alone. Among his most popular works published in English are *Don Camillo and His Flock*, *Don Camillo's Dilemma*, and *Don Camillo Takes the Devil by the Tail*.[8] Guareschi's successful books eventually drew the attention of the motion picture industry. Soon the "big priest" and "big Red mayor" were catapulted into an even wider fame through a series of popular films.[9]

The comic and yet serious antics of Don Camillo and Peppone were initially introduced to Italian and French moviegoers through a cooperative venture between French director Julien Duvivier and the Rizzoli publishing firm. The motion picture was titled simply, *Don Camillo*. One of the most influential conservative publishing houses in Italy, Rizzoli expected that a film based on Guareschi's Don Camillo would open a new venue in which its ideas and profits would flourish. This film was one of the first successful attempts by the Rizzoli firm to expand into the motion picture industry. Having profited significantly from earlier publications of Guareschi's Don Camillo tales, Rizzoli stood to make enormous profits from the film version of Don Camillo's escapades. Moreover, a much wider audience would be exposed to Guareschi's righteous depiction of how the true faith triumphed over the latest secular challenge to moral order. All that Rizzoli needed was to find talented and respected actors to play the leading roles in Guareschi's comedic morality play, Don Camillo.

As it turned out, many actors were attracted by the possibility of playing the leading characters in the Don Camillo stories. After an extensive search, the famous French actor Fernandel was chosen to play Don Camillo and the priest's nemesis, Peppone, was given to the Italian actor Gino Cervi. Through the popularity of Fernandel and Cervi, Rizzoli hoped to ensure success in this first Don Camillo film. Working from Rome's *CineCitta* (Italy's Hollywood), Fernandel's Don Camillo and Cervi's Peppone captured the hearts of theater patrons in Europe and in the Americas. Aside from the actors' skills and fame, the widespread popularity of the adventures of Don Camillo and Peppone, whether told in print or on film, was largely a result of the fact that Guareschi had created two characters who, in the end, appealed to those who held conservative opinions and even to some whose political loyalties were attached to the more radical. The finely tuned comic talent of Fernandel and Cervi depicted to movie audiences two very sympathetic protagonists who stood at opposite ends of the political spectrum, but what they held in common included their humble origins and their very human strengths and weaknesses.[10]

Fully comprehending the popularity of Guareschi's stories necessarily requires some familiarity with modern Italian political history along with a basic understanding of concomitant social and cultural developments on the peninsula. An analysis of the relationship between the traditions of Italian agriculture, the demands of the nation's industries, and the new imperatives of Cold War politics is therefore needed. Furthermore, understanding the reasons for Guareschi's success as a writer of politicized, comedic fiction requires assessing the nexus which united the cultures of those who worked the soil and those who labored in workshops and factories. Such analyses will help illuminate how the characters in Guareschi's stories personified the Cold War ideological divisions which separated Italians into two hostile political camps and also the agricultural and social traditions which historically served to unite all those who worked.

Guareschi's writings concisely reflect the complex economic, cultural and political relations which existed among those people who toiled, prayed, and played in the countryside, towns and villages, and cities of mid-twentieth-century Italy. As Guareschi knew well, such relationships, of course, were rooted deep in Italian history. The Italian peninsula had been in the vanguard of European political, economic, and cultural life from the Roman republic through the Renaissance. Added to the seminal achievements of ancient Roman Italy were the artistic, philosophical, literary, political, economic, and technological advances which developed in the many independent territories and city-states of Medieval and Renaissance Italy. From the late Middle Ages through the Renaissance, Florentines, Genoese, Pisans, and Venetians, for example, experimented with republican government, developed new philosophical insights, discovered scientific truths previously unknown, and set artistic and architectural standards which were acknowledged throughout Europe for centuries. These same northern Italian states experienced the growth of nascent capitalism which would become an engine for economic, legal, scientific, and cultural changes which have transformed life and work first in Europe and, by the end of the twentieth century, throughout the globe. Driven by a desire to increase their wealth and power, the Renaissance entrepreneurial elites of northern Italy developed business innovations which included banking enterprises and their concomitant systems of accounting, credit, and exchange. They also fostered a jurisprudence which justified and protected the earliest forms of partnerships and corporations as well as new systems of production which introduced piece-work

manufacturing and cash crop farming. As their riches grew, wealthy Italian entrepreneurial families, such as the Medici in Florence, came to hold great political
influence which would be used to promote an unparalleled cultural and artistic
rebirth. And yet, by establishing themselves as patrons of art, Renaissance merchant and entrepreneurial elites not only hoped to foster priceless works by masters such as Michelangelo Buonarotti and Leonardo da Vinci, but they also sought
to legitimize their newly acquired political power.[11]

Although the Renaissance had transformed and modernized much of the economic, social, and political life of northern Italy, the Italian peninsula as a whole
would remain predominantly agrarian long after the dynamic economic and military centers of European power had moved across the Alps. In much of the peninsula, the centuries-old economic, social, and cultural ties which bound together its
countryside and urban areas were not seriously undermined until well into the
twentieth century, when Italy would become increasingly industrial and less agricultural. Throughout most of Italian history, therefore, agricultural and urban economies remained closely interwoven.[12] As Guareschi recognized, this was most clearly
exposed in the lives of those who lived and worked on the farms and in the small
cities and towns of the provincial Italian countryside. Even in the more advanced
economy of northern Italy, the social, political and religious culture of those who
worked the land was similar to the culture of the men and women who lived in the
sizeable cities of Parma and Reggio Emilia as well as in important Tuscan provincial centers such as Fivizzano and Aulla.[13] Townsmen and peasants, therefore, knew
first hand that Catholicism and its clerics played an important role in the social and
political life of provincial Italy. Whether religious observers or anti-clerics, the
provincial lawyers and physicians, teachers and clerks, peasants and teamsters, all
acknowledged the power and influence of the Roman Church. Yet, as Guareschi
knew, the Church's political and social influence had long been challenged by
many throughout Italian history. By writing of the daily struggles which confronted
Don Camillo and Peppone, Guareschi depicted the latest phase of that battle between secular and religious forces which has occupied the daily lives of generations of Italians from ancient times to the modern era and, concomitantly, he also
celebrated the human face of age-old agrarian and urban tensions.

Guareschi depicted both Don Camillo and Peppone as sons of Italy's rich Po
river valley. Flowing southeastward from the Alps to the Adriatic, the Po is Italy's
largest river. Since Roman times the river's waters have irrigated some of the
peninsula's most productive farmlands which, in turn, helped promote the growth
of a number of wealthy cities and towns. As the life-sustaining waters of the Po
river flowed through the most fertile soil in Italy, the northern and northeastern
provinces of the nation would be among the first in the country to experience the
development of modern, large-scale industrial production and capitalist agriculture. In the nineteenth century major northern urban centers in the new Italian
kingdom thus experienced rapid growth as larger and larger factories were built to
meet the new imperatives of the Industrial Revolution.

Agriculture in much of northern Italy underwent revolutionary changes to fulfill the requirements of the nascent yet dynamic industrial economy. Many of the farms irrigated by the waters of that same Po river which so inspired Guareschi's writing came to be characterized by the dominance of large landowners who employed *mezzadri* (i.e., sharecroppers) and/or day laborers to meet the new market demands of the expanding cities and towns. The growing population of the burgeoning industrial centers of northern Italy was in need of large quantities of wheat, rice, corn, meat, and other foods. The steady production of cash crops as well as other staples and livestock required a large and compliant agricultural work force which the region's large landowners were determined to secure and control. These local entrepreneurial rural elites found a ready justification for the manipulation of the peasant work force in the principles of nineteenth-century liberalism and *laissez-faire* economics. Requiring farm workers to labor dawn to dusk six days per week under stern and harsh working conditions established by large landowners, whose ability to make enormous profits depended on maximizing the work load of their dependents while minimizing the agricultural workers' remuneration, now found sanction in the laws of modern economic theory. All too often, therefore, arduous labor did not guarantee that the peasantry would enjoy the fruits of their labor, but only that the peasantry's efforts would be compensated according to the rules of the "free market." In the case of sharecropping contracts, the sharecroppers' portion of the agricultural production for which they were responsible grew ever smaller, since large landowners were always quick to find ample reasons to reduce the share that went to these agricultural workers whenever old contracts expired and new ones were drawn. *Mezzadri* commonly found that they were expected to bear the brunt of crop infestations and diseases, bad weather, and lower market prices, as well as accusations of poor productivity, when presented with a renewal of their contracts. The big landowners' take-it-or-leave-it offers presented *mezzadri* with little choice when refusal to renew sharecropping contracts meant that these agricultural workers would lose their livelihood and shelter as well as the soil upon which they grew the foods needed to feed their large families. The ties that bound sharecroppers to the landlords were made more burdensome still by the supplemental fees which large landowners commonly charged their sharecroppers for such items as farm implements, kitchenware, and wood for cooking and heating.[14]

Meanwhile the employment conditions faced by rural day laborers were far worse and the best that most could expect would allow for only bare subsistence. The very term used to describe these agricultural workers is indicative of the level of exploitation which they suffered. Referred to as *braccianti* (literally translated as "arms"), these farm hands, who would later form the rural backbone of Peppone's Italian Communist Party, held none of the meager privileges which sharecroppers' contracts seemed to promise. The sharecropping contracts at least guaranteed *mezzadri* that their employment relationships would last a relatively lengthy period of time. Moreover, sharecroppers had contractual rights to at least rudimentary shelter and to the use of tools and farm animals as well as a legally enforceable right to a predetermined percentage of the crops. *Braccianti*, on the other hand, were hired on a short-term basis determined by the time needed to plant or harvest a specific crop. The ready supply of large numbers of unemployed workers meant that landowners could offer *braccianti* a bare minimum daily wage as compensation. When the task was accomplished, the now unemployed workers would need to find work as quickly as possible. The conditions of employment offered by any new prospective employers were, of course, determined by the landowners themselves. Even though there were times when market demands, economic factors, or the exigencies of planting and harvesting crops resulted in more favorable terms of employment for some day laborers, the great number of unemployed and underemployed rural workers inevitably meant that *braccianti* had little bargaining strength. The best that *braccianti* could hope for was that their health remained so that they could find work more days than not. After all, a combination of sweat and toil and a measure of good luck could ensure a modest if not luxurious future for the individual *bracciante* and his family.[15]

Agricultural workers of all types knew all too well that the employment relationship dictated by the large landlords meant that their day by day exploitation came at the hands of the landlords' rural agents, who were charged with supervising both the owners' estates and those who worked the fields and tended the livestock. And yet, the peasantry who lived in the towns and hamlets in the countryside (as their fictional counterparts depicted in Guareschi's tales) understood that their world was in fact subject to forces even greater than those who owned the soil upon which they labored. During the latter half of the nineteenth century, many who worked the land came to know firsthand that the condition of the rural work force was now fully sanctioned and readily enforced by the martial and judicial forces of the new Italian state.

The successful unification of Italy under the Piedmontese House of Savoy, officially proclaimed in March of 1861, brought together under one administration most of the formerly independent states of the peninsula. No longer was king Vittorio Emanuel II simply the ruler of a small kingdom which was comprised of Piedmont, Liguria, and the island of Sardinia, but now his ancient house ruled over southern territories which included Naples and Sicily as well as Lombardy, Modena, Tuscany, Parma, and other formerly independent regions in the north. By 1866 the defeat of the Austrians freed much of the northeastern part of the Italian peninsula from Habsburg domination and added one more rich and populous region to the new kingdom. With the addition of the Papal States in 1871, the House of Savoy extended its authority from the Alps to Sicily.[16]

After centuries of political fragmentation and foreign rule, many Italians in the nineteenth century were ready for the union of Italy's multiple states and territories into a single nation. Indeed, when reading Giovanni Guareschi's writings, one can better understand the loyalty which he and many other Italians continued to give the House of Savoy, even after experiencing the Fascist dictatorship and World War II, only in light of the long struggle for Italian unification and the hardships later experienced in keeping the union strong and its economy prosperous. During the *Risorgimento*, for example, a significant portion of the popular support for the Savoyard monarchy came from the peninsula's urban middle classes and entrepreneurial elites who maintained the kingdom through their resourcefulness and also identified with the ideology and goals of nineteenth-century liberalism. From an economic perspective, this support proved not to have been misplaced. The unification of all of the northern and northeastern parts of the peninsula into an expanded Italian kingdom, for example, promoted a general economic progress which greatly benefitted the entrepreneurial classes, urban middle classes and, especially, the large landowners of Lombardy, Reggio Emilia, Parma, Piedmont, Tuscany, and the Veneto. The economic advances which occurred after the incorporation of formerly independent states and territories into the new kingdom were the result, in part, of the cancellation of the innumerable tariffs which those states had enforced. Removing these significant governmental impediments to the profitability of trade and commerce certainly benefitted the entrepreneurial elites, urban middle classes, and large landowners. Peninsular unification thus ended political and economic disunity which historically had limited the growth of Italian industry, trade, and agriculture. Economic activity and profits also increased because the more progressive Savoyard rulers and their political leaders inaugurated a policy of structural modernization. Within a relatively short time after unification, the policy of modernization, along with the single economic market provided by national unification, resulted in the construction of more modernized roads and railroads as well as the introduction of new methods of production in both agriculture and industry. Domestic demand for industrial and agricultural goods continued to expand throughout most of the nineteenth century as the national market matured under the direction of a modernized state whose officials sought to ensure economic expansion by promoting the rights and privileges of the propertied elites. The great profits which were made from this economic growth, therefore, were certain to find their way into the purses of the nobility, entrepreneurial elites, merchants, large landowners, and urban middle class.[17]

While the expanding economy of the new Italian kingdom clearly benefitted the economically and politically privileged classes, it also provided more jobs in Italy's industrial and agricultural sectors as well as in the nation's workshops. Great numbers of factory hands, artisans, and rural workers were needed to meet the demands of the enlarged domestic market. Increased employment, however, continued to be accompanied by a serious and lasting discontent, the results of which, eventually, would be captured in Guareschi's tales. Those who labored in the urban factories and workshops and in the countryside would long remain dissatisfied with the new order. In part, their initial dissatisfaction can be traced to the frustration which arose when expectations that Italian unification would inaugurate the dawn of a new era where a progressive national government would improve their lives were soon shown to be exaggerated. Under the direction of political leaders who adhered to the principles of economic liberalism and the enlightened bureaucrats who administered their policies, the Savoyard dynasty did promote economic growth. Yet, state-sanctioned attempts to ensure a more equitable distribution of wealth and political power remained absent from Italian unification through those all-too-real Cold War struggles in which Guareschi placed his fictional radical and conservative characters.

During the nineteenth century rural and urban workers responded to their plight in varied ways. At first mutual aid societies were established, often under the auspices of the Church or local philanthropists, to ensure that peasants and workers (and in the case of death, their families) who suffered injury and disease could turn to the societies in which they were members for financial help and social services. Yet rising discontent among the lower orders eventually led to more radical alternatives. The creation of labor unions in Italy's cities and countryside in the second half of the nineteenth century, along with the increased influence of Anarchism and Socialism, evidenced the growth of significant popular discontent. These radical social and labor movements attracted those who were not content with merely ameliorating the condition of the working classes. While those who formed Anarchist circles and those who joined the Italian Socialist Party were often at odds over theory and methods, they were united in the belief that the riches held by the few rightfully belonged to the creators of wealth, the laboring classes. Anarchists and Socialists, therefore, proposed revolutionary changes which would inaugurate a new age in which the destruction of the power and privilege of the propertied elites would ensure political equality and economic equity. Once organized into unions and workers' leagues, factory and rural workers, whether Socialist- or Anarchist- inspired, turned to strike actions and even violence to promote their interests. Responding to the challenge from the left, the forces of order defended the status quo with legal coercion and the organized armed violence of the police and army.[18]

At the start of the twentieth century, the House of Savoy seemed besieged by a radicalized work force intent on building a new society on the ruins of the old kingdom. The workers' demands were focused both on short-term and long-term goals. Factory workers demanded collective bargaining rights and better wages and working conditions, as well as a shortened workday and workweek. In the countryside, while agrarian laborers generally mirrored some of the basic demands of the industrial work force, rural workers' needs varied according to the region and to the type of farming in which they were employed. In Tuscany, for example, *mezzadri* demands for a greater share of the agricultural wealth which their labor produced called for a complete revision of sharecropping contracts. On the other hand, the *braccianti* of Lombardy and Reggio Emilia, which Guareschi later would depict in his stories, were more immediately focused on increased wages and the reduction of the workday.

In the face of the innumerable strikes in the nation's factories and the scores of agrarian strikes which sought to force concessions from employers, national and regional governmental officials called upon the army, *carabinieri* (a national police force associated with the military), and local police to suppress the radicalized work force. The often violent clashes which ensued polarized the nation. With each new clash, the forces of order and their supporters all too often concluded that greater repression still was needed to thwart the serious nature of the threat to the status quo. The blood which was spilt, however, served to bolster and further radicalize the workers. More and more, workers openly supported Socialist ideals. Throughout much of the late nineteenth and early twentieth centuries, the Socialist Party swelled with new members. Many of these Socialists, such as Guareschi's father, were content to support their party's attempt to win more seats in parliament, while others were not averse to displaying their militancy in more violent ways. In short, Italian radicals remained much divided over the goals of the labor movement as well as over the means to employ to improve their lives and their society. While some left-wing groups which sought to revolutionize society believed in the necessity of an armed struggle against the state, others trusted an evolutionary policy which hoped to revolutionize society by achieving incremental gains in the workplace through strikes and in the parliament through the ballot box. Nevertheless, what generally united the nation's labor unions and left-wing political parties and associations was the call for both political and economic democracy. Though this was never clearly defined, many in the left believed that true democracy could be achieved only through the expropriation of private property, elimination of the privileges and wealth of the monied elites, abolition of monarchical and aristocratic power and, but for the Anarchists and the most radical revolutionaries, universal suffrage.[19]

Italy's entry into World War I in 1917 on the side of the British and French brought a momentary pause to the serious labor unrest which the nation had experienced for almost two generations. The wartime authorities made it perfectly clear that now the state would deal even more harshly with strikes and any other labor unrest, which were deemed inappropriate in this time of national crisis. In short, any act which could undermine the effectiveness of Italy's military efforts would be treated as treason by the political leadership. And yet more than coercion was needed if the state was to marshal popular support in the fight against the German and Austrian forces. The nationwide conscription which the war mandated would require the cooption of Italy's working classes. In order to gain the wider popular support needed for a successful struggle against Germany and Austria-Hungary, the Italian government did not discourage the growing popular sentiment that at war's end returning veterans and their families would be treated equitably for their patriotic sacrifices. Popular expectations in the countryside, for example, revealed themselves in the form of calls for land redistribution while urban workers anticipated that the end of the war would inaugurate, at a minimum, an era of fair labor contracts.

In fact the end of the Great War would mark a time when it seemed that Italy was closer than ever to revolution. The situation was particularly volatile in the northern Italian regions in which Guareschi later would set his fictionalized Cold War tales describing the clashes between the radical left and the conservative right.

As Guareschi knew, among the causes for the Cold War struggles of his day were the inequities which World War I had crystallized. The Italian working classes had numerous reasons for postwar dissatisfaction. Although the termination of hostilities and the era of peace which followed initially brought about increased unemployment, the government did little to provide work for urban workers or landless rural laborers. Moreover, even though Italy had emerged from this war as one of the victorious powers, the state continued to use the full force of both military and police forces against striking factory workers and farm laborers. Many urban and agricultural workers therefore felt justified in believing that wartime expectations of jobs, good salaries, and land would never be realized under Italy's old political leaders. From the foot of the Alps to the Mediterranean islands further south, more and more Italian workers were driven to conclude that the only hope for a more equitable future lay in revolutionary political and economic changes. These sentiments were put to the test in 1919 when Italians experienced their first elections under universal male suffrage. As a result of this initial step toward building a modern political democracy, two new mass political parties received the greatest number of votes. In this historic election, the Italian Socialist Party emerged as the strongest single political party in the nation, followed by strong electoral support for the new Popular Party (*Popolari*).[20]

The leader of the Popular Party (the forerunner of the Christian Democratic Party which ruled Italy after World War II and whose most prominent Cold War literary champion was Guareschi), Don Sturzo, was a Catholic priest from Sicily who was conservative on some issues and moderately radical on others. While Don Sturzo's views were not always reflected in the party's platform, the platform did make clear that the chief bond which united the *Popolari* was a determination to end the monopoly of power which anticlerical political leaders had held since the creation of the kingdom of Italy. The *Popolari*, however, were far from being united in their goals or tactics. Much of the initial Popular Party program, such as the support for women's suffrage and the condemnation of imperialism, reflected political beliefs promoted by the party's more moderate leaders. More radical *Popolari*, on the other hand, openly supported agrarian strikes and demanded an equitable division of some of Italy's largest agricultural estates among the peasantry. In the end, however, the conservative and reactionary elements in the party managed to direct the party along political lines favored by the Vatican by emphasizing the threat of moral disorder and violence posed by Socialism, Bolshevism, and social anarchy. Therefore, though there was no official connection with the Catholic Church, the *Popolari* would emerge as a potent political weapon in the Vatican's battle against those who called for Marxist revolution as well as against other secular forces which were seen to threaten the power and influence of the Church.

The Holy See determined that the most immediate threat to the Church and to the moral order of the nation came from the Socialist Party. Italian Socialists, after all, seemed ready and able to overthrow the old order, both clerical and secular.

Within the Socialist Party, the Maximalist faction was in the majority. The Maximalists called for the party to adopt a maximum program of immediate socialization. However, while Maximalist leaders were skilled at talking revolution, they lacked a clear sense of direction and ultimately proved unable to bring about any significant changes at the national level. Notwithstanding their ineffective leadership, Maximalist revolutionary rhetoric mirrored working-class discontent while also adding fuel to a political atmosphere already charged with a renewed revolutionary spirit sparked by the writings of V. I. Lenin and the toppling of the Romanov regime.[21]

The Bolshevik success in establishing a Marxist government in Russia fostered a further radicalization within Italian Socialist ranks and ultimately helped spark the emergence of the Italian Communist Party, that very organization which later would become the main target of Guareschi's pen. In postwar Italy heightened left-wing calls for the nation's proletarians to break the chains of capitalist domination and concomitant demands for expropriation of the ruling elite's wealth gave the illusion of inevitable historical change. The Italian Socialist Party's leadership along with the leaders of the newly formed Italian Communist Party, however, did not fully recognize that such provocative pronouncements, coupled with the revolutionary left's inability to act decisively, foolishly ignited counterrevolutionary reprisals from Italian nationalist groups as well as from the growing Fascist movement.

Fascism was a new right-wing political force which proved itself ready to use violence and intimidation to destroy the left and to achieve political power. The nascent Fascist movement made great strides under the leadership of Benito Mussolini. The son of a blacksmith, Mussolini had become the editor of the Italian Socialist Party's newspaper, *Avanti*. Soon after the outbreak of World War I, however, Mussolini lost this important position and his party membership because he renounced the party's neutralism. Starting his own newspaper, *Il Popolo d'Italia*, Mussolini ardently called for intervention on the side of the British and French. With Italy's entrance into the war, Mussolini found himself in uniform fighting on the Austrian front. After the war, Mussolini marshaled his journalistic talents to promote the growing number of paramilitary Fascist squads.[22]

In its earliest phase, Fascism was a political movement which attracted people from different social and economic classes and who held varied political ideals. Fascism found ready support from discontented veterans, nationalists, industrialists, and middle-class bureaucrats and, in general, it was supported by those who believed that a Marxist revolution was a very real threat. (Fascism, it should be noted, found strong support among landowners, veterans, and middle class, and clerical supporters in the regions of northern Italy in which Guareschi would later place his fictional characters.) While these groups may have held different interests and ideals, they were united in calling for radical action against all who were seen as subversive. In short, these disparate groups were all drawn to Fascism's strident nationalism and its appeals for violent action against antinationalist and leftist forces which were depicted as harmful to the nation's economy and status as a great power. Rising unemployment, for example, inspired many veterans to turn toward Fascism as it seemed to be the only movement which was ready to address their economic plight and patriotic sentiments. Since the Italian government proved incapable of subduing the Socialists and Communists and unable to achieve the annexation of Dalmatia, Trieste, and Fiume as payment for Italy's war efforts as well, nationalists were attracted to Fascism's strident demands for territorial acquisitions as well as to Fascism's promise to crush Marxism. Industrialists too yearned for a regime led by a party which could put an end to strikes, defend the political status quo, and ensure managerial control of the workplace. Similarly, each Socialist Party electoral gain, and every strike and leftist demonstration, created more middle-class support for Fascism as growing numbers of the nation's clerks, small shopkeepers, lawyers, doctors, and government bureaucrats came to view it as the only force capable of checking the growing leftist threat. Newspaper accounts of the violent acts of Fascist *squadristi* (armed civilians organized into paramilitary squads) who assaulted Marxist labor and political leaders, vandalized their offices and presses, and attacked strikers and leftist rallies were thus welcomed as necessary actions by growing numbers of Italians from the middle to the upper classes.

In the too-often-chaotic years which followed World War I, Mussolini proved ingenious at holding together this heterogenous and often contradictory movement. As the Fascist Party leader, or *Duce*, Mussolini was also skilled at capitalizing on the charged political atmosphere of postwar Italy, for much of the nation was permeated by fears of Marxist revolution. The more the government seemed incapable or unwilling to take the necessary steps to maintain domestic peace and defend the status quo, the easier it was for Mussolini to portray himself as the only leader ready and able to restore law and order. The more numerous and violent Fascist attacks against Socialists and against all those were seen as opposed to Fascism became, the more Mussolini was able to manipulate the growing fear of Fascist squads to his advantage. He skillfully depicted himself as a determined leader intent on destroying Fascism's enemies on the left. At the same time, Mussolini also portrayed himself as the only Fascist leader who could restrain the most ardent members of his party who, disgusted with the government for its inability to crush the left, were ready to overturn the old order itself.[23]

The fact that the Fascist movement could be used to repress the left, but could also successfully challenge the power long held by the established political leadership and even challenge the monarchy itself was not lost on King Vittorio Emanuele III. In October 1922, Mussolini's Fascists organized a "march on Rome" which confirmed to the Savoyard king the danger of an unbridled Fascist movement. The crown and its supporters were alarmed that so many thousands of Fascists from all over the country planned to openly demonstrate their power and counterrevolutionary ardor in the nation's capital. Weakening the left in Italy was one thing, but what was now needed, the king concluded, was to contain the Fascist movement so as to ensure that it could not challenge the monarchy and its political allies.

Wishing to maintain his power and influence, the king was coming to believe that the cooption of the Fascist movement might be achieved through the traditional levers of political power, the monarchy and parliament. While the Fascist Party did not gain a significant number of seats in Parliament in the free elections held after World War I, the party did gain some electoral victories. Mussolini and other Fascist Party leaders, for example, were elected to office. Once elected, Mussolini and the other Fascist Party political leaders were able to use this acquisition of parliamentary seats and provincial and local offices to gain some legitimacy with the monarchy. Furthermore, the *Duce* was able to manipulate the growing suspicion that Fascists might pose a threat to the continued existence of the old regime to his advantage by depicting himself as the reasonable leader of an increasingly radicalized movement which only he could control. In the end, Mussolini's maneuvers worked well. Convinced that the Fascist Party could be coopted through its more reasonable leaders and not wishing to risk his crown to a movement which was increasing in size and militancy, King Vittorio Emanuele III offered Mussolini the opportunity to form a government.[24] The fear of the left and the belief in the growing strength of the Fascist Party were so dominant that the king's decision was accepted as a necessary political maneuver by many of his contemporaries. Moreover, the fear of Marxist revolution was so great that this momentous decision by Italy's last king later would be defended by Monarchists such as Guareschi even after the harsh dictatorship and horrors of war which Italians experienced under Mussolini's regime.

Idealized by those who felt threatened by Marxism, and supported by the crown, Mussolini, not yet forty years old in 1922, had become the youngest Prime Minister in Italian history. Early on in his tenure, Mussolini began to gradually restaff government positions and offices with Fascists. By entrenching Fascist Party members in positions of power at every level, the *Duce* helped build the necessary groundwork for a dictatorship which would not be overthrown until the peninsula was invaded by enemy armies during World War II. The foundations for this dictatorship, however, also required cementing a working relationship with the monarchy and its supporters, reconciling with the Roman Catholic Church hierarchy, and working to defend the interests of the large landowners and industrialists.

After a leading Socialist parliamentarian, Giacomo Matteotti, was murdered by Fascists in the summer of 1924, Mussolini moved to definitively crush first the left and, thereafter, all opposition to his regime. By the end of that year, for example, his government ordered the seizure of all opposition newspapers. In addition, Socialists and Communists were arrested and antifascist worker unions and associations dissolved. Within the following three years the Fascist government consolidated its power by: establishing that all state employees had be acceptable to the regime; threatening antifascists with the loss of citizenship; placing Fascist Party members in charge of all municipalities; dissolving all political parties except the Fascist Party; creating a secret police force; tightening control over labor through the "Law on Corporations" which was based on the fiction of Fascist Party-led class collaboration; and restoring the death penalty. Of all the changes brought about by Mussolini, the one which would survive the dictatorship was the agreement which his government made with the Catholic Church. In 1929, Mussolini and Pietro Cardinal Gasparri solemnly signed the Lateran Pact. This state-church accord acknowledged the sovereignty of the Pope over Vatican City and the official primacy of the Catholic religion in Italy. Armed with the Church's official sanction of the Fascist Party, Mussolini seemed to emerge stronger then ever.[25]

Having fully secured domestic control, Mussolini now turned his attention toward expanding his influence overseas. During the late nineteenth and early twentieth centuries, Italy had established colonies in northern and eastern Africa. The *Duce*, however, was not content with the acquisition of Libya after the Italian victory over the Ottoman Empire in 1911, nor with Italy's other colonies and foreign dependencies. By the 1930s, Mussolini was becoming interested in expanding Italy's empire in east Africa by adding Ethiopia to the older Italian colonies of Eritrea and Somalia. Italy had failed to gain control of Ethiopia in 1896, but now Mussolini was determined to put an end to her independence. Less than eight months after ordering the invasion of Ethiopia with a large military force armed with modern weapons and mechanized forces, Mussolini was able to announce that Italy had conquered Ethiopia and that this once independent nation, now officially called Abyssinia, was the newest addition to Italy's African Empire.[26] Influenced by Fascist propaganda, many of the landless farm laborers and unemployed workers which Guareschi later would depict in his stories had seen the acquisition of new imperial territories as regions which could provide land and wealth to Italian emigrants.

On the diplomatic level, the quest for imperial territories and great power status would reach its climax with an alliance between Italian Fascism and Nazi Germany. Yet the German-Italian alliance would come only after Mussolini's failed foreign policies helped drive the *Duce* to conclude that he had little choice but to ally with the Third Reich. The Italian Ethiopian campaign, for example, had helped to further isolate the Italian government from its former World War I allies, Britain and France. Moreover, the tensions which had arisen from Italy's Ethiopian conquest would be exacerbated by the bloody Spanish Civil War. As a result of Italian hostility toward the Spanish Popular Front government as well as France's role in the Mediterranean, Mussolini decided to support the overthrow of the left-wing Spanish government, which the Italian leader saw as a possible ally of France. Eventually, over 70,000 Italian soldiers were sent to aid the Spanish fascist forces of Francisco Franco. General Franco would be victorious, but Italy's growing isolation from Paris and London helped convince Mussolini to look to Berlin. Mussolini and Hitler recognized that their respective totalitarian regimes held common foreign policy goals which involved the attainment of territorial acquisitions not favored by the British and French governments. Moreover, by the latter half of the 1930s, a personal bond developed between these two dictators which also worked to facilitate the creation of a formal alliance between Italy and Germany. During the early years of the Nazi movement, the struggling leader of German fascism looked to the well established *Duce* with envy and respect. Long before he would become Germany's *Fuehrer,* Hitler attempted to emulate Mussolini's success. By studying the *Duce,* Hitler learned much concerning the ways to master political crisis and the public with well-orchestrated propaganda and coercion. Soon after Hitler came to power in 1933, he surpassed his Italian mentor in propaganda and brutality. Both men were drawn together by the similarity of their political beliefs and by their unbridled quest to achieve and maintain power. The totalitarian regimes which these two dictators had inspired and directed saw violence and threats of violence as legitimate and effective ways to achieve their goals in domestic politics. The same coercion and threats of violence which had worked so well domestically also were seen as weapons which could be successfully used against other nations. Moreover, both Mussolini and Hitler believed that foreign conquests were valuable not only for the land and plunder they could provide, but also because war and the militarization of society would allow them to maintain an even tighter control over their respective populations by directing people's energies away from the harsh realities of daily life towards defeating alien enemies. Mussolini and Hitler thus recognized that foreign conquest was vitally important to the continued existence of dictatorship in both Italy and Germany.[27]

The resulting German-Italian alliance would immerse the Italian people in the bloodiest war in history. Mussolini's foreign policy and military adventures resulted in a world war in which Italy, allied with Nazi Germany and Imperial Japan, was forced to fight against the combined forces of Britain, France, the Soviet Union, the United States, and their allies. During World War II, Italian troops fought from the frigid Russian steppes to the barren deserts of Africa. The extreme hardships and heavy casualties they suffered were largely the result of inadequate preparation for such an extensive and sanguinary war. In short, the Fascist government simply failed at marshalling the national resources needed to sustain the demands of this first true total war. After Allied armies landed on the peninsula, Mussolini was removed from power and placed under arrest by a coalition of forces which included dissident Fascist Party leaders and the crown and its supporters. Unwilling to accept the *coup d'etat,* Hitler ordered German troops to rescue his friend and former mentor. The *Duce* was later saved from his mountaintop imprisonment in a surprise raid by German paratroopers. Mussolini was then brought to northern Italy near the Swiss border, where he formed a new Fascist regime which was to govern a new state which, referred to as the Republic of Salo, officially broke all ties to the old Savoyard kingdom of Italy.

Mussolini's last government and fictitious republic proved to be no more than a puppet controlled by Berlin. Directed by his German liberators, Mussolini and his loyal Fascist circle sought to create a purely Fascist armed force composed of Italian soldiers from the old Savoyard army and new recruits in order to fight the Allies alongside Nazi troops throughout northern Italy. Those Italian soldiers who refused to join the new Fascist army and fight for the Fascist-Nazi cause were, if captured, either executed or, as in the case of Guareschi, transported to German concentration camps where they would be used as slave labor. Meanwhile, as the war in Italy progressed, the Allied armies which had moved up the southern regions of the peninsula were halted in central Italy. Concomitantly, Italian antifascists in northern and central Italy had formed independent partisan military units which fought a bloody war against both the German occupying forces and Mussolini's troops. The fighting men in the Italian partisan forces held varied political beliefs. While some identified with a new antifascist Catholic political agenda and others were antimonarchist republicans or Socialists, many partisans were Communists. Notwithstanding these significant political differences, what held together the Italian partisan forces was their antifascism and the brutality of the Nazi occupation. Fighting in the northern Italian countryside and in the region's many hamlets, towns, and cities, partisans dealt heavy blows to the Nazis and to Mussolini's forces from 1943 through 1945. The human costs of this struggle were high. In the Tuscan province of Massa-Carrara, for example, Nazi soldiers aided by Italian Fascist troops tortured and/or killed hundreds of persons. Some were tortured and shot simply for being suspected of aiding partisans and others suffered a similar fate because Nazi policy mandated that for every German soldier killed, ten Italian civilians would be executed. To this day, the Massa-Carrara countryside bears witness to this bloody war as plaques, flowers, or crosses mark the locations where German troops executed partisans, those suspected of partisan sympathies, and even civilian hostages and other noncombatants. Such sanguinary Nazi and Italian Fascist retributions were carried out countless times throughout northern and central Italy for the duration of the hostilities. With every savage Nazi and Italian Fascist reprisal, however, more and more antifascists came to believe that Communism provided the only avenue to the freedom which the Fascist Party and the Savoyard crown had conspired for so long to deny them. As increasing numbers of anti-fascist partisans were drawn to the Communist movement, the tide began to turn against the Nazi and Italian Fascist troops in Italy. Mussolini was eventually forced to recognize that his days were numbered. Fleeing for the Swiss border, Mussolini was captured and executed by a partisan detachment. Later Mussolini's body was brought to Milan, where his corpse was hung by its feet for all to see. After twenty-three years of dictatorship, war in Africa and in Europe, and the ferocity of the fighting and Nazi reprisals in Italy, the *Duce* had come to a brutal end.[28] Few Italians, however, could be long comforted by the dictator's death or even the official end of World War II, for they now faced a monumental task, one which involved rebuilding the social, economic, and political life of their devastated nation.

Guareschi wrote of this Italy, a nation worn down by Fascist dictatorship, ravaged by World War II, occupied by foreign troops and now, once again, polarized by the age-old struggle between secular and religious forces newly intensified by the Cold War. After World War II, Italy's political climate was radicalized on both the national and local levels. The end of the war brought the first free elections since the establishment of the Fascist dictatorship by Mussolini in 1922. As a result, the country experienced an all-out electoral battle for political power. Among the most popular of the parties of the left was the Italian Communist Party (PCI). Since Communist partisans and their leaders were to a large degree responsible for the liberation of northern and central Italy from Nazi and Fascist Party control, the newly formed PCI found favor among blue-collar workers throughout northern and central Italy. Many Italian workers had come to believe that whether the peninsula was ruled by the House of Savoy, by Fascist dictatorship, or by the parliament of the modern Italian republic, the fact remained that they had been and were still denied basic freedoms as well as an equitable share of the wealth they produced while laboring in the nation's factories and shops or on its soil. As Guareschi knew, these radical sentiments were particularly well established in the Po valley, for this region was the home of a deeply rooted left-wing tradition which first had drawn inspiration during the nineteenth century from the early Socialist movement and now found renewed vigor in the postwar Italian Communist Party.

Yet, Guareschi was also intimately familiar with how the growth of support for the Italian Communist Party was accompanied by a groundswell of support for the nascent Christian Democratic Party (DC). The Christian Democrats soon proved to the left that they were more formidable opponents than the *Popolari* had been after World War I. Openly supported by the United Sates government and American labor unions as well as by the Vatican and its army of local parish priests, Christian Democratic politicians were ready to battle the forces of the left in local and national elections. The Christian Democratic leaders, the Vatican, and their foreign allies saw this struggle as a war which needed to be won at all costs. Victory, therefore, required more than the standard political debates and simple moral approbation from Vatican City and the pulpits of thousands of local churches.

The United States of America was ready to step in with its immense financial resources to aid the Christian Democrats in this Cold War struggle for the Italian peninsula. In short, while the new Italian Republic was propped up with Marshall Plan monies, the CIA secretly financed the Christian Democratic Party and anticommunist Italian labor unions were given advice and dollars by various U.S. labor unions. Meanwhile, the Roman Catholic Church in Italy put its full weight behind the Christian Democrats. While the Vatican Radio applauded the United States government for its support, thousands of parish priests throughout the country proclaimed in countless homilies the sacrosanct status of the Christian Democratic Party and openly attacked all those who favored any of the parties of the left. The clerics reserved a special condemnation for supporters of the Italian Communist Party as it was viewed with the greatest alarm. After all, the rising popularity of the Communist Party in regions such as Tuscany, Reggio Emilia, Liguria, and Lombardy was a fact which could not be denied. Throughout northern Italy, numerous Communist Party candidates won local and national elections. By the early 1950s, for example, much of Guareschi's Po River valley was "Red." And yet, elected left-wing officials and Communist Party strategists at national and local levels alike were forced to recognize the continued religiosity and conservatism of many Italians.[29]

Italian religiosity and the strange relationships and uneasy coexistence which had developed out of the Catholic-Communist struggle was captured in a profound manner by Guareschi's two main characters, one a Catholic priest and the other a "Red" mayor. Using these two fictional, simple protagonists, Guareschi was able to personify average Italians and the polar ideologies which divided the peninsula into two hostile camps. Moreover, throughout the Don Camillo stories, Guareschi used comedy and satire to promote an anti-communist and pro-Christian political message. Guareschi's Don Camillo was ever ready, for example, to strike a blow against the forces of "godless Communism" which had invaded his Po River valley town. Lacking any fear of reprisal, the courageous priest, Don Camillo, proclaimed the truth of the Gospel in simple yet direct ways. Whether in print or on the screen, Don Camillo was shown to be a rough-and-tumble cleric of peasant origins, one whose actions could be understood by the average worker. Therefore, whenever the parish faithful were coerced by the threats of rowdy Communist party toughs, Guareschi had Don Camillo exchange more than a few well-placed punches with the local party's boys in scenes reminiscent of barroom brawls in early Hollywood Westerns. In the end, the Guareschian message is that Don Camillo was respected by common folk of the left and right for the blackened eyes he caused as well as for those he suffered. Guareschi offered readers and theater patrons a no-nonsense priest who would not shy away from the good fight, ready to roll up the sleeves of his vestments and take on the local Communists, one by one, in an arena recognizable to all workers and peasants. Indeed, Guareschi's straight-talking, bare-knuckled Don Camillo character personified the idealized virtues of the Italian working man, which were deeply rooted in the respect which industrial workers and rural laborers had for hard work, honesty and, if the need arose, readiness to physically defend one's interests and principles. Therefore, whether laboring in the fields or in the factory, a workman was a good man if he put in an honest day's labor, did not mince words, and stood ready to defend, by force if necessary, his principles and good name.

Don Camillo was similarly direct and forceful when faced with political elections and their results. Undaunted by the repeated election of "Reds" to local office, the priest sought to chastise the Communists in the public piazza and in private. During May Day celebrations, for example, Don Camillo would seek to disrupt the local Communists singing the *Internationale* and *Bandiera Rossa* (*The Red Flag*) and arouse their indignation by loudly ringing the village church bells. The bells which rang from the church steeple affirmed with holy music the primacy of the church to the faithful while ridiculing the apostate. When not struggling with the Communist Party, the good priest spent much of his time planning ways to bring ridicule to the party's leaders. Peppone, the mayor and most vocal spokesperson for the left, was the natural target. Guareschi had the rambunctious cleric challenge Peppone in countless bouts meant to test strength, willpower, intelligence,

and hunting and sporting skills. Being strong, wise, determined, and good at hunting and sports were commonly recognized as assets by the average worker and
peasant. Guareschi therefore made certain that in all the contests between Peppone
and Don Camillo, the representative of God was triumphant over the agent of
Communism.

Yet God's champion was also subject to human frailties and sin. Like many
others in his flock, Don Camillo was given to excessive pride. The priest's attempts to humiliate Peppone personally by excessively parading his victories in
public were checked by Christ himself. High above the main altar of the parish
church, the Redeemer, speaking from the cross, would warn Don Camillo of the
sins of pride and remind him of the Christian virtue of humility. Again and again,
Don Camillo would have to learn that while defeat of the "Reds" in electoral or
private contests was worthy of celebration, humiliating Peppone, the man, was
giving in to the sin of pride.

While Christ often chastised Don Camillo from the cross above the altar for
his human frailties, others less privy to the Savior's guidance were more likely to
fall from God's favor. Guareschi constructs a number of scenes in which the ideal-
istic claims and ideological pronouncements of Peppone and, implicitly, other Italian
Communists were put to the test. In every instance the mayor proved not to be so
"Red." Guareschi works to make clear that all too often men seek to better themselves at the price of others. Human avarice was often the culprit from which not
even Communists could escape. Thus one finds Peppone playing the state lottery
under a false name, as participating in it would not be proper in the eyes of his
comrades. Much to his surprise, the Communist mayor discovered he had won the
equivalent of thousands of dollars. Unable to collect the winnings without losing
face with his comrades, Peppone secretly asked Don Camillo to claim the money
as if he had been the lucky player. Hoping to use Peppone's good fortune to disgrace the "Red" mayor, Don Camillo agreed to collect the money in his own name.
Once again Jesus spoke to Don Camillo. From the heights above the church altar,
Christ, looking down from his cross, gently criticized Don Camillo for wishing to
destroy the reputation of another. At first, Don Camillo objected. What was the
purpose, he asked, in allowing Peppone, a sworn enemy of the Holy Mother Church,
such good fortune? Certainly, Don Camillo reasoned, Peppone must have won the
state lottery so that all could be made aware that Communist leadership was corrupt and hypocritical. Christ refused to allow the priest to expose Peppone. Whether
Communists or Christians, all people are sinners, Jesus reminded Don Camillo.
The parish priest reluctantly accepted his Savior's personal directive and handed
over the money to the mayor without a word. Peppone put the money in a bank in
another town and no one was the wiser. Yet a heavy tax on these winnings came
due when the mayor forced to agree to his wife's demands that their newborn son
receive the sacrament of baptism. Unable to publicly participate in such an event
because of his stature as a leader of the local Communists, Peppone worked out
an agreement with Don Camillo that his son would be secretly baptized in the

local parish. The price which Don Camillo exacted from Peppone was a high one: Peppone's son would be christened Giuseppe Lenin Camillo Bottazzi. Thus Don Camillo sought to ensure that the sins of the father could work in favor of the son's salvation.[30]

Perhaps the work which best reflects Guareschi's long struggle against the "Communist menace" is his *Comrade Don Camillo*.[31] First published in 1964, this book tells of how Don Camillo was able to force Peppone to include him in a delegation of Italian workers chosen by the Italian Communist Party to visit the Soviet Union. The tale, once again, starts with a most common human frailty, greed. Using a pseudonym, Peppone had secretly purchased a ticket in the national soccer sweepstakes. Through Peppone's small gambling vice, Jesus would provide the country priest with an opportunity to do good. After Peppone, seemingly through blind luck, won the ten million *lire* prize, Christ's plan slowly began to unfold. Peppone, of course, could not openly collect the winnings because his party's stance against the bourgeois decadence represented by state-sanctioned gambling was all too well known. Unable to collect the prize himself, yet not trusting just any man with his winnings, Peppone appealed to the parish priest to secretly collect the money for him. After considerable hesitation, Don Camillo agreed and later, with even greater reluctance, handed the money over to Peppone.

Having such a large sum sitting idle in his home, however, caused Peppone to return to the village church, a traditional sanctuary for both the faithful and sinners. Peppone asked Don Camillo to arrange a meeting between him and a nearby cleric who had connections to a savvy entrepreneur who could invest the communist mayor's money. The meeting, which Don Camillo duly arranged, culminated in a secret investment accord between Peppone and the businessman. With the passage of time, Peppone became a Senator, but his profits, good name, and high office were all threatened when the entrepreneur and his business dealings were investigated. Seeking political advantage from the scandal, Peppone foolishly denounced the Church and its ties to corrupt businessmen. Don Camillo met the challenge by privately reminding the Senator of his secret investment and threatening exposure if Peppone would not meet his demands. The simple priest had come to realize that Peppone's lottery winnings, secret investments and subsequent events all had been part of Christ's plan to send him far from his little church to proselytize in the most distant and unlikely places. Strengthened with a missionary zeal, the country priest firmly announced to the Communist Senator that he would assume the false identity of a loyal card-carrying Communist and join Peppone and the small band of comrades which the Italian Communist Party leadership had chosen to visit the Soviet Union. The price of Don Camillo's silence was high, but Peppone had little choice.[32] Thus Guareschi's characters, Don Camillo and Peppone, once again became the chief actors in the latest phase of God's ever-present plan of redemption.

Guareschi started his protagonists on their colorful adventure with a chance encounter on a Roman bus between Peppone and a man reading the communist daily, *L'Unita del Popolo*. Much to Senator Peppone's surprise the reader sitting next to him was Don Camillo disguised as a worker. The comrade priest explained that, as had been agreed, he was now all set to accompany Peppone and the other chosen party members to the Soviet Union. Father Camillo had somehow obtained the necessary papers to prove that he was Comrade Camillo Tarocci, the linotypist whom the Communist Party had chosen to visit the USSR with Peppone. Since these forged documents provided Don Camillo with the false identity he needed to join the tour, Peppone now was forced to fulfill his end of the bargain and admit the counterfeit comrade to the band of political tourists.

Once in Mother Russia, Peppone and his comrades were greeted by Nadia Petrovna, an attractive Italian-speaking interpreter, and Yenka Oregov, an official from the government tourist bureau. Little did their Soviet hosts realize that the scheduled week of visits to collective farms and the Soviet capital was to be highlighted by the machinations of Comrade Tarocci, God's own secret agent. Disguised as Comrade Tarocci, Don Camillo undertook his duties with great resolve. Under the watchful eye of Peppone and his Russian hosts, he had to exercise due caution, but every day provided him with new opportunities to plant the seed of faith and salvation in this "godless land." The first opportunity which Don Camillo saw presented itself in the form of a tractor. During the Italians' visit to one of the collective farms, their Soviet hosts proudly announced that the farm's high productivity was the result of their agrarian workers' political commitment, selfless hard work, and the advanced state of Soviet farm technology. Don Camillo could not help noticing, though, that a nonworking tractor he had just observed was of the same make which the Soviet government had earlier given to an Italian farm collective in his native region. Before Don Camillo could underscore the point that the tractor the Soviets had given to the Italians was also not in good working order, Peppone interrupted and announced just how grateful the Italians were for the Soviet gift. The Italian guests then visited another large farm, but this one turned out to be more productive and its machinery was in working order. This farm's high production levels and its well-maintained machinery resulted from the fact that its workers were allowed to sell their respective shares of the farm's crops in the marketplace. Just as Peppone and the members of his group saw the dilapidated state of the agricultural equipment on the collective farm, they could not but note the higher production and better-maintained equipment on the farm in which agrarian workers had a direct stake. Not content with underscoring the connection between the profit motive and productivity, Guareschi pursued one further point. The writer from Emilia had his simple peasant priest illuminate a paradox. All too many had foolishly put faith in this Communist motherland which could send men into space but could not ensure that tractors sent into the fields would make it back on their own power.[33]

Another opportunity to undermine misdirected faith was provided by the attractive Comrade Petrovna herself. Though outwardly cold and official, she was in fact attractive and personable. These traits were enough to inspire Comrade

Scamoggia, a Roman who was by nature drawn to beautiful women. Tactfully, Don Camillo encouraged Scamoggia's attempts to make friends with their Soviet translator. With every passing day, Nadia's coldness melted slowly away as the Roman comrade sought her attention and affections. Success would come after their Soviet journey's end when Nadia, on an official visit to Italy, decided to seek asylum and to stay with Scamoggia in Rome. But Comrade Nadia was not content with a simple living arrangement. She wanted to be married in a church. Agreeing to her demands, Scamoggia willingly left the Communist party and the two former communists were later married in the eyes of God. Thus Don Camillo acted as God's own marriage broker who also managed to bring two new souls into the bosom of the Church. The Guareschian message is clear. The immutable laws of initial sexual attraction, once transformed into divinely inspired mutual love, would overcome even the most committed Communists, whether they were tied to the Soviet state bureaucracy or the Italian Communist Party. That is to say, ideological and party loyalties as well as the much older human instincts were but a veneer which could be pierced by Christian virtues of love, friendship, compassion, and faith.[34]

Guareschi's priest discovered just how deep the faith of the common folk was in a modest house in a Soviet collective farm. Peppone and Don Camillo had made the acquaintance of Citizen Stephan Bordonny, a skilled mechanic who spoke fluent Italian. Bordonny revealed that he was the son of an old mechanic who had a shop just down the road from the hometown of Don Camillo and Peppone. As fate would have it, Bordonny continued to explain, he had been an Italian soldier when his unit was dispatched to aid the Nazis in the invasion of the Soviet Union. After some terrible battles he was captured. Unlike hundreds of thousands of Italian soldiers who were captured and later killed or worked to death in Soviet concentration camps, Bordonny was saved from summary execution and the labor camps. Bordonny explained that the Soviet soldiers who had captured him quickly recognized his mechanical skills and put him to work on a collective farm. By the end of the war, the captive Bordonny became enamored with a Polish woman and, since he had come to realize escape was impossible, he married her in a civil ceremony and later lived with her, their children, and her aged Polish mother on the collective farm. Just as his mechanical skills had made him valuable to the Soviet troops, these same abilities, Bordonny pointed out, made him indispensable on the collective farm. Both Comrade Tarocci and Peppone remained speechless while Bordonny told his story. As the tale continued, the incognito priest came to know that Bordonny's mother-in-law was on her deathbed and that his children had never been christened. Don Camillo, the priest, could not remain silent and inactive any longer. Not stopping to consider the penalty if discovered to be a cleric admitted into the Soviet Union with false papers, the comrade priest ordered Peppone to keep guard while Don Camillo celebrated mass, united Bordonny and his wife in the sacrament of marriage, and baptized their children in their house. Thus both Don Camillo and an astonished Peppone witnessed that faith was stronger than all the sufferings of war and even Soviet imprisonment.[35]

By having Peppone keep guard and later remain silent, Guareschi meant to show that religious faith and the Communist Senator's personal relationship with Don Camillo were even stronger than contemporary political ideology. Guareschi also narrated this sad tale to remind Italians both of the horrible fate suffered by their nation's troops at the behest of the Communist leadership of Soviet Union and of the refusal of the Italian Communist Party to acknowledge the plight of these unfortunate soldiers and their grieving relatives in Italy. In short, the author hoped that Italian voters would not forget the inhuman treatment to which the Soviet government had subjected Italian soldiers and the shameful abandonment of these troops by left-wing political candidates who wished to govern Italy. Guareschi thus waved the bloody flag of Italian patriotism in the face of what he believed were disingenuous claims of Communist internationalism and Communists' false proclamations of respect for justice and human rights.

Throughout Guareschi's stories his audience was provided with what he believed was the true path toward justice. In *Comrade Don Camillo*, for example, the author told of how the Soviet tour brought the Northern Italian Comrade Tavan to the realization that his Communist ideals rang hollow compared to the traditional social and religious values of his simple peasant parents. Guareschi began this tale by having the incognito priest take every opportunity to remind the farmer, Comrade Tavan, of the orthodox Communist view that peasants were reactionary. Tavan responded by outwardly agreeing with the Marxist assessment of the peasantry. He added, however, that the old people in the countryside were those who were most conservative and that these agrarian workers had great influence there because they worked like dogs from childhood to old age. Thus, Comrade Tavan's response hinted at a widespread belief that those agrarian workers who had survived a lifetime of hard labor deserved both respect and the right to material acquisitions which, after all, they had more than paid for by their toil and sweat. In fact, Guareschi hoped that readers would recognize what he believed were the true sentiments of Italian agrarian and urban workers hidden in Tavan's recitation of the official Communist Party explanations of the backwardness of the peasantry. Tavan explained, for example, that though the Communist Party had the answers, in the countryside the old people held on to all sorts of wrong ideas about property ownership and religion. In other words, Tavan continued, while the party appealed to reason, the old country folk were more willing to follow their hearts than their heads. Through Tavan's assessment of the workings of peasant society, Guareschi also unveiled his antimodernist distrust of the claim that truth and justice could be discovered only through the exercise of a cold and detached reasoning process. As if in open rebellion against the influence of the Enlightenment, Guareschi promoted, through his fictional peasants and workers, the belief that what was just and true could not be found solely through the imperatives of logic and reason. What was needed to discover truth and to realize the full potential of social and political justice, Guareschi maintained, was adherence to those traditional values whose worth had been made evident through countless generations. In addition, central to the Guareschian message was the need for an unabashed acknowledgement of the spiritual component inherent in humanity. Dig deep enough, Guareschian fictional characters seemed to say, and one would find a deeply rooted religious faith even in the most committed Communist. Though Tavan, for example, had outwardly rejected spiritual truth in favor of a false secular ideology, Don Camillo discovered that beneath the political radicalism of this proud comrade rested his Christian brother. This revelation was made clear after Comrade Tavan expressed his secret wish to Don Camillo.

Tavan explained that his peasant parents had suffered years of anguish, not knowing what had happened to one of their sons who had been shipped off to fight on the Russian steppes during the height of the war. The compassionate priest, enlisting the aide of the Communist Senator, then took Comrade Tavan to a wheat field where Bordonny had earlier shown Don Camillo and Peppone the forgotten graves of some thirty Italian artillerymen and *bersaglieri* who had been captured and machine-gunned by Soviet troops in 1942. Moved by the realization that his brother had been a member of one of these units, Tavan picked three tender stalks of wheat from the grave site to bring back to his parents. Tavan then carefully put a votive candle on the very spot from which the wheat had been taken. Meanwhile, Don Camillo said the Mass for the Dead in Latin while an understanding Peppone kept guard to warn of any intruders. As they left the graves and turned to look at the flickering candle, Don Camillo reminded Tavan that he had pleased his mother but not the Communist party. Tenderly touching the stalks of wheat, Comrade Tavan emphatically declared that he no longer gave a damn about the party.[36] With these three stalks of wheat, Guareschi united religious faith, as symbolized by the Christian trinity and promoted by the ancient rites of the Catholic Church, with Italian patriotic sentiments and human compassion for the dead and their grieving relatives.

Guareschi continued to describe the profound powers of faith and the shallowness of Communist ideology throughout *Comrade Don Camillo*. To drive the point home, Guareschi placed Don Camillo in the very heart of Communist power, Moscow. While visiting what Don Camillo called the capitol of melancholy, where people wore ill-fitting clothes and gloomy expressions, the incognito priest was surprised to find himself recognized by an Italian who was sitting beside him in the crowded waiting room of a major Moscow hotel. The Italian introduced himself as none other than an old acquaintance named Comassi. Comassi then related that now he was a broadcaster of government propaganda from a radio station in Prague. During the man's explanation, Don Camillo interrupted and explained that he remembered that when Comassi had been a young Communist toward the end of the war, the youthful comrade had been accused of killing an old wealthy property owner along with other members of his household. Denying culpability for this crime, Comassi implored Don Camillo to hear his confession so that once the truth was confirmed through the sacrament of confession, the priest could tell Comassi's parents of their son's innocence. As a priest, Don Camillo was unable to turn down the penitent even though they were sitting in the middle of a crowded hotel lobby. Surrounded by hundreds of eyes and ears, Don Camillo thus heard Comassi speak the truth in a confession whispered through a copy of *Pravda* which the exile held before him, feigning that he, as all too many party faithful, believed that truth was to be found in the Soviet newspaper.[37]

As part of the long voyage traveling about the Communist holy land in planes, trains, buses, trolleys, and subways, Guareschi has Peppone's pilgrims discover eternal truth on the Soviet ship named *Tovarisch*. Moreover, in this tale Guareschi again appealed to nationalistic sentiments by having Comrade Bacciga, whose knowledge of ships was part of his Genoese inheritance, bitterly point out that this very same vessel had been the *Cristoforo Colombo* before it and the *Giulio Cesare* had been taken by the Soviets at the end of the war. After chastising Bacciga for embarrassing their Soviet hosts, Peppone and his Italian comrades set sail under the watchful gaze of Comrades Oregov and Petrovna. No sooner had they left port, than all hell seemed to break loose as a ferocious storm tossed the proud ship about as if it were but a child's toy. Wave after wave broke over the ship's deck, threatening to send crew and passengers to their death in the darkened sea. At the height of the tempest, Peppone turned to Don Camillo and pleaded that he, for the love of God, do something. Don Camillo reached for his hidden crucifix. As he held it up and began to pray for God's mercy, the Italians, Comrade Nadia Petrovna, the Soviet ship captain, and his crew fell to their knees before him. Comrade Oregov, however, watched in anger as Don Camillo said *Ego vos absolvo a peccatis vestris, in nomine Patris et Filli et Spiritus Sancti.*[38] When the ship safely reached shore, the captain informed the Italians that the last massive wave had swept Comrade Oregov into the sea. Comrade Nadia would later explain to Don Camillo what the captain had told her immediately after the storm. According to the captain, she said, shortly after the worst of the storm, Comrade Oregov raved about betrayal and Vatican spies and threatened a board of inquiry. At that point, he and the captain came to blows and as the captain knocked him against the rail, she continued, a wave swept Oregov away.[39] While Guareschi wrote that Don Camillo chose to accept this explanation, he knew that his readers would assume that while the instrument of Oregov's death may have been the hand of the captain, this political zealot had been brought to his dark end by his own blindness to religious truth.

Giovanni Guareschi believed that the best way to check the rising popularity of Communism among the Italian urban and agrarian working classes was to use humor as a weapon in the quest for truth. Guareschi's writings show that he understood that humor walks the path of paradox, and that on this path one may find a shortcut to truth. Guareschi recognized the importance of a shortcut to truth, for in the Cold War struggle for political power, victory would be assured to those who captured both the hearts and minds of average Italian urban and agrarian workers. The task, however, would not be a simple one, for in the modern marketplace of ideas, Italians of all classes had become consumers of a new and complex popular culture whose songs and films, romance magazines and novels, as well as radio and television broadcasts, filled people's leisure time. In short, from the late 1940s through the 1960s, Italy had become more and more inundated with innumerable attractions of foreign and domestic origin which competed for the reading, listening, and viewing public. However, favored by an inherent skill and natural wit, Guareschi had just the formula needed to capture the public's attention. By employing satire and humor, the author's enchanting stories became widely popular among readers and film patrons in Italy and then throughout the world. This success was due, in large part, to the imagination, humor, sense of irony, and finely tuned narrative skills of Giovanni Guareschi. And yet, behind the folly and humor which the author skillfully exposed in telling of the daily lives of his fictional characters was Guareschi's clarion call. Recognizing that the definitive defeat of the Communists at the polls required their defeat in the cultural arena of images and ideas, Guareschi wrote of fictional characters whose political and religious beliefs reflected the convictions of those who actually lived and worked in Italy's cities and countryside. By depicting both the humanity and hypocrisy of his Communist fictional characters with humor and irony, the Emilian writer attempted to expose what he believed to be the errancy of Communist ideology while underscoring the mitigating virtues of honor and compassion which, nurtured by centuries of religious and cultural traditions, could still be found in every person. Thus implicit in Guareschian tales was the promise that as Communist ideas had been defeated in the fictional life experiences of the characters in Don Camillo's little world, the eternal spiritual truths celebrated by the Catholic Church and defended by traditional political and cultural norms would prove triumphant in the real-life struggles of the global Cold War.

Notes

1. In Italy, the title *Don* has been used to indicate the clerical status of the person so addressed. For an interesting assessment of the life of Giovanni Guareschi and its relationship to the fictional characters, Don Camillo and Peppone, see Alessandro Gnocchi, *Giovannino Guareschi: una storia italiana* (Milan, Italy: Rizzoli, 1998).

2. For an overview of U.S. activities in Italy during the postwar period see James Edward Miller, *The United States and Italy: 1940–1950* (Chapel Hill: University of North Carolina Press, 1986). For the impact of U.S. initiatives on Italian labor see Ronald L. Filippelli, *American Labor and Postwar Italy, 1943–1953* (Stanford, Calif.: Stanford University Press, 1989).

3. For an interesting analysis of Italian comic film see Jean Gili, *Arrivano i mostri: i volti della commedia italiana* (Bologna, Italy: Cappelli, 1980).

4. Peter Bondanella, *Italian Cinema: From Neorealism to the Present* (New York: Ungar, 1988). Professor Bondanella provides the definitive English-language monograph

on the Italian film industry. Along with his assessments of the aesthetic qualities of Italian films, Professor Bondanella's analysis of the relationship between the industry and political events is particularly enlightening.

5. Guareschi's work was roundly criticized by leftist political and literary leaders who saw his political views as reactionary and his writings as mediocre at best. Yet, the fact remains that the tales of Don Camillo and Peppone found some favor among some ordinary Italians who identified with either communist or, more generally, left-wing political movements. Paradoxically, Guareschi received criticism in pro-Catholic circles where some, such as Father Lorenzo Bedeschi, saw in the Don Camillo-Christ-Communism dialogues heretical notions inspired by Guareschi's sense of irony which suggested that the differences between Christian and communist ideals were not so great. For a concise description of the varied assessments of Guareschi's work see Gnocchi, *Giovannino*, 13–16.

6. Giovanni Guareschi, *Don Camillo's Dilemma*, trans. Frances Frenaye (New York: Pocket Books, 1966). This work was originally published in Italian as *Il Dilemma di Don Camillo* (Milan, Italy: Rizzoli, 1953). In the U.S. the book was first published as *Don Camillo's Dilemma*, trans. Frances Frenaye (New York: Farrar, Straus & Young, 1954) and also, in the same year, by the New York house of Grosset and Dunlap. Unless otherwise noted, all citations to *Don Camillo's Dilemma* will refer to the Pocket Books edition.

7. Guareschi, *Don Camillo's Dilemma*, 1–4. One could suggest that Giovanni Guareschi's family history nurtured his literary ambitions. Although Guareschi (born in 1908 and died in 1968) held a deep affection for his father, Primo Augusto Teodosio, who had been a small landowner and largely unsuccessful merchant, the author's mother, Lina Maghenzani, was a teacher and as such she had a seminal influence on his writing career. After receiving a university degree in Classical Studies from the University of Parma, Guareschi pursued his writing ambitions with the blessing of his mother. Between 1929 and 1936 he wrote and drew pictures for the humor magazine *Bertoldo*. This was followed by freelance work for *Oggi* (1945–1968). Throughout the post–World War II period (1945–1968), he continued his association with *Candido*, a periodical which he had founded and worked on as editorial director. *Candido* was associated with Savoyard political aspirations and thus was a promonarchist publication. See Gnocchi, *Giovannino*, 14–16.

8. Guareschi, *Don Camillo's Dilemma*, 4. The first English-language publications of Guareschi's work titled *Mondo piccolo: Don Camillo* (Milan, Italy: Rizzoli, 1948) were numerous and they included: *The Little World of Don Camillo*, trans. Una Vincenzo Troubridge (New York: Pellegrini & Cudahy, 1950); *Little World of Don Camillo* (New York: F. Watts, 1950); and *The Little World of Don Camillo* (New York: Farrar, Straus & Giroux, 1950). In English alone, this single work was published six more times by 1974. Guareschi's work, *Mondo piccolo: Don Camillo e il suo gregge* (Milan, Italy: Rizzoli, 1953), was quickly published in the U.S.A. as *Don Camillo and His Flock*, trans. Frances Frenaye (New York: Grosset & Dunlap, 1952) and in Britain it was published as *Don Camillo and the Prodigal Son* (London: Gollancz, 1952). The publication history of other Guareschi works includes: *Il dilemma di Don Camillo* (Milan, Italy: Rizzoli, 1953) which was published in English as *Don Camillo's Dilemma* (New York: Grosset & Dunlap, 1954) and *Don Camillo's Dilemma*, trans. Frances Frenaye (New York: Farrar, Straus & Young, 1954) and

also printed in John Kennedy, *Light on the Mountain* (Garden City, N.J.: Catholic Family Book Club, 1957); *Don Camillo prende il diavolo per la coda* (Milan, Italy: Rizzoli, 1956), published in the U.S. as *Don Camillo Takes the Devil by the Tail* (New York: Farrar, Straus & Cudahy, 1957), while in Britain the book was published as *Don Camillo and the Devil* (London: Gollancz, 1957). Guareschi's work titled *Mondo piccolo: Il compagno Don Camillo* (Milan, Italy: Rizzoli, 1963) was published in English as *Comrade Don Camillo* (New York: Farrar, Straus & Giroux, 1964). The last Don Camillo book, published the year after the author's death, was *Mondo Piccolo: Don Camillo e i giovanni d'oggi* (Milan, Italy: Rizzoli, 1969), was printed in the U.S. as *Don Camillo Meets the Flower Children* (New York: Farrar, Straus & Giroux, 1969) and in Britain it was published as *Don Camillo Meets the Hell's Angels* (London: Gollancz, 1970). Literally translated, the Italian title of this last work would read "Don Camillo and Today's Youth." This Italian title had certainly a wider thematic range than the title of either English edition. Yet, one could observe, the difference in the English edition titles simply reflects different marketing strategies. Nevertheless, by choosing different titles in order to make the book more attractive to the English-speaking public on their respective sides of the Atlantic, the New York and London based publishing firms also gave evidence to the particular cultural stereotypes dominant in the U.S. and Britain. Another interesting work which offers a humorous insight into the family life of the Guareschi clan is Giovanni Guareschi, *The House that Nino Built,* trans. Frances Frenaye (New York: Farrar, Straus & Young, 1953).

9. Spanning the Cold War period, the films (all but the last of which were produced between 1950 and 1974) were titled *Don Camillo, Il Ritorno di Don Camillo, Don Camillo e l'onorevole Peppone, Il compagno Don Camillo, Don Camillo monsignore, Don Camillo e i giovanni d'oggi,* and, finally, a 1984 motion picture simply called *Don Camillo* in which the internationally known Italian actor Terrence Hill was also the director. This last film presented a composite of some of the more famous scenes from the earlier films. While Italian was the original language of the films, eventually all were subtitled and/or translated into French, English, German, and Spanish.

10. Finding a director for the first Don Camillo film was not an easy task. Many Italian directors refused because they believed that they would be chastised for making a film which was so clearly antileftist in tone and theme. Among the Italian directors who refused to make the first Don Camillo motion picture were Mario Camerini, Vittorio De Sica, and Luigi Zampa. The situation was deemed so serious that the American director Frank Capra was asked to take on the film, but since his contract with Paramount Pictures would not permit him to accept until after 1953, Rizzoli looked elsewhere. Throughout the various films made of Guareschi's works, the author had serious difficulties with the directors and the scripts they used. From the very start, Guareschi had particular difficulties with the first director of the Don Camillo film series, Jean Duvivier. Duvivier directed *Don Camillo* (1952), and *Il ritorno di Don Camillo* (1953). Both of these motion pictures, Guareschi bitterly complained to Duvivier and then to Angelo Rizzoli, made a mockery of his characters and deviated too radically from his original stories. Guareschi even argued that in order to appeal to a larger audience, his stories had been depoliticized. These protestations only increased when Carmine Gallone directed the third film in the series, *Don Camillo e l'onorevole*

Peppone (1955), and then the fourth, *Don Camillo monsignore . . . ma non troppo* (1961), and finally when Luigi Comencini directed the fifth film, *Il compagno don Camillo* (1965). It is also interesting to note that in 1950 Guareschi worked on another film, *Gente Cosi*, which was loosely based on some of his short stories that had been published in *Candido*. This picture had little success at the box office. See Gnocchi, *Giovannino*, 181–204.

11. For the best English-language overview of Italian history and the contribution of Italians to Western civilization see Giuliano Procacci, *History of the Italian People* (New York: Harper & Row Publishers, 1968); George Holmes, ed., *The Oxford History of Italy* (Oxford, U.K.: Oxford University Press, 1997); and Harry Hearder, *Italy: A Short History* (Cambridge, U.K.: Cambridge University Press, 1997).

12. For descriptions of the nexus between economic, social, and political life in both urban and rural Italy see: Rudolph M. Bell, *Fate and Honor, Family and Village: Demographic and Cultural Change in Rural Italy since 1800* (Chicago: University of Chicago Press, 1979); James C. Davis, *Rise from Want: A Peasant Family in the Machine Age* (Philadelphia: University of Pennsylvania Press, 1986); David I. Kertzer, *Family Life in Central Italy, 1880–1910: Sharecropping, Wage Labor and Coresidence* (New Brunswick, N.J.: Rutgers University Press, 1984); Roland Sarti, *Long Live the Strong: A History of Rural Society in the Apennine Mountains* (Amherst: The University of Massachusetts Press, 1985); and David I. Kertzer and Richard P. Saller, eds., *The Family in Italy: From Antiquity to the Present* (New Haven, Conn.: Yale University Press, 1991).

13. See Michele Angeli, *Aronte Lunese* (Pisa, Italy: Prosperi, 1835); Antonio Bernieri, *Carrara* (Genoa, Italy: Sagep, 1985); Antonio Bernieri, *Cento anni di storia sociale a Carrara: 1815–1921* (Milan, Italy: Feltrinelli, 1961); Antonio Bernieri, *Il Porto di Carrara: storia e attualita* (Genoa, Italy: Sagep, 1983); Antonio Bernieri, *Storia di Carrara Moderna: 1915–1935* (Pisa, Italy: Pacini, 1983); Massimo Bertozzi, *Massa* (Genoa, Italy: Sagep, 1985); Ernesto Bigi and Alessandro Guidoni, *Massa nella Storia* (Massa, Italy: Tipographia Sociale Apuana, 1961); Luigi Campolonghi, *Pontremoli: Una Cittadina Italiana fra L'80 e il '900* (Venice, Italy: Marsilio, 1988); Amelio Fara, *La Spezia* (Bari, Italy: Laterza, 1983); Ferrando Cabona, Isabella Crusi and Elizabetta Crusi, *Storia dell' Insediamento in Lunigiana, Alta Valle Aullela* (Genoa, Italy: Sagep, 1982); Ferrando Cabona, Isabella Crusi, and Elizabetta Crusi, *Storia dell' Insediamento in Lunigiana, Valle del Rosario* (Genoa, Italy: Sagep, 1982); Carlo Lazzoni, *Carrara e le sue ville: Guida storico, artistico, industriale seguita da brevi cenni su Luni e sue rovine* (Carrara, Italy: Drovandi, 1880); Pietro Lorenzini, "Tyranny of Stone: Economic Modernization and Political Radicalization in the Marble Industry of Massa-Carrara (1859–1914)" (Ph.D. diss., Loyola University of Chicago, 1994); Giorgio Mori, ed., *Storia D'Italia Le Regioni Dall'Unita a Oggi: La Toscana* (Turin, Italy: Giulio Einaudi, 1986); Emilio Palla, *Massa e la sua gente* (Massa, Italy: Uliveti, 1984); Raffaello Raffaelli, *Monografia storica ed agraria del Circondario di Massa Carrara compilato fino al 1881* (Lucca, Italy: Rossi, 1882); and Giulivio Ricci, *Aulla e il suo Territorio Attraverso i Secoli* (Pontremoli, Italy: Artigianelli, 1990).

14. See Stefano Jacini, *I Risultati della Inchiesta Agraria* (Turin, Italy: Piccola Biblioteca Einaudi, 1976). For an analysis of local developments see Renato Mori, *La Lotta Sociale in Lunigiana: 1859–1904* (Massa, Italy: Le Monnier, 1958).

15. For a general understanding of *mezzadria* and the use of *braccianti* in various areas of Italy see Giuliana Biagioli, "La diffusione della mezzadria nell' Italia centrale: Un modello di svilupo demografico ed economico," *Bollettino di demografia storica* 3 (March 1986): 219–235; Aldo Pagani, *I braccianti della valle padana* (Rome, Italy: N.p., 1932); Jacini, *Inchiesta Agraria*; G. Mori, *Storia: La Toscana*; Bell, *Fate and Honor*; Kertzer, *Family Life*; and Sarti, *Long Live*.

16. For a general overview of Italian unification see Denis Mack Smith, *Cavour* (New York: Alfred A. Knopf, 1985); Denis Mack Smith, *Italy* (Ann Arbor: University of Michigan Press, 1959); Denis Mack Smith, ed., *The Making of Italy: 1796–1870* (New York: Harper & Row Publishers, 1968). For more focused and still classic studies see George Macaulay Trevelyan, *Garibaldi and the Thousand*, (London: Longman, Green and Co., 1912), William Roscoe Thayer, *The Life and Times of Cavour*, 2 vols. (Boston: Houghton Mifflin Company, 1911); and also Raymond Grew, *A Sterner Plan for Italian Unity: The Italian National Society in the Risorgimento* (Princeton, N.J.: Princeton University Press, 1963); and Mack Walker, ed., *Plombieres: Secret Diplomacy and the Rebirth of Italy* (London: Oxford University Press, 1968). See also John A. Davis, "The Age of the Risorgimento," in Holmes, ed., *Oxford History of Italy,* 235–263; Derek Beales, *The Risorgimento and the Unification of Italy* (London: Longman, 1981); and A. William Salomone, "The Risorgimento and the Political Myth of the Revolution that Failed," in *Italy from the Risorgimento to Fascism: An Inquiry into the Origins of the Totalitarian State*, ed. A. William Salomone, (London: David & Charles Publishers, 1971), 5–22.

17. A seminal contribution to the literature on the economic history of modern Italy is found in Shepard B. Clough, *The Economic History of Modern Italy* (New York: Columbia University Press, 1964); see also Christopher Seton-Watson, *Italy from Liberalism to Fascism: 1870–1925* (London: Methuen & Co., 1967), 78–80; Adrian Lyttelton, "Politics and Society 1870–1915," in *Oxford History of Italy,* ed. George Holmes (Oxford, U.K.: Oxford University Press, 1997), 235–263; Gianni Toniolo, *An Economic History of Liberal Italy: 1850–1918* (London: Routledge, 1990); and Mack Smith, *Italy*, 43–51. For an analysis of the localized impact of the general movement towards economic reform in Tuscany see David G. LoRomer, *Merchants and Reform in Livorno: 1814–1868* (Berkeley: University of California Press, 1987), 247–272.

18. See Richard Hostetter, *The Italian Socialist Movement: Origins: 1860–1882* (Princeton, N.J.: D. Van Nostrand Co., 1958); Martin Clark, *Modern Italy: 1871–1982* (London: Longman, 1984), 69–90; Giovanni Manacorda, *Il Socialismo nella storia d' Italia* (Bari, Italy: Laterza, 1966). For examples of local developments see Orazio Pugliese, Caterina Repetti, and Giulivio Ricci, eds., *Movimento Socialista in Lunigiana tra la fine dell' Ottocento e il Novecento* (Pontremoli, Italy: Artigianeli, 1990); Mori, *Lotta Sociale*; Raffaelli, *Monografia;* and Giorgio Sacchetti, *Sovversivi in Toscana* (Todi, Italy: Altre Edizioni, 1983).

19. D. L. Horowitz, *The Italian Labor Movement* (Cambridge, Mass.: Harvard University Press, 1963). For a concise summary of Italian anarchism see James Joll, *The Anarchists* (London: Longman, 1964); and for an analysis of the relationship between workers and politics on a local level see David H. Bell, "Worker Culture and Worker Politics: The Experience of an Italian Town," *Social History* iii, (March 1978): 1–21. See also A. William

Salomone, *Italy in the Giolittian Era: Italian Democracy in the Making: 1900–1914* (Philadelphia: University of Pennsylvania Press, 1945). For an interesting and humorous reference to political and economic activities on the part of northern Italian farm workers as interpreted by Guareschi see Giovanni Guareschi, *Comrade Don Camillo*, trans. Frances Frenaye (New York: Pocket Books, 1964), 73. Here Guareschi has Peppone proudly announce to the Russian hosts who had escorted him through some Russian collective farms that in the first decades of the twentieth century some of Italy's first and most successful people's cooperatives had been established in the province of Emilia.

20. See Anthony Cardoza, *Agrarian Elites and Italian Fascism: The Province of Bologna: 1901–1926* (Princeton, N.J.: Princeton University Press, 1982), 209–274; Seton-Watson, *Italy from Liberalism*, 413–560; Mack Smith, *Italy*, 281–337; Lyttelton, "Politics and Society," 235–263. On the development of the Catholic political movement see Mario G. Rossi, *Le Origini del Partito Cattolico: Movimento cattolico e lotta di classe nell' Italia liberale* (Rome, Italy: Editore Riuniti, 1977); and Sandor Agocs, *The Troubled Origins of the Italian Catholic Labor Movement: 1878–1914* (Detroit, Mich.: Wayne State University Press, 1988). For insight on the impact of immigration and emigration on Italian workers in Italy and host nations see Dino Cinel, *The National Integration of Italian Return Migration: 1870–1929* (Cambridge, U.K.: Cambridge University Press, 1991); and Madelyn Holmes, *Forgotten Migrants: Foreign Workers in Switzerland before World War I* (Cranbury, N.J.: Associated University Presses, 1988).

21. Seton-Watson, *Italy from Liberalism*, 413–560; Clark, *Modern Italy*, 180–213; Mack Smith, *Italy*, 321–328; and Cardoza, *Agrarian Elites*, 209–274. For assessments of the emergence of Italian communism and its leaders see Antonio Gramsci, *Selections from Political Writings 1910–1920* (New York: International Publishers, 1977); John M. Cammett, *Antonio Gramsci and the Origins of Italian Communism* (Stanford, Calif.: Stanford University Press, 1967); Martin Clark, *Antonio Gramsci and the Revolution that Failed* (New Haven, Conn.: Yale University Press, 1977); and Paolo Spriano, *L' Occupazione delle fabbriche* (Turin, Italy: Giulio Einaudi Editore, 1975).

22. Gaetano Salvemini, *The Fascist Dictatorship in Italy* (New York: Howard Fertig, 1967); Angelo Tasca, *Nascita e avvento del fascismo*, 2 vols. (Florence, Italy: La Nuova Italia Editrice, 1950); and Max Gallo, *Mussolini's Italy: Twenty Years of the Fascist Era* (New York: Macmillan Publishing Co., 1974), 3–120. For a concise and thoughtful analysis of Italian Fascism see Alexander De Grand, *Italian Fascism: Its Origins and Development* (Lincoln: University of Nebraska Press, 1982), 3–37; and Elizabeth Wiskermann, *Fascism in Italy: Its Development and Influence* (London: Macmillan, 1970). For another view on the debate concerning Mussolini's early radicalism see also G. A. Borghese, "Mussolini the Revolutionary: The Intellectual Flux," in Salomone, *Italy from the Risorgimento*, ed., 167–181.

23. Donald H. Bell, *Sesto San Giovanni: Workers, Culture, and Politics in an Italian Town: 1880–1922* (New Brunswick, N.J.: Rutgers University Press, 1986); Clark, *Modern Italy*; David D. Roberts, *The Syndicalist Tradition and Italian Fascism* (Chapel Hill: University of North Carolina Press, 1979); Seton-Watson, *Italy from Liberalism*, 561–577; and Cardoza, *Agrarian Elites*, 290–339.

24. Alan Cassels, *Fascist Italy* (Arlington Heights, Ill.: Harlan Davidson, 1985), 5–36; Salvemini, *Fascist Dictatorship*, 19–54; Mack Smith, *Italy*, 347–364; Denis Mack Smith, *Italy and Its Monarchy* (New Haven, Conn.: Yale University Press, 1989);

25. See Adrian Lyttelton, *The Seizure of Power: Fascism in Italy, 1919–1929* (London: Weidenfeld and Nicolson, 1973). For a general overview see Mack Smith, *Italy*, 357–387; and also De Grand, *Italian Fascism*, 41–57. For Marxian analysis see Palmiro Togliatti *Lectures on Fascism* (New York: International Publishers, 1976); and Nicos Poulantzas, *Fascism and Dictatorship: The Third International and the Problem of Fascism* (London: Verso, 1979). See also Frank J. Coppa, *Planning, Protectionism, and Politics in Liberal Italy: Economics and Politics in the Giolittian Age* (Washington, D.C.: Catholic University of America Press, 1971); Richard Collier, *Duce: A Biography of Benito Mussolini* (New York: Viking Press, 1971); and Clark, *Modern Italy*, 203–242. Adrian Lyttelton, ed., *Italian Fascism from Pareto to Gentile* (London: Cape, 1973) provides insight into leading Fascist intellectuals. See also Federico Chabod, *A History of Italian Fascism*, trans. Muriel Grindrod (London: Weidenfeld and Nicolson, 1963). For insight on how the Fascist regime tried to shape the political values of Italian youth see Tracy H. Koon, *Believe, Obey, Fight: Political Socialization of Youth in Fascist Italy, 1922–1943* (Chapel Hill: University of North Carolina Press, 1985). A definitive analysis of the relationship between Fascism in the countryside and in the city in the early days of the movement is provided by Alice A. Kelikian, *Town and Country under Fascism: The Transformation of Brescia, 1915–1926* (Oxford, U.K.: Claredon Press, 1986); and see also Paul Corner, *Fascism in Ferrara: 1915–1925* (London: Oxford University Press, 1975). For an analysis of how the regime attempted to achieve popularity among the Italian workers see Victoria de Grazia, *Consenso e Cultura di Massa nell' Italia Fascista: L' Organizzazione del Dopolavoro* (Bari, Italy: Editori Laterza, 1981); and for a review of the social context of Italian Fascism see Edward R. Tannenbaum, *The Fascist Experience: Italian Society and Culture, 1922–1945* (New York: Basic Books, 1972). On the evolution of Italian industrialization before and during the Fascist period see the outstanding work of Professor Giorgio Mori, *Il capitalismo industriale in Italia: Processo d' industrializzazione e storia d'Italia* (Rome, Italy: Riuniti, 1977). For a seminal work on how European elites retained their power after the First World War and through the emergence of the Fascist movement see Charles S. Maier, *Recasting Bourgeois Europe: Stabilization in France, Germany and Italy in the Decade after World War I* (Princeton, N.J.: Princeton University Press, 1975). For an analysis of European Fascism see Stuart J. Woolf, *Fascism in Europe* (New York: Methuen, 1968).

26. A good overview of Italian Fascist foreign policy is provided by Denis Mack Smith, *Mussolini's Roman Empire* (New York: Viking Press, 1976). For insight into Mussolini's Ethiopian venture see G. W. Baer, *The Coming of the Italian-Ethiopian War* (Cambridge, Mass.: Harvard University Press, 1976) and for a more detailed analysis see Brian R. Sullivan "A Thirst for Glory: Mussolini, the Italian Military and the Fascist Regime: 1922–1940" (Ph.D. diss., Columbia University, 1981). Roberto Battaglia, *La Prima Guerra d'Africa* (Turin, Italy: Einaudi, 1958) provides a most interesting view of the Italo-Ethiopian War of 1895–1896.

27. For a general review see Mack Smith, *Mussolini's Roman Empire* and Collier, *Duce!: A Biography of Benito Mussolini* (New York: Viking Press, 1971). A more detailed analysis of Mussolini's foreign and war policies is provided in Macgregor Knox, *Mussolini Unleashed, 1939–1941: Politics and Strategy in Fascist Italy's Last War* (Cambridge, U.K.: Cambridge University Press, 1982).

28. For the Italian-German alliance and the relationship between Mussolini and Hitler see F. W. Deakin, *The Brutal Friendship: Mussolini, Hitler and the Fall of Italian Fascism* (New York: Harper and Row Publishers, 1962); and also Knox, *Mussolini Unleashed*. For insight into the economics of Fascist imperialism see Enzo Santarelli, "The Economic and Imperial Background of Fascist Imperialism," in *The Ax Within: Italian Fascism in Action*, ed. Roland Sarti (New York: New Viewpoints, 1974).

29. For a favorable interpretation of the rise of the Christian Democratic Party see Elisa A. Carrillo, *Alcide de Gasperi: The Long Apprenticeship* (Notre Dame, Ind.: University of Notre Dame Press, 1965). A seminal political history of this period is provided in Giuseppe Mammarella, *Italy after Fascism: A Political History, 1943–1963* (Montreal, Canada: Mario Casalini Press, 1964). For more recent critical analyses see Joseph LaPalombara, *Democracy Italian Style* (New Haven, Conn.: Yale University Press, 1987); Paul Ginsborg, *A History of Contemporary Italy: Society and Politics, 1943–1988* (London: Penguin Group, 1990); and Donald Sassoon, *Contemporary Italy: Politics, Economy and Society since 1945* (London: Longman, 1986). For an assessment of the modern Italian political system and culture see Mark Gilbert, *The Italian Revolution: The End of Politics Italian Style?* (Boulder, Colo.: Westview Press, 1995); and also the somewhat dated but still useful work by Frederic Spotts and Theodor Wieser, *Italy: A Difficult Democracy: A Survey of Italian Politics* (London: Cambridge University Press, 1986).

30. The references to the tales mentioned above were taken from *Don Camillo's Dilemma*. The stories in this book neatly summarize both the humor and general theme found throughout Guareschi's best works.

31. Giovanni Guareschi, *Comrade Don Camillo*, trans. Frances Frenaye (New York: Pocket Books, 1965).

32. Guareschi, *Comrade Don Camillo*, 12–17.

33. Guareschi, *Comrade Don Camillo*, 19–36.

34. Guareschi, *Comrade Don Camillo*, 48–61 and 162–163.

35. Guareschi, *Comrade Don Camillo*, 72–86.

36. Guareschi, *Comrade Don Camillo*, 99–107.

37. Guareschi, *Comrade Don Camillo*, 122–26.

38. Guareschi, *Comrade Don Camillo*, 150. Here, Don Camillo gives absolution to the ship's passengers, who are facing death, in Latin, the traditional language of the Catholic Church. In English, Don Camillo's words would read, "I absolve you of your sins, in the name of the Father, Son, and Holy Spirit."

39. Guareschi, *Comrade Don Camillo*, 141–153 and 164.

4

From Guthrie through Dylan to Springsteen: Losing the Working Touch

David S. Sims

A particular succession of notes created a tune. Certain notes started it, you rec-
ognized them but the music immediately carried you someplace else, behind the
notes, between them. The meaning of the notes was where they took you and how
you felt to be there, behind them, feeling again what you felt another time when
you heard the notes played. A fast, jumpy tune makes you sad. A slow song thumps
you between the shoulder blades and you remember the wings folded back there
and they open and fly you away.[1]

—John Edgar Wideman

Tuning

Myth and consciousness are two linguistic constructs dangerous in their mallea-
bility, yet tenable definitions of both are first necessary in order to understand the
linkages between the music, lyrics, and—most importantly—*presences* of Woody
Guthrie, Bob Dylan, and Bruce Springsteen. On surface levels, connections between these three iconic performers are readily apparent. Musically speaking, the
influence of Guthrie upon Dylan has long been noted, and the profound traces
of the first two artists in Springsteen's solo work readily detectable. In one sense
—that being how written language must always follow whatever music actually is, and whatever music does or might do intellectually or emotionally to par-

ticular members of certain audiences—there is little to suggest that has not already been noted. Even a cursory review of titles from the available interdisciplinary literature will provide a general understanding of the myriad ways academic and popular paradigms have already been applied to all three artists, both individually and collectively. Yet my focus here is concerned less with the rather obvious intellectual or aesthetic similarities, and more with what such connections might reveal about the transformation and subsumation of a collective, working-class identity.

Myths of various kinds both inform and surround the development of identity. As Jerome Bruner writes, "the mythologically instructed community provides its members with a library of scripts upon which the individual may judge the internal drama of his multiple personalities . . . Personality imitates myth" and "myth becomes the tutor, the shaper of identities."[2] Thus, myth is first of all a relational term. Generally speaking, it is one manifestation of the natural human attempt to weave a coherent and encompassing story—a metanarrative, if you will—regarding the possible roles for the individual within collective experience. As Joseph Campbell writes, "The second function of a living mythology is to offer an image of the universe that will be in accord with the knowledge of the time, the sciences and the fields of action of the folk to whom the mythology is addressed."[3] In general terms, myths by their nature must remain flexible and adaptive—characteristics that are shared not only by many popular songs, but also by theoretical frameworks.

Secondly, all myths must inevitably employ a language that is subtle, symbolic, metaphorical, associative. If enough individuals find their own internal, often inchoate, utterances either echoed or answered within the particular structure, codes, and rendering of a tale, then that tale has at least the potential to evolve into myth.

It is obvious that Guthrie, Dylan, and Springsteen are all tellers of tales, and that at least some of their musical stories—certainly "This Land is Your Land" for Guthrie, "All Along the Watchtower" for Dylan, and "Born in the U.S.A." for Springsteen—have achieved what I would term a mythic status. Interpretations of what particular mythic stances these songs encircle and what those mean are, of course, dependent upon an ever-changing rhetorical context (See, for example, curious endnote #19 in Rauch, *op cit.*).[4] But more significantly than the individual works of each artist, by now it is obvious that all three figures *themselves* have come to occupy iconic niches within the popular imagination. It is nearly impossible for people to listen to works from any one of these bards without carrying some sort of foreknowledge regarding their creator's past or current status in the pantheon of American popular music. What this knowledge might consist of, how accurate or extensive it may or may not be, and how it was acquired, are nearly moot questions. The point is that all three figures, in some form, swim inside the framework of popular music, one cultural arena where the dialectics of the individual and the group are clearly at issue. That being the case, each has long been fair game for academics—not to mention journalists, politicians, reviewers, and a score of other arbiters of public discourse. But now, given the current intellectual climate which asks us to question some of our most deeply held myths, not the least of which is the seemingly objective impartiality of academic discourse, the primary questions are not only *what* do we discuss when we put Guthrie, Dylan, and Springsteen together, but also *how* do we discuss them?

Nicholas Bromell, concerned with the creation of a new vocabulary of meaning to diffuse the rigid distinctions between private and public, explores the role of imagination in politics. In *Tikkun*, he writes that "The meanings of Bob Dylan (and I believe, of all popular culture) are essentially latent, to be understood as Potentialities rather than as determinants of meaning. They do not cause the listener to articulate certain propositions in the mind . . . but they provoke the listener to experience one or more such relations."[5]

No matter how we interpret the isolated, syntactical intent of individual works within the extensive canons of Guthrie, Dylan, and Springsteen, at least one of the propositions all three bards ask us to consider has a lot to do with being isolated, powerless, and forgotten workers entangled in the web of a voracious capitalistic spider. Regardless of his or her economic circumstances, the conscious listener would have to be deaf not to hear such a surface similarity within the works of the three artists. All three lyricists have—in one way or another—given voices, names, and faces to those theretofore recognized yet inevitably innocuous people. Mythologically speaking—given the admittedly loose private/public component of the term posited here—such utterances become political statements. Why? Because myth always must precede politics, no matter how either word is defined. Whereas politics is always a conceptual endeavor (since it always, linguistically speaking, seeks to contain rather than verify the isolated experience), stories provide and define the specifics, the actualities, that invite listeners into the tensions that comprise the inner lives and outer worlds of particular human beings.

When it comes to the mythic dimensions of Guthrie, Dylan, and Springsteen, the essential and enduring questions will always remain: What do any of their words/performances *mean*? Who is speaking of what and to whom? What aspects of human experience are shared and what aspects will remain forever unknown? What are the limitations of verbal/musical communication? Who hears what, when and how? How much is a matter of interpretation and how much has to do with essential truths about being workers in a capitalistic society?

Bromell creates a profound and useful construct when he states earlier in his essay:

> when I write "Bob Dylan," I do not mean that particular flesh and blood person; nor do I mean the sum total of his works. I mean the composite figure created when we put these two together with the act of listening to his songs. This Bob Dylan exists when the music is on and a person is in the room listening. What this Bob Dylan has to say about the renewal of democracy and the relation of the private to the public sphere cannot be read directly from his words. Nor does he bury a message beneath or within the manifest meanings of his lyrics. Rather, his songs are best understood as a resource used by listeners to sort out their ideas

about such matters. Dylan pushed forward certain moods, attitudes, stances and his listeners have an opportunity to try them on for size.[6]

Seeing as how Bromell's language invites rather than discourages dialogue, it should be apparent by now that my "Woody Guthrie" is a similar construct, as is the "Bruce Springsteen" performing on albums such as *Nebraska* and *The Ghost of Tom Joad* (1996), songs from the latter compilation which will concern us later. Given the constraints of this paper, the musical sources for most of my "Bob Dylan" are found in recordings from his early career, specifically the compilations *The Times They Are A'Changin'* (1963) and *Freewheelin' Bob Dylan* (1964). My "Woody Guthrie" is composed from a pastiche of several recordings of his work, performed by himself as well as others, including *The Early Masters: Woody Guthrie* and *Pastures of Plenty: An Austin Celebration of Woody Guthrie* (1993). There are, finally, more than a few unattributed bootlegs underlying and motivating my words.

Poise

Two points now require emphasis. First, one of the essential paradoxes of music is that it will remain forever inviolate to the probings of anyone's written language: How does what must essentially remain a private web of intricate and layered evocations—on the parts of both individual creators and recipients—ever manage to translate into some sense of collective identity? No one has or will ever be able to tell a public group once and for all how such vital, continuing, and concurrent processes operate.

Secondly, it should be obvious that this discussion is already operating well within the current theoretical fray. In spite of the usage of many semiotic constructs, this relatively brief discussion is not intended to be a defense of, or attack upon, either structuralist or poststructuralist concerns. In addition, the difficulties with writers who speak from the third person to claim how "this essay steers a middle course between those formalists who claim too much for structure, those opponents of structuralism who admit too little"[7] also remain beyond the present scope. Nontheless, Paddy Whannel's statement (one that might easily be applied to the later work of Bob Dylan) that "Semiotics tells us things we already know in a language we will never understand"[8] sounds relevant and considerably similar to Doris Lessing's famous definition of education, that being what happens when we hear something we've known all along but in a different way. Certainly Saussure's linguistic dialectics will continue to permeate academic discourse regardless of discipline (just as Guthrie's achievements will continue to reverberate within popular music), if on nothing other than the obvious levels and tensions between constructs such as *parole* and *langue,* or sign and signifier. Lacan, Foucault, Derrida, Wittig, Barthes, Irigaray—these are just a few of the major theorists who have quite a bit to say about how our minds are infiltrated, consciously or not, by language and the social constructs that both precede and follow it.

But popular music is one rather obvious arena where distinctions between content and context sooner or later inevitably fade—which is not the same as say-ing that they disappear or never were. Popular music reminds us that life and lan-guage are always in process, will always be changing. Fisk and Hartley's warning that "we are . . . produced by the environment of signification that we have collec-tively produced"[9] must always be held in the forefront of our (those of us who risk speaking *of* music rather than *inside* it) discourse. Unfortunately, certain aspects of popular culture when viewed as the target of academic attention often result in discussions that in many ways turn evasive; writing becomes an escape, if you will, into an arena where the implicit contention is that only by closely analyz-ing—through written discourse, of course, and via all the implicit conventions that come therewith—the artifact at hand, can we bring ourselves closer to actually understanding what those products mean to their individual recipients.

This of course is a dangerous and false stance. When it comes to music, is any of what we write somehow "truer" than what people hear? How do we write about music and its effects? Presenting static, written lyrics from "All Along the Watch-tower" really has little to do with what happens when anyone listens to a *rendition* of Dylan's words. Under the mask of academic impartiality often lies the scarred face of the one that claims to be the final arbiter of meaning.

All of this is relevant to the mythic presences and works of Guthrie, Dylan, and Springsteen. When it comes to academic discussions of music, what exactly does it mean to be "impartial"? Who are those people that dare to place themselves in the gatekeeping position to control not only the language but also the reception of such language—no matter how any point of this process is defined—that has such incontrovertible impact and creative potential upon others?

In other words, I have to ask who am I, here now, to dismiss the opinion of a nameless woman in Kalamazoo concerning Bruce Springsteen, she who told Nicho-las Dawidoff in a recent *New York Times Magazine* profile, that "By now we'd come to see this guy sing about anything, even about walking out to the driveway in the morning to pick up his newspaper"?[10] Part of me wants to scream at such a state-ment. Yet another part realizes even though I want to, I cannot elevate, for example, Jane Flax's more possibly precise, yet somehow generalized, assertion that "a prob-lem with thinking about (or only in terms of) texts, signs, or signification is that they tend to take on a life of their own or become the world, as the claim that noth-ing exists outside of a text; everything is a comment upon or a displacement of an-other text, as if the model of human activity is literary criticism (or writing). . . ."[11] Music reminds us that one of the tricks of living is to balance a multiplicity of inner voices, to strive for integration of our increasingly fragmented inner voices, to at least attempt to transform all of those into one that has more to do with whole-ness, continuance, and courage. To paraphrase Allen Ginsberg, "It's not enough to say your heart is broken, since everyone's heart is broken these days." What do we do with the heartbreak of injustice and institutionalized disparities that permeate the songs of Guthrie, Dylan, and Springsteen? Concurrently, we might ask what do they do *about* them?

It is not for evasive reasons that I repeat this is not a theoretical paper. To return to my opening statement concerning myth and consciousness, this particular temporal- and text-bound utterance is one attempt to forge a language that allows us to contain perhaps a different sense of what it means to name Woody Guthrie, Bob Dylan, and Bruce Springsteen in the same breath.

Attack

Now consider the following tripartite definition of a working-class consciousness: 1) The individual becomes aware that he/she is not separate or alone regarding his/her public needs, wants, and desires; 2) an understanding of such potential for belonging is also often immediately accompanied by the awareness that while basic needs can often be met by the prevailing economic forces, additional wants and desires can only be obtained through direct and systematic dialogue, interaction, and inevitable confrontation with representatives of those controlling economic forces; and 3) in order to make progress toward the attainment of these wants and desires, such dialogue, interaction, and confrontation require resources that are beyond the capacity of the lone individual.

Some amplifications are necessary for each branch of the definition. First, the act of an individual mind somehow coming to realize relationships with others of like sensibilities is a layered process that occurs continuously and simultaneously on conscious and subconscious levels. How individuals come to feel a sense of belonging; to whom or what; and the linguistic, rational, intuitive, and emotional webs that coalesce to create that sense of belonging are intricate and infinitely variable.

Secondly, the tendrils of the prevailing economic forces that can both create and defy further union are sensed by a great many people long before their language comes to contain, let alone explain, even the brushes of such affinity, the "potentialities" that Bromell recognizes. In other words, the necessary conditions for any sort of "belonging" are both forged and consequently limited by inherited social conditions. It should go without saying how these conditions, in twentieth-century popular music at least, have always been inextricably bound up with economics. Members of the listening audience at a Bruce Springsteen concert, for example, undoubtedly feel connected to each other; regardless of what they each think about or receive from the performance, they are bound by the fact that they form a community of consumers: it cost them each thirty bucks or so to gain entry to the collective. In contrast, it seems obvious that their sense of belonging is considerably different from that experienced by the patrons in the audience of a New York City coffeehouse when Bob Dylan first sang "The Times They Are A'Changin'." And finally, their experience of community is considerably different from that experienced by the fellow tramps with whom Woody Guthrie traveled on hundreds of Depression boxcars.

It is no surprise to say that audience *sensibilities* shift over time. Increasingly, it seems we can belong to groups in which we are equal participants, only if we first engage in processes that somewhere along the line reinforce institutionalized inequality. Distancing occurs on multiple levels, not the least of which is that between the audience and the performer. The economic forces implicit in the commercial music industry, the agents/producers/distributors who carry the sound—in one form or another—further outward to more listeners have also infiltrated our very sense of what it means to belong. That is our concern on the audience side; but what about the concerns of the artists on the other side of the performance context? What about the *texture* of works produced inside those continuing constraints?

Finally, to allow for one last amplification: having arrived at some point of awareness that others are in situations similar to our own, that we belong to something larger, and that powerful injustices and disparities deny human dignity and connection, what do we *do* with the understanding that only through wider and more reflective collective action will changes ever result that might lead to individual betterment? Since the forces which seek to discourage human growth and authentic public debate are so subtle and often insidious, what do we do with our knowledge that the achievement and maintenance of justice and respect for all people will occur only through struggle? How do we engage in dialogue? Using what language? What actions are effective? When is confrontation necessary? What kind of confrontation?

Certainly some of the answers to these questions have a lot to do with faith, with hope, with strength, with endurance, and, finally, with compassion and responsibility. They also have a lot to do with music. Given this admittedly raw yet functional definition of a working-class consciousness, it should be apparent that popular music can be perceived as a political instrument in several ways.

First, certain songs can and do express sentiments and impulses that provide individuals with a sense of belonging, the potential for an instant of recognition that most of us are living lives that are, for better or worse, in many ways created and defined for us by larger social forces. So what else is new?

No one who has ever punched a jukebox in a bar expects to hear anything he/she has not heard before. Ditto for anyone who slaps x amount of dollars down to hear a concert by a popular musician. Just because we are not surprised by what we hear, just because we expect to hear, and in most cases receive, some kind of verification for whatever it is we are feeling at the instant we drop the coins into the slot or give our Visa number to a Ticketron operator, does not mean the actions which precede and follow the sounds we hear in the air, our minimal rewards, so to speak, are any less political than, say, voting. Conceptions of romantic love and the lack of job opportunities, to take but easy examples, have been embedded into culture and language long before the advent and proliferation of recorded music. Countless musicians, including the three gathered here, write and perform songs whose interpretive codes have already been embedded into their listeners. Since the broad social constructs of unrequited emotion and lack of success obviously cut across the boundaries of gender, race, education, and class, what musicians *do* with that embedded language and the receptivity it poses has a lot to do with the maintenance of or challenges to the status quo.

So even if popular music is perceived as little other than "entertainment," or "mindless distraction" or "simple amusement," those who both produce and listen to the myriad manifestations of this construct share at least one point of awareness: performers know that if they punch the right buttons, a common response on the part of the listener will be, "Hey, at least I'm not alone with having a *cheating* (or fill in the blank) partner . . . " or "At least I'm not alone with wanting to escape from my sorrow through a bottle/needle/shotgun, etc. . . . " or "At least I'm not the first person to be feeling whatever it is I'm feeling. . . . " Not so incidentally, a vast majority of blues songs operate in this category: they provide innumerable opportunities for the listeners' recognition of some public expression of romantic, social, racial, spiritual, and/or economic difficulty.

But then what happens to the listener after hearing the song? And what happens to the performer after writing such a song? Given the musical and/or lyrical powers of the performer, these public—and most often somehow commercially controlled—expressions may or may not shift to the next level of political efficacy.

The political stakes get raised and consequently complicated upon this second level of popular music as political instrument. Certain songs can reveal either explicitly or implicitly the economic disparities and social injustices that permeate American society. Explicit songs of course can be categorized as protest songs, the academic treatment of which has filled volumes. Regardless of the fine rhetorical qualifications and particular distinctions that have been offered, however, I am not the first person to note that blatant didacticism in popular music has always had rather limited emotional appeal and even less temporal staying power. It's rare that anyone these days listens to hot radio stations or the CD player to intentionally learn more about, say, gender inequality, global exploitation, or the influence of Pepsico in Burma. It should go without saying that the commercial value of blatant protest songs is nearly nonexistent. If we get any sort of awakening, it is only because the message has been coded in such a way as to strike some deeper aspects of our humanity—aspects that go beyond the simple recognition that one is not alone in believing life to be a difficult process because . . . We can all fill in that pause with our own particular statements.

It is at this level that the implicit, subconscious, intuitive impacts of Guthrie, Dylan, and Springsteen upon political identity are most noticeable. Certain kinds of popular music can be viewed as political instruments in that they at least begin to posit definitions for the parameters between thought and action. An individual who comes to understand a sense of belonging to a larger group of people—all of whom are enduring the consequences of the systematized immobility of self-sustaining structures of disparity and injustice—must then begin to at least glimpse possible approaches toward altering such conditions. Beyond saying that one can connect with others (first level), beyond saying that something has to be done to change the social geography (second level), we must begin to ask what popular musicians have begun to suggest necessary actions toward those aspects of society that need to be challenged and changed (third level).

But, hey, we're talking about music here, don't forget, and what I have termed mythic music, at that. To clarify this progression of music as a political tool, let me offer one specific example where writing about what one of these artists has done seems to have little to do with the reality of what actually happens when people listen.

In "Bruce Springsteen and the Dramatic Monologue," Alan Rauch provides a fine discussion of the ways Springsteen employs the device of the dramatic monologue to attempt to achieve a level of connection with his listeners. After a thorough explication of songs from *Nebraska* and other selected stanzas from Springsteen's canon, Rauch writes in his conclusion that:

> the accomplishment of Springsteen's lyrics is that they sensitize listeners to very real contemporary problems. Rather than glorified heroes, the characters of Springsteen's songs are models of flawed, but understandable, behavior. As we hear them tell their very personal stories, we not only learn about the social problems that bring them down, but about the way that we might, by recognizing their flaws in ourselves, avoid being defeated by similar circumstances. To identify with the characters in Springsteen's lyrics would be to admit to defeat to a system that the activist Springsteen knows very well can appear insurmountable. Rather than offer songs with messages that are hollow in their optimism, Springsteen offers hope in the form of the dramatic monologue of the kind of improvement that requires initiative, discipline, and a sense of self.[12]

Yet somehow, this positive assessment seems a form of intellectual sleight-of-hand, in that Rauch first establishes the parameters of his discussion by stating earlier that "the dramatic monologue is a very active and intellectually demanding genre,"[13] (which it is not) and that "the challenge for the audience is to penetrate the credibility of the narrative voices, and hear exactly what they are saying: in short, the challenge is to resist the seductive appeal of the tone in order to analyze content."[14]

Here Rauch seems to set himself up as the arbiter of meaning. Who is the "we" he so smoothly addresses in his conclusion? The line of argument seems to run: "Listen more closely, work at Bruce, and you'll hear what he's *really* saying. Then you, too, can change."

But working people already know life is tough. It seems like it is always been. Springsteen is not vital in that he keeps reminding his listeners of those facts. Most working people do not have the luxury of doing what Rauch asks. When listening to music, the last thing most people want to do is to work hard to achieve the sort of understanding Rauch wants us all to experience. Most people would agree that the first requirement of efficacious music is emotional; listeners need to be moved by a song, to escape from themselves for at least a transcendent instant, and in order for that leap to occur, one cannot make a split between tone and content. The texture of a piece implies a unity that, in actuality, has little to do with the analytical distinctions between stylistic elements.

Delivery

In other words, when it comes to the impact of music upon individuals, the relationships are considerably more complicated than many scholars have made them appear. Songs enter into human beings in ways that will remain forever mysterious; music and lyrics strike and form aspects of individual identity that can never be fully explained to ourselves, let alone others.

At least one reason for such continual shapeshifting elasticity has to do with the experiential nature of the listening process. As Chris Weedon writes in *Feminist Practice and Poststructuralist Theory*, "experience is perhaps the most crucial site of political struggle over meaning since it involves personal, psychic and emotional investment on the part of the individual. . . . The power of experience in the constitution of the individual as social agent comes from the dominant assumption in our society that experience gives access to truth. It is assumed that we come to know the world through experience."[15]

While much of contemporary poststructuralist theory attempts, in many cases admirably, to attack the dangers embedded in foregrounding experience as the determinant of truth, music becomes one arena that seems immune to such charges. For but one example of such an attack, Weedon goes on to state, "It is assumed that we come to know the world through experience. There is little question of experience being open to contradictory interpretations guaranteed by social interests rather than objective truth . . . We learn that as rational individuals we should be non-contradictory and in control of the meaning of our lives. This understanding of subjectivity is guaranteed by common sense and the liberal-humanist theory of meaning which underpins it . . . The distinguishing feature of humanist discourses is their assumption that each individual woman or man possesses a unique essence of human nature."[16] She then goes on to suggest that cultural constructions of identity in many cases subsume that essence.

It is difficult to claim that individual people do not possess unique essences, in spite of the enormous and undeniable power of socialization. The exact manner in which human beings live within the given cultural and historical constructs reveals an incredible diversity of emotion, if nothing else. And the experience of listening to music can be nothing except experience. One either listens to music or one doesn't; one experiences a song or one doesn't. Whoever hears that song interprets it in his/her own inimitable way, using the language and operating within the frameworks previously established by culture. One one level, it all seems ridiculously simple. Many poststructural theorists all too often seem to pick the wrong fight, since certain facts remain regardless of an infinitude of interpretations.

The arena of contention, then, occurs on the interpretive plane. Embedded language, the words we have or do not have, the concepts we use or choose not to use to shape and mold what it is that we experience, inevitably determine our consequent experiences. Popular music is but one of the many forces that help to create the palette of our interpretive language. In this sense, whatever the music of these artists *means* to individual listeners has never been static. Alternative and contradictory interpretations have always been present regarding the works of Guthrie, Dylan, and Springsteen. Context—private and public both—determines meaning.

Yet what they collectively sing about, at their best, the stories they transmit, in many ways has been less open to interpretation. We can avoid the question regarding this sort of verbal, discursive context by simply acknowledging that all three mythic icons have produced stories that have tried to touch us, to get us to listen, and that what we do with what we hear is up to us. Guthrie, at least, continues to remind us that such a response will not ever be good enough. The forces of oppression are gnarly and enduring giants, their language a powerful and intricate weapon, and we had best figure out a way to go for their tendons before we tackle their jugulars.

My main premise is that something has been lost in the progression of the working-class sensibility depicted by these three bards. What is this "something" and how has it been "lost"? How can I say it? More importantly, how can I say it in such a way that you will not just hear me on an intellectual level, but listen to the echoes?

As previously mentioned, the common academic approach to writing about music—that is, extracting passages from song lyrics, presenting them on the page, and then subjecting them to certain kinds of critical inquiry and investigation—is highly dissatisfying. Tom Waits, when once asked by a listener why he does not write a book of poems, replied "A book's so quiet; it just kind of sits there." Extracted lyrics to prove interpretations of a song in many ways have little to do with how the song operates in the development of individual meaning.

To best understand the loss of texture in working-class songs by Guthrie, Dylan, and Springsteen, one would have to listen to certain performances in a particular arrangement, at a particular time. To leave text behind is the only way this process can occur, and in order to at least approximate such a contextual situation on paper, one would have to don the guise of the written equivalent of a disc jockey, someone who can craft a musical space that allows for linkages and connections on levels that include but immediately move beyond the merely verbal or intellectual.

I have recorded such an arranged compilation, but obviously you cannot listen to it by simply reading these words. What I can do, however, is offer the titles and order, and hope that a sense of the erosion comes across. If you are already familiar with the works and the performances, the linkages should come through the next time you play them when you are ready to think about working-class consciousness and the mythic nature of these artists. If you are unfamiliar with the performances, I could write volumes and the words on the page would still at best only come to an approximation of what remains to be heard.

Open up a conscious listening space for yourself, one which allows time for reflection, for both close attention and ranging associations. Give yourself an hour, sixty minutes when you can listen with your heart as well as your head. All the while you might in some part of your mind be holding up a couple of questions: What do you hear? How will you explain to yourself what it is you are experiencing? How will you later find the language to tell others?

What follows is a a taste of potential answers, offered in a hybridization of liner-note style:

Begin with Dylan's "Ballad of Hollis Brown." The basic twelve-bar blues structure is relentless, the hammers and pulloffs elegant reminders of a strong and enduring folk tradition. Dylan doesn't let up with his narrative of a desperate man living on the "outskirts of town." There's no room in this dark story for chorus, no need for repetition, no pause for the kinder tonal stitching from his harp. It's a story of a man stripped and alienated. "Is there anyone that knows, is there anyone that cares?" A beautiful cause/effect relationship is established: the reason not even God can answer his prayers to send him a friend is because his pockets are empty. He's haunted by responsibilities signaled by the crying of his children, "so hungry that they don't know how to smile." The crying pounds at Hollis' brain, his wife's screams stab him. The guitar never lets up, Dylan's voice remains strong. The world outside is is marked by dead grass, a dry well. Hollis's last economic exchange is to spend his last dollar on a gift for every member of his family: seven shotgun shells. The howl of something older and larger outside, one of Dylan's coyotes, permeates the night. Hollis's brain is bleeding as he contemplates his seemingly inevitable actions. Then Dylan does a rapid narrative shift, addressing the listener as "you." All at once it's not Hollis's story. No intermediary is present. The listener is living in the man's head as he first takes the shotgun off the wall, then holds it in his hand. Then the sound of the wind, seven breezes, seven shells, "seven people dead on a South Dakota farm." And then, at the end, an upward movement, a suggestion of continuance—but the unstated question of continuance in what circumstances. What kind of world are we living in where this occurs? Pure working-class Dylan.

Move ahead thirty or so years and then listen to the second cut, Springsteen's "Ghost of Tom Joad." The voice here is a lament, a sense of defeat is palpable and it profiles another alienated man, this time nameless, one of Springsteen's drifters on the lam, with helicopters and police cruisers chasing him. The desert of the southwest forms the brooding landscape, and the shift to Steinbeck's mythic story occurs. Is the man Preacher or someone else? The lyrics tells us we can take it both ways, nothing's changed from the dustbowl days—"no home, no peace, no rest"—and what's worse is that even the promise of the road has disappeared. Springsteen focuses primarily on his narrative, uses the harp to reinforce the lament of the end of some American dream, repeats that while the highway is alive, "everybody knows it's headed nowhere." But unlike the character's claim in Steinbeck's powerful closing scene from *The Grapes of Wrath*, the contention is that Tom Joad is not going to continue in the working-class consciousness, not in the America Springsteen is chronicling. Something has faded; the folkhero, after all, is nothing but a ghost, Springsteen reminds us. And that's just the way it is.

Compare this version with Guthrie's "The Ballad of Tom Joad," the third cut on this compilation. Here the folk tradition is, of course, much more vibrant, much more noticeable. In one of Guthrie's classic artistic thefts, he transposes the entire Steinbeck storyline upon an old fiddle tune. The song jumps, it moves, and even while violence, death, and injustice are present, there is an honesty from the instant Tom Joad hitches his first ride after being released from prison until he makes the famous claim at the end: "I think everyone might be just one big soul . . ." Steinbeck, Joad, and Guthrie are, of course, still right. There's no false optimism here, since the forces that erode the human spirit are clearly identified. But unlike Springsteen's Tom Joad, Guthrie's response to those forces is one continuance no matter what. An adamant refusal to give in to despair, no matter where or when one is living, rises up clean and clear from this song, its relevancy to the America of today apparent and necessary.

The fourth cut on the compilation, "The Lonesome Death of Hattie Carroll," is a song that reveals Dylan's working-class politics quite clearly. Here the story of a black kitchen maid killed "for no reason" by the cane of a wealthy white son of Baltimore is told to the listeners in a nearly didactic way. Dylan uses the progression of the chorus to remind us—"You who philosophize disgrace, and criticize all fears"—that we need to cry not about the unwarranted deaths of so many individuals like Hattie, but more about a system in which the best legal retribution to one who commits such a crime—made all the more heinous because of its casual nature—is a six-month sentence. Pay attention also to the odd repetition of "the table." What's the playing field, Dylan keeps asking, when the rich can get away with so much and the workers have only themselves and their labor to survive? What kind of world is this, Dylan asks again, but this time with the implicit charge that we're not asking ourselves what we're doing about changing it. The guitar work here is a rhythmic strumming, a near-dirge that pounds the story into the listener's heart.

"Lonesome Road," Guthrie's classic paean to the sense of motion in the face of adversity, follows Hattie's story. The generality of the metaphor is applicable to anyone, and it's apparent that the speaker believes in someplace better, and that only by first believing in a world where "the dust storms never blow," will anybody ever find themselves in a better place. Here the road that Springsteen told us was dead is still vibrant as an option. We may not know where we're going, but at least setting off on the journey to greener pastures isn't diffused as an option.

Such a belief that the world can be better elsewhere is what forms the core of the story that follows, Springsteen's "Sinola Cowboys." But once again, the teller informs us that the dreams of two Mexican brothers to cross the border to a better life will turn out to be naught. The advice the father tells Luis and Miguel before they leave, "For every gift the North gives, it takes something else in return," sets up the impending sense of loss. Springsteen follows Guthrie's lead in addressing the concerns of migrant workers, updates the options now offered them by the illegal drug trade, and reminds us that some things haven't changed in half a century: "You can make as much on a ten-hour shift" in the methamphetamine lab "as a year working in the fields." A brother's life is exchanged for ten thousand dollars, all that they'd managed to save. But again, as with most of the songs on *The Ghost of Tom Joad*, the delivery of the story is so low-key, so soft, so prone to being unheard and overlooked, that how many listeners are able to absorb the full impact of the lyrics? And for those of us who do listen, what do we then do with the story? How do we absorb it into our sensibilities? A sense of defeat remains predominant.

Compare the response of the unemployed worker in Guthrie's "Buffalo Skinners," two versions of which follow. Here the actualities behind the promises of a "good job" killing buffalo offered by "a well-known drover" or a man named "Kriegle" are detailed in lyrics expansive and visual. Guthrie attacks the circumstances which have always put the survival of workers upon the less than tender mercy of exploitative employers. We taste the dust, peel the hides, feel the cut thumb of the speaker, which all allow us to participate in a historical drama that exposes the particularities of the wide chasm between the real and the ideal. Yet when the season is over, the worst experience stems not from the conditions the workers agreed upon but the denial of promised wages. Instead of the workers being defeated by their experiences in a land of danger, death, and latent violence, they take matters into their own hands. After all the speaker had experienced along with his companions, the only fair option is to kill the lying boss rather than to kill themselves or walk away. The two versions provide interesting musical and lyrical variations, but Guthrie's determined stance comes across loud and clear in both. "The cowboy never had heard such a thing as a bankrupt law."

Dylan's classic "North Country Blues" seems a good followup to the story of the buffalo skinners in the 1830's. A hundred and thirty or so years later, the same forces that seek to cheat workers out of their labor are here chronicled by an orphaned woman who watches the world that was all she knew crumble around her by the decisions made by faceless corporate institutions. How does anyone fight a system that creates the very world in which he or she lives? "With three babies born the work was cut down/ to half a day's shift with no reason" quickly advances to the notification that the entire Number 11 mine will be closed within a week. An entire way of life is ended because of economic decisions; their ore "ain't worth diggin" because "it's much cheaper down in the South American towns/ where the miners work almost for nuthin'." Don't people who develop policies like NAFTA or GATT listen to these songs? The resultant inner silence, the response of alcohol, the woman's sudden despair that stems from the knowledge that—having already lost her father, mother, and brother—even her children will leave her soon, "cause there ain't nothing there now to hold them," are all captured in Dylan's high plaintive tonal range and sustaining notes. The voice lingers and holds to the point of nearly breaking.

The transition is obvious to Springsteen's "Youngstown"—in my opinion the best cut on his *Joad* album. As he states, "From the Monongahela Valley to the Masabai Iron range/ the coal mines of Appalachia/ the story's always the same." It's the same story that Dylan sang, that Guthrie sang, and here Springsteen uses the fiddle strains to etch such a lasting temporal and historical truth upon the listener's spine. The Whitmanesque vision runs across the origins of industrial development, and the subtext of wars as the motivating engine is quickly and forcefully anchored. Here Springsteen's voice is strong, rising well above the sad lamentation that marks his other pieces. His closure, when the speaker addresses the faceless forces of the system, hammers home his message simply and force-fully: "Once I made you rich enough, rich enough to forget my name." The song is chilling, the pulse driving, the anger justified and manifest and comprehensive. The promises of heaven aren't a fair enough replacement for a good job at honest wages in a world that the forces created and destroyed around him; the collective voice claims how he'd rather rather work in hell than go for some promised land.

By this point, you'd be hearing a wealth of interconnections and relationships on rational, intuitive, and emotional levels. You'd be seeing faces, witnessing ac-tual lives and responses to social conditions. You'd be sensing something rising up generation after generation—something about promises and exploitation and at least one lasting truth being the simple doing, the hard continuance in the face of adversity.

The tape would close with Dylan's poem "Last Thoughts on Woody Guthrie." In this spoken piece, these relationships between voice, instrumentation, charac-ter, speaker and audience—some of what you'd have been engaging in for fifty or so minutes, would be stripped down to the essentials of a five-page spoken tribute. When Dylan explains what Woody Guthrie means to him, he also encompasses what the man means to other musicians such as Springsteen. He offers us a better summary of what the man might mean to us all.

Progression

Additional cuts from different artists and some observations about the way certain performers have selected from and advanced the tradition inherited from these three bards could of course be added to this compilation—Chris Albert's haunting version of Guthrie's "Pastures of Plenty," say, or Arlo Guthrie's version of his father's "1913 Massacre." But those might be other valuable directions for inves-tigations within this particular type of discourse approach.

But to cut to the heart of the argument, first consider how Woody Guthrie and his music once served as an instrument of social change, an efficacious medium in the transmission of worker solidarity, and perhaps most crucially as an adaptive vehicle to expose the injustices suffered by human beings at the brutal, wringing hands of corporate interest. (Simply read Jim Longhi's excellent *Woody, Cisco and Me* to hear several first-person accounts of such a process occurring.)[17] It is not

Guthrie or his works that changed, but rather his listeners. He lived a life that allowed him to sing in a way that lets us know—years and bad recordings later—that reality is still close as his boyhood antics, his disturbed mother, the next freight train, the voices of two girls and a guitar in a migrant camp. He asks if our lives are at least that real to us. Guthrie was not too concerned with top-forty hits when he crafted his works, and we hear such continuing sustenance when we listen to them now. To dismiss them as artifacts from the past says more about the shift in listening sensibilities than it does about the enduring stance he strikes in his songs. The public good—the public betterment—always seemed and still seems more important to him than his own private continuance. He knew he would always survive—in one way or another—and we can continue to hear how his own individual survival was never a matter of question for him, and how the forces he chose to contend with are still, with variation, with us now. The land and its people—always something truer than the bottom lines of dollars and cents—and yes, the *essence* of an individual—must always remain more important than any one individual self.

The turbulent social and political changes brewing in the 1950s set the stage for the emergence of Bob Dylan in the 1960s. Dylan's early awareness regarding the power of the American bardic tradition, his intuitive understanding of the nature and causes of social injustices and the embedded forces of hypocrisy, which form a strong thematic focus of his early work, allowed Dylan—for a time—to directly continue Guthrie's legacy, reaching people, uniting them and even rallying them. But times, yes, they were a'changin' and Dylan opted for private retreat. Withdrawing into lyrics and sensibilities obscure for even aficionados, Dylan cultivates the perspective of the outsider; whatever political sensibilities might have motivated his aesthetic lyricism later became, at the least, publicly inaccessible to the majority of people who even have a marginal connection to what I have defined as working-class consciousness. In a recent *New Yorker* profile, Alex Ross provides a fine discussion of how Dylan still continues to escape the myriad applications of meaning that his own mythic status continues to invite. As Ross writes of witnessing Dylan in concert, "It's hard to pin down what he does: he is a composer and a performer at once, and his shows cause his songs to mutate, so that no definitive or ideal version exists."[18]

Finally, having attained a public status and potential far exceeding those of either of his predecessors, Springsteen and his works are less reflective and considerably less capable of transformations in regards to working-class identity. In Springsteen's explorations of the modern American worker, one primary characteristic that arises is a disturbing distance, a near-mythologized cynicism and despair that collectively combine to create a prevailing sense of nostalgic lamentation and even defeat. Springsteen's recording career has been marked by a consciousness long since explored by critics of all stripes. Academic articles concerning his work continue to proliferate, and *The Ghost of Tom Joad* is hailed as one of the best statements of populism that has emerged from the music industry in the past decade. As Michael J. Bader writes, "*The Ghost of Tom Joad* represents the evolution of Springsteen's interests and values from the purely personal to the politically personal."[19] Perhaps the defeat I hear is simply the defeat of unions in an increasingly corporate world. Yet given his enormous popularity and influence, shouldn't such a shift have occurred long before? All along, his lyrics have been saying that economic conditions are tough for the average American worker; how can his works be termed politically efficacious in the same way as those of Guthrie or Dylan when the hypocrisy of his own media-created and -controlled celebrity status is painfully apparent? He is continuing the tradition, certainly, pulling us back to the simply stated stories that Guthrie knew would appeal to more people, and he has become quite wealthy doing so. Lyrically he has not retreated into the obscurity of the later Dylan, but there rises from inside his songs a troubling uncertainty concerning where we all go from here—an uncertainty that also affects the tone and textures of his performances. In this sense, perhaps, his music duplicates the uncertainty felt by all working-class Americans.

Closure

How does one attempt to forge a language capable of addressing the myriad and complex interrelationships between music, myth, politics, and discourse against the context of popular music? Such a task is impossible to do justice to employing written words alone, yet nonetheless some conclusions seem in order.

The mythic presences of these three artists collectively make a claim about the conditions and sensibilities that both surround and comprise working-class experience. Guthrie, Dylan, and Springsteen all agree that the forces which subtly destroy the wants and desires of so many people have been able to transcend the lives of a great many individual men and women. All three recognize the need to continually acknowledge, reveal, and transmit vital, important, and most of all human portraits of human beings who experience such continual loss.

But once we have tuned our sensibilities to recognize and relate to these conditions, what happens next? For the performers, the answers are obvious. Woody Guthrie ends up dying in the Brooklyn State Hospital. Dylan continues to tour the countryside even today, continually reinventing himself for the scores of "Dylanologists" that Ross describes in his recent article, as well as the thousands of admiring fans who see and hear in him something that they still need. Bruce Springsteen shows up on *Entertainment Weekly*, and through the years keeps trying to strip down his music in quest of some secret, lurking bone that always seems just out of his grasp.

The recording industry is young, yet it seems apparent that over the course of its hundred-year-old life, the corporate forces have managed to effectively silence scores of independent voices, until today popular music is anything but an instrument of political change. How can it be, when the musical tastes of listeners, their social group identities, are spawned, molded, targeted, and reinforced by the forces of mass cult and consumer society? Maintenance of the status quo is achieved through an elaborate web of prepackaged "choices" that in reality are anything but. What sells gets recorded, and what gets recorded is what gets listened to. Whatever is listened to in some way helps to shape the private life of the audience. Seeming messages of dissent are vital only in that they serve to provide the illusion of difference, but in effect there remains little to no room within the industry for an authentic form of debate and critique. Ani Defranco? Dan Bern? Who listens to them, really? How many people in comparison to the benumbed fans of the Spice Girls and the Backstreet Boys? And in one of the most laughable postmodern absurdities, even Rage Against the Machine sells t-shirts at their concerts.

By looking at Guthrie, Dylan, and Springsteen, we can easily see the erosion of working-class consciousness. Of course this returns us to the idea of myth, and the question of whether or not there ever was a time when working-class identity was aided and abetted by the music and lyrics of performers. Perhaps the idealized world of America that Guthrie loved so deeply and so well was already slipping away when he took to the rails, and by the time Dylan came along, and later Springsteen, all that remained for them were the hollow empty mills, looming darkly in their aesthetic consciousness, crying out in silence for a time that never was.

In any case, for popular music to serve as a galvanizing force of political resistance and reform, its creators, as mentioned earlier, must demonstrate two primary characteristics: compassion and responsibility. Their compassion—for those they sing of and about as well as to—must be deep and abiding and real; their responsibility must be for the words and music they call forth from the void and set into motion. Of the three artists discussed here, it seems apparent that only Woody Guthrie demonstrated such commitment and concern. With his passing, succeeding generations of artists and listeners need now to somehow account for the losses they both witness and imagine. And therefore, the enduring questions remain: What sort of instrument is anyone—personally, popularly, academically—using to challenge the politically dominant forces, and in what ways? What happens now?

Notes

1. John Edgar Wideman, *Philadelphia Fire* (New York: Henry Holt and Co., 1990), 83.

2. Jerome Bruner, "Myth and Identity," in *Myth and Mythmaking*, ed. Henry A. Murray (Boston: Beacon Press, 1969), 268.

3. Joseph Campbell, *Myths to Live By* (New York: Viking, 1972), 214.

4. Alan Rauch, "Bruce Springsteen and the Democratic Monologue," *American Studies* 29, no. 1 (1988): 29–49.

5. Nicholas Bromell, "Both Sides of Bob Dylan: Public Memory, the Sixties, and the Politics of Meaning," *Tikkun* 10, no. 4 (1996): 15–16.

6. Bromell, "Both Sides of Bob Dylan," 15.

7. Darryl Hattenhauer, "Bob Dylan as Hero: Rhetoric, History, Structuralism and Psychoanalysis in Folklore as a Communicative Process," *Southern Folklore Quarterly* 45 (1981): 69–88.

8. Ellen Seiter, "Semiotics, Structuralism, and Television," in *Channels of Discourse, Reassembled*, ed. Robert C. Allen, (London: Routledge, 1992), 1.

9. John Fiske and John Hartley, *Reading Television* (London, England: Methune, 1978), 68. See also Janet Wollacott, "Messages and Meanings," in *Culture, Society and the Media*, ed. Michael Gurevitch, et. al. (London: Routledge, 1982).

10. Nicholas Dawidoff, "The Pop Populist," *New York Times Magazine*, 26 January 1997, 30.

11. Jane Flax, "Postmodernism and Gender Relations in Feminist Theory," in *Feminism/Postmodernism*, ed. Linda B. Nicholson (New York: Routledge, 1990), 47.

12. Rauch, "Bruce Springsteen and the Dramatic Monologue," 46.

13. Rauch, "Bruce Springsteen and the Dramatic Monologue," 32.

14. Rauch, "Bruce Springsteen and the Dramatic Monologue," 33.

15. Chris Weeden, *Feminist Practice and Poststructuralist Theory* (New York: Basil Blackwell, 1987), 79.

16. Weeden, *Feminist Practice*, 80.

17. Jim Longhi, *Woody, Cisco and Me: Seamen Three in the Merchant Marine* (Chicago: University of Chicago Press, 1997).

18. Alex Ross, "The Wanderer," *The New Yorker* (10 May 1999): 58.

19. Michael J. Bader, "Bruce Springsteen, Tom Joad and the Politics of Meaning," *Tikkun* 11, no. 2 (1997): 32–33.

Partial Discography

The recorded compilation mentioned in the text follows this particular order:

Dylan: "The Ballad of Hollis Brown"
Springsteen: "The Ghost of Tom Joad"
Guthrie: "The Ballad of Tom Joad"
Dylan:"The Lonesome Death of Hattie Carroll"
Springsteen: "Sinola Cowboys"
Guthrie: "Buffalo Skinners"
Bootleg: "Buffalo Skinners
Dylan: "North Country Blues"
Springsteen: "Youngstown"
Dylan: "Tribute to Woody Guthrie"

The fact that these ten recorded performances alone initiated the text of this paper, not to mention all the specific critical treatments consulted and used within this particular academic treatment, should suggest something about the evocative power of music and the sadly ineffectual ability of written language to contain this power. It all looks rather simple on the page, doesn't it?

As also mentioned, additional selections that reveal further reinforcements and amplifications of the ideas suggested would also be useful. I state in the text which of the following recordings contain the above songs, but I also include other recorded performances which reveal still further relationships among Guthrie, Dylan, Springsteen, and the many musicians they have influenced. Finally, it is apparent that I have not bothered to locate the original sources for my bootleg tapes. People die and move away; I hope it is enough for me to say that this type of music finds its way into people's lives in a variety of ways, not the least of which might be academic contexts.

Bob Dylan, *The Freewheelin' Bob Dylan*, prod. John Hammond, CK 8786, Columbia, 1963.

———, *The Times They Are A-Changin'*, prod. Tom Wilson, CK 8905, Columbia, 1964.

———, *The Bootleg Series, Vols. I and II*. Bootleg copy: details unknown.

Arlo Guthrie, *Alice's Restaurant*.

Woody Guthrie, *The Early Masters: Woody Guthrie*.

———, *The Early Years*. Bootleg Tape: details unknown.

———, *Woody Guthrie by Others*. Bootleg Tape: details unknown.

Pastures of Plenty: An Austin Celebration of Woody Guthrie, prod. Steve Wilkinson and Greg John, DJD 3207, DejaDisc. Recorded live at La Zona Rosa, 18 July 1993.

Bruce Springsteen, *The Ghost of Tom Joad*.

———, *Nebraska*.

5
A Struggle for Hearts and Minds:
Labor Age and the Popular Press, 1920–1930

Cynthia Gwynne Yaudes

"What we've got here is . . . a failure to communicate."
—Strother Martin to Paul Newman in the film *Cool Hand Luke* (1967)

A few months before the stock market crash of 1929, labor economist William M. Leiserson privately fumed over the failure of organized labor in the United States. He had good reason for his muted despair. The 1920s, the "Golden Age of American Capitalism," had seen the triumph of crass materialism in national labor policies and the development of a hardened social conservatism among the top leadership of the American Federation of Labor. As a whole, industrial union organization fell into disarray during the decade, and powerful collective bodies among workers in most mass-production industries were simply nonexistent.[1]

In short, the apparent listlessness of organized labor during the 1920s disturbed those, like Leiserson, who quarreled with the underlying assumptions that defined and sustained the New America as a corporate society. He complained to industrial engineer Morris L. Cooke: "What the labor movement . . . now needs is a lot of strong criticism showing up their weaknesses and their stupidity. That is the only way . . . in which they can be awakened and stimulated to perform the functions . . . which they ought to be performing."[2]

The activists and scholars who wrote for the League of Industrial Democracy's journal *Labor Age*[3] did not need such advice. For nearly ten years (at the time of Leiserson's writing) they had played the role of critic of the New America and especially of its hardened Labor Establishment. Channeling their anger, frustration, and despair into the pages of their "little magazine," they challenged the burgeoning conservatism of many trade union organizers, the waning socialist movement, and the increasing isolation of radical critics. Their work drew attention; *Labor Age* gained notoriety for its solid reporting of labor events on the local and national scene, its in-depth and articulate analyses of the "failure" of American labor as an institution, narrative essays describing workers' personal experiences under labor's "industrial depression," and editorials decrying "attacks on the worker by the employing interests."[4] As one of the most widely-read journals among "labor progressives"[5] between 1920 and 1930, it functioned on one level as a kind of forum for the projection of authors' cultural idealism, the development of ideas about social change, and the discussion of tactics for worker organization. On another level, *Labor Age* served as a conduit for news and information about the labor movement in general. The editorial board made an effort to report to their readers "the up-to-date happenings from the battle line of struggle" more thoroughly and more widely than any other labor publication of the period.[6]

Underlying the magazine's internal and external work were echoes of Leiserson's complaints about the labor movement; *Labor Age* criticized the stagnancy, lethargy, and the seeming incapability of its administrative structure. Nevertheless, the magazine's appraisals stopped short of reflecting Leiserson's belief in the existence of a weak, stubborn, and stupid labor force. Instead, they dressed their critique of the worker and the description of his plight in optimism, humanism, and altruism. They penned messages of recognition and support for workers' struggles, attempting to adequately and accurately portray individual and group experiences. Moreover, insisting on the possibility of a national worker identity and class solidarity, they provided advice and direction to laborers and organizers. "Only by safeguarding ourselves through the organization of our own culture will we help to promote the happiness of the greatest number—the goal of social development."[7]

Contrary to such ideals, however, *Labor Age* never fully realized its great expectations. Despite the enthusiasm of all those connected with the enterprise, the journal was never able to perfect its editorial mission or realize its goals. The reasons for this lack of success were framed by the journal's own editorial identity, which was out of sync with the identity of many of the workers it attempted to reach and organize. Drawing upon *Labor Age* news presentations and editorial commentary, this essay will suggest that the journal actually had within its structure the seeds for its own failure.

Many labor journals of the Progressive Era fell short in their efforts to create a national labor movement. But the fact that *Labor Age* in particular failed to unify and organize workers stands out among these because of the journal's unique design and its broad-based reader solicitation. From the beginning, *Labor Age* promised to secure and disseminate information among all ranks of the labor movement. The journal vowed to be "wherever the leading issues and events in the world of labor in the United States are occurring" and to "interpret those events through the eyes of every section or group."[8] Despite these wide-ranging editorial plans, however, *Labor Age* never achieved the inclusivity for which it strove. The magazine was able to attract attention and participation from activists at all levels of the labor movement, but it could not draw a substantial and loyal readership from among the rank and file. This realization puzzled and frustrated the writers and editors of *Labor Age*, as their best efforts to create and distribute a magazine that would capture and hold the attention of laborers continually failed.

During the past decade, numerous historical studies have been undertaken to chronicle the breadth of experience of American working people: how they have defined their lives and jobs, how they have interpreted their experience within the larger events around them, and the ways in which they have attempted to create an identity and an ideological space for themselves.[9] While such studies are able to bring the personal perspective of working people to the fore, they are, nevertheless, quite limited in their ability to demonstrate how workers perceived the labor organizers who petitioned them to join the movement. This is because the workers who are their sources did not discuss to any great degree the external impetus to action they were receiving. The absence of this discussion has led some scholars to conclude that workers, by the millions, gave little credence to the unifying anti-capitalist message brought to them by activists.[10] Certainly, laborers registered specific complaints and grievances to themselves, to each other, to their families, and to union organizers and representatives. Yet, workers never fully embraced a conscious rejection of capitalism nor voiced a unified negation of bourgeois society.

The reasons offered as to why such a phenomenon occurred in the American past are as complex as they are many and will not be considered, for the most part, in this essay. What will be addressed is how a media publication, in its attempt to realize a workers' movement, actually prevented it from happening. Contributing to this predicament is the connection between a cultural and personal identity that helped to shape workers' perceptions of their own experiences, in addition to profound community and social identities that brought substance to individual and group life. Such a connection often stood to challenge the editorial ideas, primarily driven by the "socialist cause," of those who ran *Labor Age*.

There were, indeed, other issues and influences besides the evocation of a classless society that commanded workers' attention and influenced their social understanding. Often, these competed with the ideological focus of *Labor Age*; in the process, the journal's projected importance in the lives of workers was lessened and its ability to realize its goals was challenged. More to the point, when push came to shove, many in the rank and file ignored the solidarity that *Labor Age* espoused along with the need to overthrow capitalism because such a mission was alien to them. In the first place, workers identified with more than just the proletarian role assigned them by *Labor Age*. They were divided by skill. They were also distinguishable by social roles and interests. Workers were spouses, parents, immigrants or new citizens, seekers of recreation, and spiritual beings. To this extent, when confronted with the anticapitalism and the class solidarity of *Labor Age*, most saw too little of themselves in its pages to feel compelled to adopt and/or act upon the linguistic or pictorial direction. Instead, workers turned to other written sources not just to explore and understand their labor experiences, but, perhaps more importantly, to see and feel themselves in all their extended identities.

Probably the most popular sources of information, enrichment, and even identity for workers were the local "mainstream" newspapers that circulated in their respective and primarily urban communities. Such papers were important as accessible sources of information about a variety of local and national events. These "popular dailies" provided a means of entertainment and escape, they articulated cultural and personal identities, and they played a key role in the formation and maintenance of a recognized notion of the "American community."[11]

The front-page stories gave workers a sense of what was occurring in "their" nation and "their" city (places into which they were desperately trying to fit). The sports section allowed them the relaxation and escape of following the scores of national and local teams; it also allowed them to see those of the same original nationality who (in their mind) had realized the "American Dream." The community pages made them aware of local events of popular, if not traditional, interests and provided them with a sense of belonging and a developing sense of historical continuity. In addition, the sensationalism that defined the journalism style of many of the newspapers allowed workers to engage in a bit of vicarious adventure, stoking the fires of individual imagination. Most important, however, the overall focus of these papers was to stress agreement rather than conflict, emphasizing values and interests on which there was a high degree of local or national consensus. To this extent, the papers were not prone to challenge the existing American system of production or political accountability.[12]

In stark contrast, *Labor Age* focused on making workers aware of the labor issues of the day that were splitting towns and cities across the nation, as well as emphasizing the need for all workers to see the ills of capitalism and to understand the nature of reality in purely economic terms. As these efforts were driven by socialist ideals, *Labor Age* understandably privileged class over all other identity traits. In so doing, the journal created an impression of hierarchy in its editorial message, marginalizing all except class characteristics. The writers and editors, therefore, and not the workers, became the vanguard for socialism. Potential *Labor Age* readers were thus drawn to other sources of popular culture, whose depiction of worker issues extended into areas of local and national citizenship, family life, and community culture. Ultimately, any consciousness of class that *Labor Age* had hoped to foster and utilize became blurred into these other identities, thereby losing its power to unify and create change.

In 1921, the League for Industrial Democracy (LID) was organized. The group owes its heritage, in part, to an earlier twentieth-century movement organized to promote Socialist learning at American colleges and universities. The earlier movement was guided by the belief that reading and talking about socialism would make the ideology more familiar and, by extension, acceptable, thereby creating a generation of socialist-minded citizens who would be the foundation for a utopian social order. The LID accepted this tradition, but also extended it beyond the campus to the workplace. Its mission was to reveal to workers the evils and inequities of the American system of politics and economics and to show how socialist ideals might remedy those disparities.

The direct predecessor to the LID was the Intercollegiate Socialist Society (ISS), a national association of study clubs begun in 1905. Over its 15-year lifetime, the ISS established chapters at more than 100 colleges and universities across the United States, and attracted as members and administrators some of the most illustrious personalities, socialist and nonsocialist, of the period. These included Upton Sinclair, Charlotte Perkins Gilman, Morris Hillquit, Florence Kelley, Harry Laidler, Elizabeth Gurley Flynn, Jack London, Roger Baldwin, A.J. Muste, and Rose Pastor Stokes. They and their co-organizers actively encouraged "all legitimate endeavors to awaken an interest in Socialism among American college men and women, graduate and undergraduate."[13] Legitimate endeavors included campus-based reading and study groups, nationwide lecture tours, and the publication of pamphlets and a newsletter (the *Intercollegiate Socialist*) to "shed light, more light"[14] on the socialist ideal. By raising the socialist consciousness of American collegians, ISS administrators hoped to begin to reduce the acceptance of the human costs of the political, economic, and cultural institutions of the United States. Their ultimate goal was a gradual socialist revolution, one defined by a change in beliefs and values that would occur subtly over several generations.[15]

By 1921, however, in the aftermath of the First World War, ISS administrators recognized the need for reorganization in order to serve "the changing needs of the socialist movement."[16] Prior to the war the ISS had filled a void by dedicating itself to the dissemination of information about socialism among American collegians; by the end of the war, information about the socialist movement among collegians had become sufficiently widespread to obviate the need for such an organization. Instead, there now existed the need to, first, extend the study and understanding (read as acceptance) of socialism from the campus to the general public and, second, to act on that understanding. While strengthening their work in the colleges, ISS organizers directed increasing attention to the community—in particular to the labor movement on the economic and cultural fronts. Toward this end, they brought together both (skilled and unskilled) laborers and college-educated activists within a new organization dedicated not only to discussion of socialism but also to its attainment:

> while the main need of the Society hitherto has been to acquaint college men and
> women with the existence and the meaning of the world drifting toward socialism

and 'industrial democracy,' the new situation demands more than this. It demands that, added to its primary educational work, the Society shall stimulate the hardiest kind of thinking on the concrete problems of social ownership and democratic control of our industrial life. It demands that the Society shall do its part to utilize in constructive tasks the hundreds of young idealists who have aligned themselves within the past few years on the side of the new social order. . . . It requires, furthermore, that the Society enlarge its direct appeal, so that it may include not only the small minority of the population that has received a university training, but the non-collegian, whose active participation in social situations is absolutely indispensable to any fundamental change in our social structure.[17]

The efforts of the ISS executive committee culminated in the official reorganization of the ISS as the League for Industrial Democracy (LID) in November of 1921; the ISS executive committee was retained as the LID executive committee and there was considerable general membership overlap between the two groups.

Despite that basic personnel commonality, the League reoriented the Society away from its purely educational objective to education-plus-activism. It encouraged members of its affiliated chapters to work for various social and economic causes and involve themselves in radical and labor activities across the country. The LID sought to "combine social idealism with economic realities and to impress upon the American people the eternal value of cooperation among every class."[18] In all of its work, the revitalized organization was guided by the concept of industrial democracy: "the principle of production for use and not for profit, social ownership and democratic management of industry."[19] They recognized, as well, that "the first essential for any step forward toward industrial democracy" was to organize "an able and energetic working class."[20]

With this new commitment to labor, the League for Industrial Democracy had officially emerged from the shadow of the Intercollegiate Socialist Society. It had evolved into an active anticapitalist organization focused on the realization of industrial democracy (socialist ideals) through the creation of producers', consumers' and credit cooperatives, the public ownership of basic utilities, the establishment of worker education programs, and the organization of all workers into industrial unions. LID administrators believed that workers would play a central role in those activities in recognition of their continuing need, as producers and consumers, for larger control over political, economic, and social forces. "There will never be efficiently operated industry until the men who have invested their lives in a given industry are made responsible for its conduct and share in its control."[21] To this extent, the League made great efforts to reach out to workers to combine them with labor progressives toward creating a nationwide labor movement that would be "the arbiter of social change, an instrument to overthrow the capitalist system and a challenger to the present structure of labor. . . . In order to develop an effective labor movement in this country, we must begin by developing a labor culture as the foundation for a completely rounded out labor movement, encompassing the organization of the workers on all important fields of human endeavor."[22]

A major way in which the LID addressed itself to the labor movement and its struggles was through the publication of *Labor Age*. This journal was an extension and reworking of the educational pamphlets and the newsletter that had been distributed by the Intercollegiate Socialist Society. *Labor Age* maintained the ISS desire to familiarize readers with socialist tenets and to demonstrate the ways in which that ideal, as reinterpreted by the LID, might bring about social and economic equality. Moreover, the journal aimed at being *the* labor news source for all ranks of the labor movement, from the pure and simple trade unionists through the skilled metal trades workers to the unskilled laborers.[23] The LID understood that "workers in America . . . [were] no longer chiefly concerned with just bread and butter. They want[ed] to know about and want[ed] something to say about the conditions and continuity of their employment."[24] *Labor Age* was created to give workers the knowledge and the voice for which the LID believed they were looking.

To give their magazine the best opportunity to reach its intended audience, the LID handed the publication and circulation of *Labor Age* to a professional press (previously, the ISS had undertaken the entire process themselves in the publication of the *Intercollegiate Socialist*). The League would control the content of *Labor Age*, but the Labor Publication Society[25] would handle the design and distribution.

> Almost immediately, the consortium examined the LID's target audience and determined that *Labor Age* should be reorganized to better fit into their image of the "modernizing"[26] lifestyles of this group. The consortium concluded that the journal should be rearranged into sections that would more effectively perform the ideological tasks of the LID. "The makeup of *Labor Age* is very important to us, as it adds much to its success or failure. We are living in an age when art is applied to business, especially to the business of printing. Small type, thin paper, minute margins—all of these tire the eyes very quickly. . . . The text of *Labor Age*, therefore, must be made readable and appealing, playing to the eye, mind, heart and ambitions of workers. . . . The editorials must contain originality; they must discuss the news of the day—that of the community and, of course, the worker—and reflect on it; and they must interpret the news in its relationship to the workers' plight.[27]

With these rules in mind, and with the goals of the LID clearly laid out, *Labor Age* was substantially redesigned.[28] The Labor Publication Society decided that the first section of the journal should provide news and narrative information concerning current labor events of national and local interest. The other sections of *Labor Age* could be more flexible and variable in their layout, but their structure was meant to provide varied interpretation and discussion of "practical" and "theoretical" labor topics, editorial opinion about the labor movement's most recent maneuvers, and personal (human interest) reports from and about the workers and organizers who were struggling to bring the goals of the LID to fruition. Photography was also to be made an important part of *Labor Age*, as a way to give visual interest and support to the news stories, and to help in putting a local human face on a huge national labor movement. As a whole, the focus was on making *Labor Age* a publication that would be attractive and useful to both labor progressives and workers across the nation and that would fill their informational and educational needs.

Distribution of the journal was to be undertaken in several ways. Sample copies were distributed at union meetings by LID representatives; samples were also distributed among those in attendance at various worker's educational seminars[29] and at luncheon conferences arranged by the LID.[30] Those workers and organizers who purchased subscriptions[31] to *Labor Age* were encouraged to pass along a copy to their comrades in hopes of obtaining new subscribers. Finally, it was hoped that *Labor Age* might eventually be made readily available nationally at newsstands.[32]

These heightened public relations activities gave LID administrators great confidence that *Labor Age* could reach workers with information and ideas that would set them on the road to instigating social change. "Never has an American labor monthly been launched with the backing of so powerful and active a group. Never has it been possible for a labor and socialist journal to play so vital a role in the labor movement as at the present time."[33]

With the publication of its first issue in November of 1921, *Labor Age* seemed well on the way to fulfilling its proposed role as "a vivid and comprehensive composite of what American labor is thinking and doing."[34] Just as the Labor Publication Society had advised and planned, the journal's 35 pages[35] were directed into two general sections: one that reported the activities of laborers and employers and one that supplied an empathetic and active voice for labor's cause. During its lifetime, *Labor Age* never wavered from this very basic organizational structure.

Much of the information that appeared regularly in the organs of international unions, local labor papers, and liberal and radical activist publications was compiled within the pages, of the first section of *Labor Age*.[36] Such information, published in separate places, had previously been available only to a limited group of readers: the members of a particular craft or the followers of a particular sectional idea. Centralizing its location, however, offered the entire nation's labor progressives and its workforce the opportunity to see the commonality of their plight and the scope of their struggle. Many pages were devoted to synopses of labor occurrences believed to be of regional and national interest. In addition to utilizing information from many local and national labor presses and offices, *Labor Age* also sent its own writers to locations nationwide to keep activists and workers abreast of conditions and activities inside and outside mines, mills, and factories.

Strikes and threatened strikes, cooperative activities, relief work, sweeping antilabor injunctions, antiunion drives, and widespread unemployment were the events most commonly detailed in *Labor Age* during the 1920s:

> Overshadowing every other question of labor and capital in the last few weeks was the threatened railroad strike among the Big Five: the Brotherhood of Locomotive Engineers, the Brotherhood of Trainmen, the Brotherhood of Firemen and

Enginemen, the Order of Railway Conductors and the Switchmen's Union. It was at first expected that the railway shop crafts would join forces with the larger groups, but these refused to go on strike as the Big Five had given them no hope of support after the demands of the brotherhoods had been met. Soon after, the strike was called off. The real struggle is yet to come. . . . [37]

No sooner was the railroad strike "settled" than rumors of war were heard in several other directions, notably in the coal and clothing industries. Federal Judge A. B. Anderson issued one of the most dramatic injunctions in the history of American labor. The injunctions prohibited coal miners from using the funds of the United Mine Workers to organize in the Williamson coal fields of West Virginia. War clouds in the industry are becoming even thicker . . .

Peace, not only in the coal industry, but in the clothing industry has been menaced by the events of the last few weeks, and the ladies' garment industry throughout the nation is now face to face with one of the bitterest struggles in its existence. . . . [38]

During the month the strike of the International Ladies' Garment Workers against the reestablishment of piece work and of the forty-nine hour week was of outstanding importance in New York and other centers. A last minute attempt to avert the walkout was made by twelve United States senators, but refusal of the employers to continue their old agreement made this attempt futile. This effort failing, the workers walked out of their shops on the morning of November 14. . . . [39]

The wage reduction of 20 percent and the proposed increase of working time from 48 to 54 or 55 hours by the mill owners of New England have led to a widespread strike among the textile workers of Massachusetts, New Hampshire and Rhode Island. Federal investigators are trying to bring about a settlement. State troops have been sent out into several mill towns in Rhode Island "to quell the rioting strikers and their sympathizers." In Pawtucket several strikers have been killed and wounded by the authorities, in an attempt to "reestablish law and order."[40]

Overshadowing all other questions in the field of labor during the past month is the strike of over 600,000 miners. The textile strike was extended to the mills at Lawrence. In the needle trades the Amalgamated Clothing Workers averted threatened strikes in Chicago and Rochester, and entered into a three-year agreement with the clothing manufacturers in these sections. The railroad workers continued their contests before the Railroad Labor Board. The month was also marked by important developments in the fields of workers' education, of politics and of co-operation.[41]

During the month of August the number of registered unemployed increased by 31,000—a hint at what the coming winter will bring. "Registered unemployed" are those out-of-work folks who enter their names for the unemployment dole at the government labor exchange. They do not represent by a great deal all the persons out of work in the country. The Labor Research Department, in its October Circular, estimates the total number of unemployed on September 1 at two and one-half million.[42]

January was another bloody month in Colorado. Two miners were shot to death in Walsenburg, making eight murdered in the state since the strike began. But high-powered rifles are not digging coal. Failing to get production, Mr. Rockefeller's Colorado Fuel and Iron Company is offering men another 50-cent-a-day raise, making $6.52-a-day. But strikers demand the Jacksonville scale, pit committees, and checkweighmen.[43]

In Pennsylvania and Ohio, the United Mine Workers' members are waiting out the winter with the aid of relief from their union and other trades. Money and carloads of clothing are going to the strike zone but the best is not enough and the life of this great union is threatened.[44]

Company doctors in western Pennsylvania, Art Shields reports, are refusing to help the wives of coal strikers through childbirth. Other districts are completely deprived of all medical attendance since the strikers are too poor and the Red Cross regards their sufferings as "their own fault." The next time the Red Cross comes into your factory with its hand out—remind them of western Pennsylvania.[45]

Like heat lightning on a sultry summer evening are the quick, fitful strikes of the unorganized workers. Flint auto workers, Bayonne oil workers, Troy collar work-ers—here and there workers, bewildered, speeded up past endurance, goaded, seek relief, protection, guidance. Troy collar girls heard about the new Bedeaux system of paying their wages. It meant speeding up and wage cuts. They struck. They didn't quit the Cluett, Peabody factories, they just cut off the motors and stayed by their machines. For three days they sat by their machines, reading, playing cards, singing, but not working. Then Cluett, Peabody gave in.[46]

Reading, Pennsylvania has put over the most dramatic labor organization cam-paign in recent times. Maybe it is because the city has a labor administration with James H. Maurer as an alderman. Maybe it's because the Hosiery Workers know how to do such things. Maybe it's because the Federated Trades Council heeded Jim Maurer's advice to can the dignity stuff, get out and make a noise, shout and talk unionism. Anyway the Join the Union drive proved big stuff for a town whose low wages and open shops are the stenches in the nostrils of all decent unionists. . . . A calliope covered with union slogans traveled up and down business streets, corner meetings were held every night, for the first time unionists spoke to non-union hosiery workers at the very mill gates. 30,000 copies of the Reading Unionist, special drive paper, were distributed every Sunday morning on every doorstep. . . . Other towns that feel they need to put a punch into union work might drop a line to Reading's trade council. It knows how.[47]

Easily the most important strike since the epochal railroad and coal struggles of the post-war period is the attack launched on the International Typographical Union by the "open shop" division of the American Newspaper Publishers Association, coupled as it is with a double threat of job elimination through the revolutionary teletypesetter. Although less than 250 union printers are involved in the first en-gagement on what promises to be a wide-flung battle line, this lockout parallels that of 300 Allen-A hosiery workers in Kenosha, Wisconsin in demonstrating that mighty issues can be rooted in apparently local fights.[48]

In the sunny, open spaces south of Van Cortlandt Park in New York stand the cooperative apartments of the Amalgamated Clothing Workers. Ground has just been broken for another unit of the buildings which will accommodate in all 500 families. Already more than 300 families enjoy the present apartments and the privileges of cooperative service. A year of success proves what organized workers can provide for themselves when they act together. Children who were born in dark little tenements of the lower east side now play in sunshine around the buildings or pile into the co-op's bus to drive over to grammar school. Cooperative stores provide all necessaries in the way of groceries, meat, fruit and vegetables. An educational committee gets up plays and the auditorium has a stage large enough to make it a little theatre. All these advantages are secured for a monthly charge averaging only $11 a room.[49]

Union miners in the anthracite are fighting hard to save their state hospitals. The fee-charging medicos are sore about the hospitals, where the miners get treatment free of charge when they are maimed in their gamble against high explosives and falling rock in hard coal mines. The coal operators, too, want to shift the burden to the miners so as to ease the taxes.[50]

While these few examples give just a glimpse of the effort that compilers and writers put into relaying all pieces of labor information to their readers,[51] they are quite representative of the overall labor situation at the local, state, and national level during the 1920s. During the decade, "employing interests" directed their efforts toward suppressing both the stronger labor organizations (such as the ones mentioned above) and the smaller labor groups and company unions. "In all their work to achieve their ends, the employing interests made a systematic use of all available weapons. The injunction, the armed guard, the state militia, and the power of hunger were employed in the fight at every opportunity."[52] Yet, in the face of such overwhelming power and without any nationally organized, class-based movement, labor did respond to these maneuvers in various ways throughout the 1920s; *Labor Age* was there in an attempt to publicize the confrontations.[53]

Labor Age also summarized the conventions and conferences that brought together workers and activists to speak their frustrations and aspirations and to plan for their alleviation or realization:

Several representatives of organized labor took part in the conference of the Public Ownership League of America, held in Chicago, from November 18 to 22. John Brophy, President of District No. 2 of the United Mine Workers, and chairman of the Nationalization Research Committee of the miners, gave a vigorous address in support of public ownership and democratic administration of the mines. He quoted Secretary Hoover as declaring that the coal industry was one of the worst governed industries in the country. The present instability of the industry, he quoted a mine president as saying, was costing the country $500,000,000 annually. He declared that the annual loss of coal was 150,000,000 tons; that transportation wastes were appalling and that the owners were engaging in gross profiteering. One West Virginia firm, he asserted, had secured a profit of $478,000 on a capital of $178,000. No less than $20,000,000 of the stock of the Pittsburgh

Coal Company, one of the largest bituminous companies, was "water." Some 2,500 miners are killed and 30,000 injured each year. The average working year of the miner during the last thirty years was 215 days. The miner's average income in the United States will probably be less than $1,000. National ownership is necessary for economy, for the conservation of the nation's coal resources and for the sake of both the producer and the consumer.[54]

The hand-picked Harding Unemployment Conference has met and adjourned without accomplishing very much practical results. However, the mouthpiece of big business took advantage of the occasion to present resolutions advocating the repeal of the Adamson law, the abolishment of the Labor Board created under the Cummings-Esch, reduction of wages, lengthening of hours of labor, granting large sums of money to the railroads, etc., and took advantage of their superior numbers on the Committee on Manufactures to recommend these things to the general conference. However, as those in charge realized that such a course would react upon the heads of those responsible, they did not act upon the recommendations of this committee. President Gompers and a couple of other delegates representing labor presented a minority report which tore the recommendations of the committee to shreds, and vigorously defended the interests of the workers. This report, like that of the majority, was read, but not acted upon.[55]

In late January, John L. Lewis, president of the United Mine Workers, sent letters to officers of the sixteen railroad unions inviting them to confer with the miners' officials "at the earliest possible date." The invitation stated that both the railway men and the miners were faced with unwarranted reduction in their wages, and that "in order to cope with this situation, and to successfully combat this frenzied hysteria, the mine workers are willing to pool their interests with the railroad organizations and stand with them in resistance to the proposed attacks on wage scales. . . ." Fifteen of the sixteen unions responded favorably, and the conference was set for February 21 in the city of Chicago. An alliance of the two groups would join together about 2,000,000 workers in these two most strategic industries of the country and make it impossible to put a wedge between these groups in the present critical situation. . . . No attempt was made at the conference to induce the railroad unions to declare a sympathetic strike in case of a miners' conflict. The delegates drew up a memorandum, however, which declared that 'the mutuality of the interests of the employees' in the railroad and mining industries 'must be recognized and we assert our purpose to apply every honorable method to secure adequate standards of living.[56]

The two great clothing workers' unions—the International Ladies Garment Workers Union and the Amalgamated Clothing Workers Union—held their conventions in early May. Each organization has grown in the last dozen years from a mere handful of scattered groups to among the most powerful, efficient and progressive labor organizations in the country. Each has revolutionized working conditions in its respective field. Each has passed through the most extensive and most bitterly fought struggles in its existence and has come out with lines intact and colors flying.[57]

Here again, the focus is on labor's news. Writers and compilers gathered the most current information to demonstrate to readers the variety of activities undertaken to bring the "good society" into existence.

In addition to providing information about timely issues, *Labor Age* revisited past national and local labor events not only to present a solid historical account of American labor activities, but also to draw lessons and inspiration from them. In most cases, these narratives reviewed nationally recognizable group actions, evaluating their positive and negative aspects and, at times, providing a reinterpretation of the outcome:

> The question is often asked: "Why did the great steel strike of 1919 fail?" As a matter of fact, the steel strike was not a failure. It taught the Steel Trust a lesson that that corporation will never forget. It gave the workers of the steel industry a taste of their own power, when used in cooperation with their fellow-workers. They will, from now on, never give up the idea of freedom in their work, which can only be attained through unionization.
>
> When the steel workers organize again—and this will not be long from now—they will profit by the five points of weakness shown in the last walk-out, and arrange their organization methods so as to bring complete victory.[58]

That example suggests how closely the LID saw *Labor Age*'s informational role blending with its role in creating a sense of class identity and solidarity among workers. Such an ideally balanced vision was carried through in the design of the journal: while section one illustrated and narrated workers' plight, section two aimed at helping readers to understand the necessary means to lessen it.[59]

The writing in the second half of *Labor Age*'s roughly 35 (on average) pages focused equally on workers and labor progressives to inspire and link them together in the movement for industrial democracy. Toward this end, the journal made a point of always backgrounding the "proletarian versus intellectual question" with which most activists of the period struggled yet few had overcome. *Labor Age*'s writers believed that their effort, above all others, would erase the ideological gap that had long separated workers from social activists.

Specifically, they took on the task of responding to critics who not only spoke openly about that ideological gap, but also clung vehemently to the idea that such a gap must be maintained. Writers William R. Sautter, M. B. Butler, and others of similar belief were vocal proponents of the need for intellectual leadership within the socialist movement. This leadership, they explained, should focus their attention and energy primarily on the "responsible, intelligent, self-respecting workers," [60] as the others were simply not worthy of help. Many diatribes appeared in other labor journals of the period, including the *Industrial Worker*, the *Call*, and the New York *Worker*:

> It is up to every local union to see that the real "slum" element, the degenerates, the drunks, and those men who are so far gone that they have lost all manhood, are kept away from the halls and meeting places. The element which make up the human race are a detriment to any association. The sooner their wretched bodies are off the earth the better chance the fighters will have. . . . It may be true that

some old barrel stiff or booze fighter is "not to blame" for his filthy condition, but neither are we to blame for it. A union is nothing, if not to fight the employing class. We have no place in our ranks for the degenerates.[61]

The American workingman is a composite of superstition, stupidity and cowardice. . . . In rare moments of lucidity, the American realizes that the wealthy leisure class is living by his toil, like a parasite sucking his blood. Yet when it is in his power to organize . . . he casts his lot unthinkingly with the fat, jolly, smiling employment shark.[62]

You say "our benevolent fathers, the capitalists, give us jobs, and we couldn't live without jobs." Did you ever stop to think that it is you who support the capitalist class . . . ? No, you never tried to think in your lives. . . . You are brutally murdered and you piously roll up the whites of your eyes in thankfulness to god for it. What infinite ignorance! What a huge but ghastly joke you are! Do you deserve pity? No, a thousand times no!. . . . Blame yourselves![63]

Why don't they see how they are oppressed and misused and ill treated? Why don't they see that there is no use in their working in poisoned, filthy, hot places in the summer, and bitter, freezing cold places in the winter? Why don't they see that no one need work for the weary long hours they do? Why don't they see that there is no need for them to do all the work while their masters live filled with beauty? Oh, we have shown them so many times! Why don't they see? If they won't see, they deserve to be slaves![64]

Labor Age writers also positioned themselves in opposition to activists and scholars at the other ideological extreme, those who revered workers, placing them above all others in society. Writings in this vein are emotionally intense, and convey a vision of heroism and immortal spirit, not securely anchored in a particular time or place. Consider the following prose essay written by a socialist novelist:

The average workingman has more sense, more logic and more heart than the average holder of the sheepskin degree, the average professor, or average editor. Man for man, the so-called "lower" class is infinitely superior to the misnamed "higher" class . . . Vive le proletaire![65]

J.S. Biscay, (another prominent organizer and writer) after a lengthy denial that intellectuals have any special claim on radicals' indulgence, pens this ode to the proletarian:

He (the worker) does everything and gets the least. It is this despised prol when he begins finally to think for himself and organize from the hole in the ground to the top of the skyscraper, before whom the very earth trembles. He is God all over the world.[66]

Labor Age made an effort to challenge both the incredibly negative and the positively mythic characterizations of the worker, to overcome the usual hierarchies created between "brain workers" and "brawn workers". The journal's writers began by universalizing the frustrations of workers and activists, arguing that although the actual life experiences of individual workers and labor activists might differ greatly, their emotional frustrations and desires were very similar. The means to create a classless society to meet the needs of all, they asserted, could be achieved through mutually understanding their labor experiences and by recognizing the commonality of their struggle. Organizer and socialist W. J. Ghent eloquently expressed the official position of the League for Industrial Democracy:

> When men in a delegate body take it upon themselves to extol ignorance and to decry knowledge or to speak contemptuously to one set of men as "proletarians" and apologetically of another set of men as "intellectuals," it is time to take stock of our principles and our personnel. . . .
> There is no room [in the movement] for the demagogue, literary or political. . . . There is no room for the plea that the man who works with his hands is better or worse than the man who writes or teaches or organizes or plans. . . . Everyone who comes into the Socialist movement comes in, or should come in, on the same terms and he remains there on the same footing as every other comrade. . . . There is no room for class distinctions in the Socialist movement, just as there will be none in the Socialist Republic.[67]

Such beliefs shaped much of the writing in the second section of *Labor Age*. The editorials, essays, fiction, and human-interest articles were undergirded by the hope of getting laborers and labor progressives to know and understand each other, and to realize that "the weakness of the labor movement is not because of the strength of the opposition on the part of the owners. The weakness of the labor movement is in our own indifference in our need to unite."[68] In the idea that unity grows from knowledge and knowledge from familiarity, personal sketches of workers and organizers from particular areas of the nation were printed in every issue.

Labor Age reporters and writers spent much time living and laboring with workers in an attempt to gain an understanding of the beliefs and values which drove them and to get a clear sense of the home and workplace conditions under which they existed. LID member and *Labor Age* reporter Dorothy Gary spent several consecutive summers in the mid- and late-1920s living with six textile mill families in Alabama; she presented their stories in a *Labor Age* series as "sketches" or "glimpses" of a "submerged South." Her tales are ones of the tenuousness of an existence defined by unemployment, abject poverty, and early mortality.

> The Crenshaws live on the edge of the village (Brandon, Alabama) where the poorest cottages stand. No trees or flowers here. Only yellow dirt, flies and sizzling heat. Around their shack runs a high chicken wire fence and the gate is locked. Inside stands grandmotherly Katy, minding twelve, half-naked squalling children while her daughter and son-in-law work in the mill.[69]

After spending several paragraphs in further describing the pallid and drawn physical presence of the town's residents and describing the squalor in which they live, Gary engages Katy in a discussion about her labor experiences:

> Roe mill (in which her daughter and son-in-law work) ain't so good for wages but

I've lived on worse. . . . Roe is got a good character 'n that means a lot. All mills ain't. I wuz in one, once, soon after we come down from the mountains. My ole man'd ceased-'ed, so it wuz jus' me to support th' babies. Every day I locked 'em in the house before I went to th' mill, 'n every night I wuz home scairt th' house had burned down. I tell you, them wuz hard days, before the hours wuz cut to ten.[70]

Gary contrasts these ideas with those of the Rhodeses, a family in a similar position physically and financially to Katy's, yet more aware of their position as laborers and of the fact that they deserved more from their employers. Sitting on her porch one evening, Sally Rhodes tells her story:

"We live in common like, us six families here." With her right thumb she indicated the houses fronting the little square of dirt before us. "Each one got a little patch. Wages bein' what they is—we cudn git along without. One raises beans 'n peas, somebody else, yellers 'n taters. And me, I raise corn. Whin meal time comes, we jes go 'n help oursefs. Now the drought 'n hot weather is killin' our crops, 'n th' mill only runnin' part time. I tell you they're gettin' us lower 'n lower. They wan us on our knees, that's what. We ain't low 'nuf fer 'em yit. Millionaires they are. They made their money out of us. I look at their fine houses whin I go into town 'n I tinks to mysef, you made that out o' us. If we warnt so poor, you'd not be so rich! And I rememba what th' Bible says about th' rich 'n th' poor. But they'll git theirs when they die.'[71]

To *Labor Age* readers, Gary related efforts to take Katy's complacence and Sally's frustration away from the personal, social, and spiritual realms and move it toward the political. Gathering the families together one evening, she told them of the struggles of other textile workers for a union: how they had suffered and been defeated, but had finally won out; what conditions were like before and what they were like now. "Mrs. Rhodes, sitting as she did in church, with unnoticed tears slipping over her twitching mouth, even Katy wide-eyed, pressing her arms to her flat chest . . . listened without a word until the story ended. Then the questions began to pour in: 'We cud do that too. Why doan somebody cum down 'n organize us?'"[72]

The desire here, in ending the article (and the series) in this manner, was that these stories would give organizers the desire to do just that (seeing how needed their efforts were), and would allow workers to see that their experiences were not unique and were changeable. A similar method was used by *Labor Age* writer Grace Burnham in her review of conditions in the Passaic, New Jersey textile mills:

Exposure to poisons, heat, steam, denial of the most elemental sanitary provisions . . . hours averaging 59 a week . . . low wages . . . such are the degrading conditions of work which produce on the one hand the brilliant display of colored silks, velvets and other attractive fabrics in our shop windows . . . and on the other hand break down the bodies of the men, women and children employed in the dyeing and finishing of textiles.[73]

Burnham highlighted the medical records of many who worked in the mill, reporting that not one of the 77 dye workers given medical examinations by the Workers' Health Bureau was free from physical defects such as heart disease, high blood pressure, tuberculosis, or severe throat and eye irritation. She allowed the workers to tell their own stories of mill conditions, and they spoke of the heat, the fumes, and the lack of "decencies" (such as a lunch hour and rest rooms).[74]

"Professional" activists and organizers like Grace Burnham were not the only ones called upon to write for *Labor Age*. Western Pennsylvania miner H. A. Armstrong was just one of the workers recruited by the journal to relate his pre-union experiences under the oppressive and unhealthy conditions created by the Consolidation Coal Company in the town of Somerset. "Life under non-union conditions is nothing more than petty slavery, because nonunion men know that if one of them does try to change conditions he will be quickly got out under the boss' orders. A man working under such conditions is naturally afraid to trust his fellow man. Eventually there is a feeling of distrust—one against the other."[75]

Physical hardships complicate this emotional struggle: As men emerge from the mine each day, "every face carries yesterday's fatigue and last year's. Now and then I saw a man who looked as if he could work a turn and then box a little in the evening for exercise. There are few men like that. The rest made me think strongly of a man holding himself from falling over a cliff, with fingers that paralyze slowly."[76]

The worsening of these circumstances forced western Pennsylvania miners to strike; such activity eventually created an active union among the Somerset miners. Armstrong and other *Labor Age* writers had great hope that such an occurrence would multiply and spread on a national level, with workers uniting not only under the banner of unionism, but (even more important for the LID) under the umbrella of socialism.

Even white-collar workers were encouraged by *Labor Age* to notice, understand, and act against their plight. Grace Coyle's article, highlighting the invasion of the office by technological advancements, warned that "until clerical workers see their common needs and will work together to meet them, the individual is helpless before the sweep of these great social changes."[77] She further predicted that if collective action would become widespread among white-collar workers, they could certainly overcome the physical and mental pressures, and the economic inequality, created by technology.

Dorothy Gary, Grace Burnham, H. A. Armstrong, and Grace Coyle (among many others) researched and wrote these worker-focused pieces with the goal of dismantling the hierarchy that placed the activist above the laborer (and consequently disrupted the possibility of a working class movement). Conversely, other *Labor Age* writers highlighted the personalities and efforts of activists who worked in various parts of the country, to challenge the placement of the worker above the activist (equally disruptive to any working class movement). "Meet Ed Crouch, Inventor and Organizer," "Hitting the Trail with 'Paul the Apostle,'" "Following the Fight with Louis Budenz," "Visiting with the Practical Idealists of the North-West" were just a few of the headlines that were used to "humanize" the activists and show the empathy (rather than mythic worship) within their work.

> Edward L. Crouch, the man behind the "Camel City" campaign,[78] is one of the most interesting people I have met in the South. It isn't often that a talented inventor[79] and a skilled union organizer are found under the same skin. Here is a workingman who would be highly honored in a more progressive society. He designs the machinery that creates wealth and organizes the workers to see that this wealth is distributed. . . . [80]

In introducing the reader to Edward Crouch, *Labor Age* writer Art Shields described the threats that Crouch consistently received from those managers and owners who felt that a union of tobacco workers was not in their best interests. "But Crouch was thinking of the girl packers getting a few dollars a week, and colored strippers getting less. He stayed with the union. . . . And he struck after the Reynolds refused to renew the contract. The inventor is a full time organizer, a "sticker," a crusader."[81]

Not all articles focused on the older, more seasoned organizer such as Crouch. Another profiled the experiences of young activists who spent almost a year living the lives of factory workers. They worked in industry to "learn labor's slant,"[82] having become impatient with the merely academic approach of most activists to labor problems.[83] They quickly

> learned the meaning of fatigue. Wage rates also exert a sobering effect upon us as "student workers." The pay envelope contains a certain satisfaction that quickly passes when we try to live upon the rest of the contents. . . . Twelve young women in the student industrial group in Chicago this summer, working from 44 to 59 hours per week, averaged $13.62 as their weekly wage. If they had not pooled their wages, the colored student who worked 49 hours for $7 would have suffered the usual disadvantages of the Negro worker. The prospects of living on even the relatively high wage of $13 per week, month after month, gave these women a vicarious shudder. . . . One of the more determined in the group has since joined the Amalgamated Clothing Workers and is now working in a tailor shop in Chicago. "I feel that working through the union is the best way of developing a better social order," she says.[84]

Other articles attempted to entertain readers with stories of novice but enthusiastic activists who "brought the gospel" to small mine and mill towns across the nation. Hastings, Pennsylvania was one of these places where "Paul the Apostle" (any nameless, faceless organizer) preached the "good news" of labor organization and industrial democracy.

Wherever "Paul" went, he spoke of the "path out of the morass—to a reorganization of the industry, to nationalization with the workers sharing in control. . . . [In a sort of socialist altar call, he asked:] 'Would any join together, in the name of Democracy, to think this thing through, to save their industry and themselves?' There were volunteers, tens of them, double that number. . . ."

If only that many would have read *Labor Age*. There is little doubt that the journal made serious efforts to raise workers' and labor progressives' awareness of each other, and of the labor-related events occurring around them. The journal also made a solid attempt to steer its audience to an understanding and adoption of industrial democracy, i.e. to reject the individual ideal and accept group unity, to choose socialist tenets over capitalist ones, to ultimately rise up and militantly express their class solidarity. Yet, *Labor Age*'s toil never came to fruition, especially among workers. Certainly the journal gained great respect and a large readership among activists and organizers, but it failed to touch substantial numbers within the working ranks.[85] While *Labor Age* could pride itself on seeing the worker as proletarian, without scorn or excessive praise, at the same time, however, it also failed to see the worker in *all* of his multifaceted social milieu (through distinctions of ethnicity, gender, age, religion, etc.).

The writing in *Labor Age* contains and promotes certain assumptions about the form and function of the worker, based solely upon his relation to the means of production. This tendency reinforces the impression that when *Labor Age* writers looked at a worker, they did not see him; they saw what he was supposed to become in their movement. Driven by class analysis, *Labor Age* did not take into consideration the other beliefs, values, and roles workers found important; no doubt, at times, the writers' goals seemed completely irrelevant to them. In short, the *Labor Age* organizers seemed completely unaware that the workers' lives included any other meaningful relationships except with the activists themselves on the one hand and with their workplace on the other. This becomes more evident through an examination of some of the letters that were sent by workers to the *Labor Age* and LID offices in New York.[86] As the journal itself had no section in which to display the thoughts of readers, this correspondence was never printed or circulated in its entirety.[87] Nevertheless, the letters are extremely important. The examples below, in particular, suggest that while the journal may not have realized the power of life's complexity and the importance of recognizing it, the workers themselves did.

> When I, a railroad machinist in the Beech Grove shops at Indianapolis, go out on strike, I am not thinking in terms of New York "revolutionists." I don't know anything about "surplus value" or the "solidarity of the proletariat." But I do know that my brothers and I have been given a raw deal.... I want the sort of talk that does no fine splitting of hairs but presents sweeping statements; that, or things that come home to me and touch upon my daily life, my home and my children.[88]

> I have learned that acquiescence is a great word. I acquiesce. Of course, I don't believe in what is going on, but what can one man or a handful of men do against the whole town, backed by the power of the state and the business interests? If you have ideas and express them, you're just bound to get into trouble, and in my present position, with a sick wife on my hands, I can't afford trouble, so I acquiesce.[89]

An examination of workers' expressions and complaints about *Labor Age* discourse reveals that an alternative meaning of *context* is employed. The worker is (as the LID would hope) seeing the *Labor Age* message as a *call-to-arms*; however, he is also seeing it as being at odds with his daily life. The worker has other responsibilities to confront beyond the commitment he has to his economic *class*. He has a sick wife; he has a need to keep his job. He has a need to get along with his neighbors. He has a responsibility to his children who also have relationships of their own. In other words, he sees the *context* of *Labor Age's* message within a framework of personal efficacy. How can he act on the challenge mounted by the writers and editors given his present state of affairs? How is he to comprehend the message alongside of his other social obligations? The *context* of *Labor Age's* message, therefore, must be joined to a notion of what James Der Derian and Michael Shapiro term *performativity*.[90] More to the point, the rhetorical dimension of the above letters is framed not only by the suggestion of *worker solidarity* but by the *Labor Age* reader's sense of *action*. The stipulated context of *Labor Age* cannot get beyond the reader's frustration at not being able to act upon it. So reading *Labor Age* becomes a *chore* for its intended audience; its goals for the workers become not only unattainable, but alien to their lives.

Mainstream media publications do not necessarily face this situation. The vocabulary used by their producers used often allows for an inexpensive[91] and comfortable joining of linguistic and pictorial context to performance on a daily basis. Many mainstream media presentations serve to promote excitement, if not inspiration, for the individual to act in consort with others to organize joint community (rather than workplace) interests. Articulated messages in either verbal or visual presentations (which appear to represent normality) draw upon such interests and thus allow the reader of the mainstream presentations to have an understanding of the happenings reported by the media even before he or she sees and reads about them.

Messages that titillate and excite the reader to action are often emblazoned in the headlines of daily newspapers. An understanding of the events or circumstances covered by the headline and its attendant article is framed by emotions and language generated by sports entertainment, by the attractiveness of advertised family activities and by the official agencies who organize and define community values. In this way, reader understanding precedes the media intent by virtue of the topic of the article being part of a culture's or community's world. The popularization of activity establishes precedent. The paring of vocabularies in the popular press enhances and/or blurs the connection between intent and comprehension. As such, the meaning delivered to the reader becomes either natural and normal or confusing and misunderstood.

An example of this can be found in connecting the word *labor* to *day*. For the LID, *labor day* was commemorated on May 1. Socialists all over the world had been celebrating the cause of labor on this day since the late nineteenth century. Parades, workshops, and other group celebratory activities within the labor movement had become an annual event. In the United States, however, the official designation of such a day was not May 1st but September 3rd. Furthermore, the activities generated on this day commemorating and acknowledging American workers' efforts extended beyond the customs inspired by traditional *Labor Day* (i.e. *May Day*) activities. A look at a *New York Amsterdam News* headline of May 23, 1923, "KEARNS SAYS DEMPSEY WILL MEET WILLS LABOR DAY,"[92] exemplifies this point. For the readers of this newspaper, *Labor Day* was the day on which Jack Dempsey was going to fight Harry Wills for the world's heavyweight boxing championship, not a day for the celebration of labor. Rather than supporting a common theme of a worker's holiday, the *News* transformed the meaning of *Labor Day* until it was analogous to the celebration of sport.

Labor Age discourse many times seemed to be at odds with the popular vocabulary and social concerns of workers. Speaking of and to the workers' strikes during 1921, *Labor Age* created discourse that was basic to organizing an interpretive frame for its ideological underpinnings. For socialists, capitalism caused unemployment, and threatened and actual strikes were the ultimate ways in which labor could confront its negative consequences. Writing in the November issue of *Labor Age,* Harry Laidler presented an intellectually reasoned argument showing how the strike and the threat of striking were the natural outgrowth of capitalistically inspired unemployment and its ally, official government. He went on to say that the individual distress caused by the government's lack of action toward rising unemployment was fundamental to the chaotic ups and downs of the American capitalistic economy.[93]

Popular media vocabulary regarding the striking activities of workers was not so refined and intellectually considered. Indeed, it was often short and simplistically arranged. Their language, in many renderings, reflected alternate considerations of social context, often eliminating the fine nuances of political and economic design. The headline and story in the *New York World* of November 9, 1921 demonstrates how the elimination of such an intellectual consideration is necessary, because of the social consequences a particular strike was creating in the New York metropolitan area: "VIOLENCE BEGINS IN MILK STRIKE; FAMINE IN HOUSEHOLDS." The short article that appears below the headline continues the rhetorical intent, "Borden Truck Attacked, Load Destroyed and Driver Beaten—Family Supply Available Only at Train Platforms—Station Possible Today."[94] Nowhere in the article is there any political or economic analysis of why the workers were striking. The meaning conveyed in the presentation is vague. The article does not overstipulate its own meaning; instead, it is direct and to the point in demonstrating social concern for violence and familial dysfunction.

An equally frank headline appeared in the *New York World* on July 30, 1922: "LABOR COSTS CUT, MORE STEEL MADE, UNDER 8 HOUR DAY." A sub-headline reads "*Colorado Fuel and Iron Company Found Workers Were in Better Condition, Too.*" The accompanying article explains that the Colorado Fuel and Iron Company had recently adopted changes in its labor policies (reducing the twelve-hour day to eight, increasing wage and piece rates). Such practices, according to "the auditing department," had greatly increased the productivity of the company, yet had simultaneously reduced its production costs. Perhaps the most important consequence of the company's changes, the article concludes, was that workers were in "better physical condition and their mental attitude [was] better."[95] To the reading audience, it would certainly seem to be a victory for workers.

Yet, a *Labor Age* article, also from July of 1922, appears to ignore the victory. Instead it gives a broader and more ideologically-based perspective to events like the one covered by the *World*. Such a rendering often served to annoy if not confuse the worker reading it as it required a deeper analysis of the state of the economy. Workers, for the most part, had little time to engage in such activity. They were too busy working their shifts, raising a family, and otherwise attending to the daily responsibilities of life. The author of the *Labor Age* article, in reviewing the progress of Industrial Democracy, appears to miss this. While he does consider many of the positive changes that were occurring in the economy across the nation, he evaluates them within a larger context. As such, he sees them as just one step in the process toward an entirely new social system—a system that identifies itself not simply through a renegotiation of the relationship between worker and employer (through increased wages or lowered hours), but by a complete overhaul of that relationship. The authors' dedication and duty to the socialist cause, therefore, leads him to conclude that "it is not a question of hours and wages. Hunger and suffering often compel men to start thinking. But once the process (understood as the move toward industrial democracy) has started, a good meal now and then cannot stop it."[96]

A similar instance of transformational grammar can be seen in another pairing of articles. The front page of the *New York World* of October 9, 1922 displayed an article entitled "UNEMPLOYMENT DROPS; LABOR SHORTAGE SEEN." This two-paragraph piece reveals the positive result of the settlement of the coal and railroad strikes: increased employment on a national scale. "The most encouraging sign of this increased prosperity," it announces, "is a threatened common labor shortage in all parts of the country."[97] Reading this, workers could see the possibility of new and better employment opportunities. Indeed, the straight-forward language of the article encourages them to do so.

This would not necessarily be the case after the worker read an article on the same topic that appeared in *Labor Age* a few months later. While the journal saw similar positivity associated with the labor shortage for workers, it again undertook a deeper and more ideological consideration of it: the labor shortage was just part of the natural cycle of capitalism. History, for the editors of *Labor Age*, bore witness to this. Therefore, instead of being complacent as a result of this new opportunity, workers were to see it as a call to action. To this extent, the labor shortage was reinterpreted as a means toward achieving the demands of the LID, rather than seen as just a factor that increased the economic prosperity of the American workforce.[98]

Popular culture influenced the transformation of meaning and the creation of social identities for workers during the 1920s in other, not so obvious ways as well. Aided by an acceptance of cultural standards, workers extended and adapted social behaviors beyond the boundaries of the socialist discourse advocated by the editors of *Labor Age*, establishing, in the process, modes of subjective identity that often stood in direct opposition to those created by the journal. Many times, addressing the lowest common social denominator, workers participated in activities that reinforced their popular image of themselves and their world. Raffles, contests, and other social events encouraging individualism and competition were commonplace in workers' daily lives. In terms of social identity, individualism was measured by popular cultural standards of participation. A psychological sense of mutual recognition evolved as more and more members of the workers' neighborhoods participated in such events sponsored by local churches, ethnic social clubs, national identity groups, and the popular press.

The *New York Daily News* was only one of many papers that paid $1 to $5 to individuals who submitted captions, limericks, embarrassing moments, and "bright" sayings. As many as 20,000 readers a day responded. In one 1926 contest, more than 100,000 people were happy to report on "The Queerest Boss I Ever Worked For." [99] (One would be hard-pressed to locate such a "fun-relationship" between workers and managers in the pages of *Labor Age* during the decade.) Readers also competed with each other to identify Presidents from scraps of pictures or match serial numbers on dollar bills. Prize amounts varied widely among the "dailies"; some offered nothing to the winner except recognition in the paper; others paid out huge sums to the skillful reader.[100] The *New York Daily News*, for example, paid $10,000 in 1922 for the best solution to a mystery story. Regardless of the size of the payout, however, reader response was overwhelming. It seems that merely the chance for an individual to compete with (and possibly triumph over) every other reader was enough to draw bags of entries for each contest.

Such ardent competition went to the roots of American thought during the 1920s: "any man, however humble, can rise as far as his talents carry him; every person received his just reward, great or small; and the success of the individual, so encouraged, contributed to the progress of the whole."[101] There is no way to know whether the workers who participated in the newspaper contests could recognize this ideology of individualism or articulate its pervasiveness in their lives. But the enthusiasm with which they participated against each other in the newspaper contests may be taken as evidence of the extent of its appeal during the 1920s.

While the popularity of newspaper contests was running high in most workers' communities, *Labor Age* was publishing articles like "HAPPINESS THROUGH GROUP ACTION," which suggested that individual efforts toward reaping personal rewards should be redirected toward the building of group movements to overthrow capitalism and its control of the social order:

> The human is the only animal which has not learned clearly and completely the lesson of cooperation . . . and it is the fault of the social order today that it does not encourage this. It [social order] fails signally enough on the economic side, with

its glaring contrasts of dazzling wealth in the hands of a few, whilst the enormous majority exist in squalor and poverty. But above all, capitalism fails to bind men together by any ideal loved by all in common. It futilely tries to supply this, dragging in some preachment from a religion which the economic order contradicts in every detail. The unifying ideal must exist within the foundations of society itself. This it will do, when we who care enough put the world upon a cooperative basis.[102]

To imagine game-playing workers digesting the fine political nuances of this call to action issued in *Labor Age* is a stretch (the call to action alone would subvert it being read by game-players). The message is geared to a presumed comrade; individual workers competing in contests did not fit such an identity. For them, happiness came not from group action, but through winning a contest.

Participation in popular enterprises also includes membership in social organizations. Friends recruit neighbors and significant others to join community alliances and other groups of fraternal enterprise. Such organizations included ethnically-based associations, fraternal benefit societies, and church-affiliated sodalities that were organized both for specific sociopolitical intent, (such as the Ancient Order of Hibernians (AOH), the American Legion, the Knights of Columbus) and groups with a less than specific design (like Saturday afternoon knitting societies, neighborhood recreation clubs and local athletic associations which merged masculinity with working-class identity). In the case of organizations with specific sociopolitical intent, newsletters and other formal means of notification were used to tie members into the goings-on not only in their respective communities but in the nation as well. Notices on bulletin boards at churches and in the community served to inform those in the less structured groups, who gathered in more local and casual settings.

Labor Age competed with such media, but this proved to be a daunting task. Not only did the journal have to compete with the rhetoric of these house organs and flyers, they had to confront the reality that the message being delivered was often replicated and mutated by stories appearing in the popular mainstream media. As the political course of action evolved in Ireland in 1922, for instance, the events were reported in the official AOH bulletins, Roman Catholic diocesan and parish newsletters and papers, and the mainstream American Press.[103] In many Irish-American working-class communities, feelings ran high and the bonds of ethnicity were strengthened. For the people at *Labor Age*, such publicity and ethnic emotion were a barrier that overwhelmed both their intellect and their energy. Indeed, the only recourse taken by the journal was to continue verbalizing the "party line." Headlines like "Let's Get Together,"[104] "Putting Up a Fight: The Capitalist as Evil to be Resisted,"[105] "Organization Begins at Birth,"[106] "Hard Times: A Social Responsibility,"[107] and "The United Working-class Front,"[108] preceded calls for alliances among workers to challenge the power of American capitalists:

Organized labor takes the offensive in many industries in their fight against reduced wages and increased hours. The miners started a vigorous campaign for an alliance between the 2,000,000 workers in the mining and railroad industries in order to cope with the present situation. The railroad workers joined with numerous labor organizations and radical and progressive groups in an effort to develop common political action among the labor forces of America, while the Amalgamated Clothing Workers began a campaign for a national reserve fund, to be used in time of emergency.[109]

A similar situation occurred with reference to Polish-American workers during the same period. Polish-American house organs across the nation were beating the drum of true "Americanism."[110] Destroying any inroads made by the left into the Polish-American working-class community and challenging any future road construction, editors of such publications as the *Polish-American Journal (Republica-Gornik)* mounted an offensive to bring Polish pride into the American community.[111] No issue during the early 1920s neglected to include a tirade against socialism abroad and its sympathizers at home.

Once again, in their struggle to place class above all other identifiers, *Labor Age* writers and editors failed to recognize ethnicity.[112] Moreover, the journal ignored or overlooked the need to understand why "Americanism" served as such an easy substitute for socialism."[113]

In the aftermath of the Industrial Revolution, American popular culture emphasized the notion that "the working class was a nonexistent, if not mythic social identity."[114] The concept of upward social mobility that the Industrial Revolution unleashed brought with it the idea that America had eliminated class warfare. Those who maintained otherwise, therefore, were thought to be foreign to the American scene, particularly within the purview of popular culture. More to the point, capitalism was viewed by most American institutions as the precursor to and defender of social mobility. This placed those who would give challenge to it into the category of being "un-American."

In the 1920s, the defending of the "realm" took on a cultural as well as a political identity; the term "nativism" helped to frame this occurrence: those who challenged capitalism became alien to the "American Way"; those who were "natives," spoke the language of America, be it of a personal or public venue. As organized labor was, for the most part, viewed (within the cultural context of upward social mobility) as not being natural to free enterprise, then those who supported trade-unionism had to walk a very careful line, balancing respect for social mobility with the desire to increase the rights of workers, lest they be viewed as alien to the culture. With this in mind most trade-union activity revolved around an acceptance of capitalism, thereby keeping the effort to organize within a certain cultural boundary. The socialist editors at *Labor Age* operated within this cultural milieu. Consequently, in their efforts to bring industrial democracy to fruition, they not only had to challenge capitalism but they had to challenge its ardent defenders as well.

One such defender was the American Legion. Founded in 1919 to "preserve the memories and incidents of [Americans'] association in the great war,"[115] the legion perfectly captured the romantic, almost chivalric memories that many veterans held of their wartime service. During the 1920s, as the United States moved further and further from World War I, the organization's raison d' etre seemed to naturally evolve away from that of human archive and toward that of defender (indeed, at times, definer) of all things American. The periodic parades held by the American Legion (and which received widespread coverage in the popular press) are a good example of this evolution in action.

In November of 1921, an American Legion reunion parade was organized in Kansas City, Missouri: 25,000 soldiers and sailors participated while 500,000 cheering spectators lined the sidewalk. The parade was made more memorable by the fact that it was reviewed by Marshal Foch and General Jacques of France, General Diaz of Italy, and General Pershing and Admiral Beatty of the United States. As viewed by the *New York World*, "it was an event the people of this city will never forget. It proved that the comradeship made on the battlefields will not die. The men who spent sleepless nights in no man's land together, faced poison gas and machine gun fire side by side are not going to forget it." Closely tied to this remembrance of war was a celebration of the nation (and the culture) that fought it. The *World* quoted General Pershing: "The parade shows the great power and dignity of the American Legion. This power and dignity was developed in the World War. During all the time that I watched battalion after battalion passing, I thought to myself, 'here is the soul of the United States. Here are the men who fought for a great principle and whose souls dominated everything in the struggle. . . . ' [They are] men of high ideals, [whose] spirit of depth and seriousness [dwells below] an exterior of gayety and youthfulness. . . . These men make a fine backbone for any nation." Here, the common character features that helped win a war are now the characteristics that make a good citizen, a good American.

Paralleling the Legion's claims to represent everything that was American were the many actions it took to support the contention. During the 1920s, the Legion engaged in many efforts in which they purported to identify true "Americanism." In an almost "chautauqua" fashion legionnaires crossed the country speaking to American communities on the evils of radicalism and socialism. One event, in particular, stands out among this activity. Members of the Industrial Workers of the World (IWW) were tried and convicted of murdering three Legionnaires in Centralia, Washington in 1920. Protests against the trial's fairness had been launched by many concerned citizens in the years following the court proceedings, most notably by those who represented the left in the fields of journalism, the arts, and the law, (H. L. Mencken, Ethel Barrymore, and Clarence Darrow to name a few).[116] The American Legion took on the role of defending the convictions of the IWW members. Calling upon all "true Americans" to support the court decision as well as to aid the government in attempting to "rid the nation of reds," the Legion commanded the attention of the mainstream media for much of the decade.[117] While the appropriate appeal courts continuously voted to uphold the decision and the vast majority of the nation's mainstream newspapers supported same, the editors of *Labor Age* throughout the decade chose not only to ignore the event but to maintain that marvelous progress toward socialism was taking place in the American northwest.[118] As the *Labor Age* audience was obtaining more and more of their news and their views from the mainstream press, the notion of the LID becoming more and more out of step with its rank and file took on greater meaning. By 1930, *Labor Age* readership had dropped to less than 1000 (most of these labor progressives). No longer able to maintain the struggle financially, and continually puzzled by the impotence of their work, the editors laid the journal to rest in 1933.

Most American citizens of the 1920s confronted popular culture in their daily lives (as Americans do today). The ideology expressed in popular culture is as concrete as it is subliminal. By administering ideology through language and visuals, the material world of mainstream newspaper publication creates an effect upon the reader that can be partisan and contradictory, satisfying and annoying, and relevant and irrelevant in the personal view of the nature of reality and the constitution of social identity. This is important to recognize. In the competition for the definition of American political culture in the 1920s, the messages expressed in *Labor Age* became vague and nondescript in the minds of many working-class Americans. Encouraged in the acceptance of an official American identity by various ethnic and religious groups, and reinforced in their individual and familial identities by other social organizations, industrial workers of the decade created meaning about their everyday lives within a framework of popular culture. To this extent, the popular press supplied something that *Labor Age* did not. Daily newspapers were satisfying. They appealed to individuals through a context for action that was not threatening to the normalcy of the worker, one that blurred the contradictions and insecurities of a multifaceted industrial society. Mainstream media preached the comfort of American values like upward social mobility and disgust with those who, in their opinion, stood against them. The message used was steeped in a rhetoric that stirred feelings of self-satisfaction. In reading it, workers began to feel good about themselves, to see that compared to others in the world, they indeed lived better lives: the relationship between populism and authority went unseen and reading the news felt worthwhile. Such was not the case in reading *Labor Age*. In the journal's message, context and performativity encouraged indecision and subsequent anxiety among its worker-readers. The fact that the journal's message was misunderstood (combined with its failure to recognize the misunderstanding) did little to draw or maintain worker readership for *Labor Age*, and indeed most likely sent the worker elsewhere for personally meaningful reading.

Notes

1. Herbert Gutman, "Introduction," in *Labor Age* (New York, N.Y.: Greenwood Reprints, 1968), 1. For a discussion of the difficulties experienced by the American labor movement during the 1920s, see Stanley Aronowitz, *False Promises* (New York: McGraw

Hill, 1973); Irving Bernstein, *A History of the American Worker: The Lean Years* (Boston, Mass.: Houghton-Mifflin Company, 1960); Paul Buhle, *Taking Care of Business* (New York: Monthly Review Press, 1999); Melvyn Dubofsky, *Labor in America: A History* (Wheeling, Ill.: Harlan Davidson, 1999); Leon Fink, *In Search of the Working Class* (Urbana: University of Illinois Press, 1994); Daniel Jacoby, *Laboring for Freedom* (Armonk, N.Y.: ME Sharpe, 1998); David Montgomery, *The Fall of the House of Labor* (New York: Cambridge University Press, 1987); Daniel Nelson, *Shifting Fortunes: The Rise and Decline of American Labor* (Chicago, Ill.: Ivan R. Dee, 1997); and Annielise Orleck, *Common Sense and a Little Fire* (Chapel Hill: University of North Carolina Press, 1995).

2. Irving Bernstein, *A History of the American Worker: The Lean Years* (Boston, Mass.: Houghton-Mifflin Company, 1960), 142.

3. *Labor Age*, the primary organ of the League for Industrial Democracy, was published by the Labor Publication Society between 1921 and 1933.

4. Gutman, "Introduction," 4-5.

5. "Labor progressives" were defined by the administrators of *Labor Age* as those who opposed the American Federation of Labor policy of the 1920s, characterized as promoting organization through union-management cooperation and convincing businessmen, politicians, Legionnaires, and the public in general that organized labor was a respectable, patriotic, and American institution. Labor progressives were not satisfied with this policy, seeing in it little direct action that aided or advanced workers. James O. Morris, *Conflict Within the AFL: A Study of Craft Versus Industrial Unionism, 1901–1938* (Ithaca, N.Y.: Cornell University Press, 1958), 86–135.

6. *Labor Age*, November 1921, ii.

7. *Labor Age*, November 1929, 19. The idea of the need for a labor culture had always been prevalent among the organizers of the LID; however, the best articulation of it was made in this article in 1929.

8. *Labor Age*, November 1921, ii.

9. See for example Debra Bernhardt and Rachel Bernstein, *Ordinary People, Extraordinary Lives* (New York: New York University Press, 2000).

10. See the work of Eileen Kraditor, specifically, *The Radical Persuasion* (Baton Rouge: Louisiana State University Press, 1981).

11. See Raymond Schroth, *The Eagle and Brooklyn* (Westport, Conn.: Greenwood, 1971).

12. See, for example, John D. Stevens, *Sensationalism and the New York Press* (New York: Columbia University Press, 1991); Robert Karl Manoff and Michael Schudson, eds., *Reading the News* (New York: Pantheon, 1986); or Richard Kluger, *The Paper: The Life and Death of the New York Herald Tribune* (New York: Alfred A. Knopf, 1986).

13. "The Call of the Intercollegiate Socialist Society," The Papers of the Intercollegiate Socialist Society, Tamiment Institute Library, New York University, New York.

14. "The Call of the Intercollegiate Socialist Society."

15. Because the ISS has only a minor role in my essay, I do not provide an extensive discussion of its goals and activities. For more information on the means and methods of the ISS, along with a list of its members over its lifetime, please see Max Horn, *The Intercollegiate Socialist Society, 1905–1921: Origins of the Modern American Student Movement* (Boulder, Colo.: Westview Press, 1979).

16. "Report of the Secretary of the ISS, September 21, 1921," The Papers of the Inter-collegiate Socialist Society.

17. "Report of the Secretary of the ISS, September 21, 1921."

18. "Report of the Secretary of the ISS, September 21, 1921."

19. LID organizer Norman Thomas wrote: "Democracy means government of the people, by the people and for the people; industrial democracy is the application of this same idea to our economic life." The LID focused itself on "Industrial Democracy" for several reasons. Foremost, it wanted to distance itself from the Socialist Party so that it was not seen as a purely political entity. Nevertheless, the LID did not want to divorce itself from the ideal of socialism, nor did they want to remain an organization that merely studied the tenet without acting upon it. Therefore, the LID took on a name that expressed its desires to focus on giving the people who functioned within industry access to the means of production and access to the profits created by those industries. He later adds that World War I left lasting imprints on American politics and culture, including a new vocabulary with which to discuss the labor question. The term "industrial democracy" had rarely appeared in American discussions before 1912. It seemed to be everywhere ten years later. See Norman Thomas, *What is Industrial Democracy?* (New York: LID Press, 1925), 10.

20. Thomas, *What is Industrial Democracy?* 15.

21. Thomas, *What is Industrial Democracy?* 17.

22. "Report of the Secretary of the ISS, September 21, 1921," and also found in *Labor Age*, November 1929, 19. The brief history of the LID presented here is a cursory one, provided only to give foundational information. For a more thorough coverage of the organization, see Norman Thomas and Harry Laidler, *The LID: Twenty Five Years of Social Pioneering* (New York: LID Press, 1926).

23. Although *Labor Age* was a monthly journal, the LID still believed that it could provide solid and current reports about labor news that would compete with the activities of the "labor dailies." The secret was thought to be the breadth and depth of coverage. Specifically, it was believed that *Labor Age* would be distributed nationwide (unlike the daily or weekly labor newspapers that covered only a certain city or narrow national region); further, *Labor Age*, it was thought, would provide unique and varied insight into these events that could draw together laborers and labor progressives into a national movement. It was simply impossible for labor dailies to give so much opinion, interpretation, and analysis.

24. Harry Laidler correspondence, The Papers of the Intercollegiate Socialist Society.

25. A consortium of representatives from labor and socialist groups.

26. David E. Shi, "Advertising and the Literary Imagination During the Jazz Age," *Journal of American Culture* 2, no. 2 (Summer 1979):167–175. Shi describes the modernism of the 1920s as a growing economic and intellectual independence, and a craving for excitement in a world dull and standardized.

All of these values began to be reflected in the popular press, and *Labor Age*, too, recognized its need to do so.

27. The Papers of the League for Industrial Democracy, Tamiment Institute Library, New York University, New York.

28. In relation to its predecessor, the *Intercollegiate Socialist*.

29. Some were run by Brookwood Labor College, an institute for labor education. See Jon Bloom, *The Voice of Labor Educators* (Katonah, N.Y.: Brookwood Labor College, 1997).

30. Much of the funding for the startup of *Labor Age* came through the benevolence of monied activists like millionaire Gaylord Wilshire, prosperous politician Morris Hillquit and insurance mogul Rufus Weeks. These, among others, had been benefactors of the Intercollegiate Socialist Society, and continued their support as the organization evolved into the LID.

31. Between 1921 and 1925, each *Labor Age* subscription was $2.00 per year or .20 per copy; between 1925 and 1930, the subscription rate rose to $2.50 per year or .25 per copy.

32. Indeed, by 1929 the journal was available at six newsstands across the nation, including Portland, Oregon; Indianapolis, Indiana; and Pittsburgh, Pennsylvania.

33. The Papers of the League for Industrial Democracy, Tamiment Institute Library, New York University, New York.

34. *Labor Age*, November 1921, ii.

35. Each month's issue ran between 30 and 40 pages.

36. *Labor Age* drew upon the Federated Press for much of its information. Begun in 1920, the Federated Press (an "impartial labor news service") gathered news through its organized bureaus, staff correspondents, occasional correspondents, and the central Chicago office. The central office distributed the news every day through its printed service sheet, which contained about 6,500 words and went to all papers and individuals subscribing. In addition, *Labor Age* also solicited information from local and national labor union newsletters and other labor journals.

37. *Labor Age*, November 1921, 18.

38. *Labor Age*, November 1921, 18.

39. *Labor Age*, December 1921, 20.

40. *Labor Age*, March 1922, 26.

41. *Labor Age*, May 1922.

42. *Labor Age*, November 1923, 27.

43. *Labor Age*, February 1928, 23.

44. *Labor Age*, February 1928, 23.

45. *Labor Age*, April 1928, 23.

46. *Labor Age*, August 1928, 13.

47. *Labor Age*, August 1928, 13.

48. *Labor Age*, January 1929, p. 13.

49. *Labor Age*, February 1929, p. 21.

50. *Labor Age*, February 1929, 21.

51. There were usually no less than 30 events listed in each issue of the journal.

52. *Labor Age*, March 1929.

53. Harry Laidler reviewed *Labor Age*'s news gathering and reporting at the thirty-fifth anniversary celebration of the League for Industrial Democracy. In his summary, he outlined the extent to which the "employing interests" went to maintain the subservient

position of workers and praised the efforts of workers and organizers to overcome such oppression. Norman Thomas and Harry Laidler, *The League for Industrial Democracy: Thirty Five Years of Educational Pioneering* (New York: LID Press, 1941).

54. *Labor Age*, December 1921, 19.

55. *Labor Age*, January 1922, 22.

56. *Labor Age*, March 1922, 24.

57. *Labor Age*, June 1922, 23.

58. *Labor Age*, November 1921.

59. *Labor Age* was not as clearly divided and labeled as a newspaper. The journal's two sections performed separated core functions, but the way in which these functions overlapped and mutually reinforced made the publication, as a whole, quite seamless.

60. See Ira Kipnis, *The American Socialist Movement* (New York: Monthly Review Press, 1972).

61. Kipnis, *The American Socialist Movement*. This is attributed to the organizers of the Industrial Workers of the World and was printed in the New York *Call* during 1912.

62. Willliam R. Sautter, "The American Workman," *The Industrial Worker*, 12 February 1910.

63. M. B. Butler, "Stand Up, You Humble Slaves," *The Industrial Worker*, 10 September 1910.

64. The *New York Worker*, 13 October 1906.

65. George Allan England, "Our Hopeless Highbrows," *The Call*, 30 January 1911.

66. J. S. Biscay, "What Would Marx Say," *Sol*, 19 March 1910.

67. Ghent worked through an early draft of this argument in a letter to the editor in the *Worker* as early as 1907. This fully developed idea appeared in correspondence with other LID members throughout the 1920s. The Papers of the League for Industrial Democracy.

68. This became one of the mantras of *Labor Age*, and it appeared in the front matter of each issue, beginning in 1923. See any table of contents. Also appeared as an article in *Labor Age*, January 1925, 18.

69. "Another Glimpse of the South," *Labor Age*, November 1927, 8.

70. "Another Glimpse of the South," 8.

71. "Concluding Sketches of a Submerged South," *Labor Age*, January 1928, 17.

72. "Concluding Sketches of a Submerged South."

73. *Labor Age*, April 1928, 11.

74. *Labor Age*, April 1928, 11.

75. *Labor Age*, December 1922, 18.

76. *Labor Age*, December 1922, 18.

77. *Labor Age*, January 1929, 21.

78. This was a 1920s campaign to organize the workers who processed, manufactured, and packaged cigarettes in North Carolina. The LID played a major role in this movement.

79. Crouch designed an automatic bottoming machine that "eliminated all risk" to tobacco workers who placed the bottom on cans of Prince Albert tobacco by hand. Often their fingers were gashed badly by the sharp tin. Crouch's machine was "fool proof, highly efficient and conserved the operator's strength." *Labor Age*, April 1925, 13.

80. *Labor Age*, April 1925, 14.

81. *Labor Age*, April 1925, 14.

82. *Labor Age*, July 1928, 10.

83. Many of these young people had been student participants in the ISS. Those who expressed frustration at not being able to put the socialism they had read and discussed to practical use found membership in the LID refreshing.

84. *Labor Age*, July 1928, 10.

85. The circulation of Labor Age never reached over 5,000 at its peak. See The Papers of the League for Industrial Democracy. Compare this to the circulation figures of mainstream newspapers of the era: The *New York World* (300,000); *The American and World* (600,000), *The American-Journal* (300,000) and the *Daily News* (1 million). For more specificity, see James Wyman Barrett, *Joseph Pulitzer and His World* (Vanguard Press, 1941) and Stevens, *Sensationalism and the New York Press*.

86. It is not clear whether these workers were recipients of a sample copy of Labor Age or whether they were subscribers. Regardless, the extent of their comments suggests that they engaged the journal on more than one occasion.

87. Pieces of these letters were used in fictionalized accounts and to "make" arguments. See *Labor Age*, August 1922, 1 and 8.

88. The Papers of the League for Industrial Democracy.

89. The Papers of the League for Industrial Democracy.

90. James Der Derian & Michael Shapiro, *International/Intertextual Relations* (New York: Lexington) 1989, xviii.

91. The cost of an issue of *Labor Age* was between .20 in 1920 and .25 in 1930, whereas newspapers could be purchased for a few cents.

92. *The New York Amsterdam Press*, 23 May 1923, 1.

93. *Labor Age*, November 1921, 18-20.

94. *New York World*, 9 November, 1921, 1.

95. *New York World*, 30 July 1923, 26.

96. *Labor Age*, July 1923, 4.

97. *New York World*, 9 October 1922, 1.

98. *Labor Age*, April 1923, 15.

99. *New York Daily News*, 20 July 1926.

100. Skill, more than luck, was involved here. Rules set by the postal authorities governed the mailing of contest entries to newspapers. To be mailable, a contest had to involve skill and not mere luck. John D. Stevens. *Sensationalism and the New York Press*, 130.

101. George Brown Tindall and David E. Shi, *America: A Narrative History* (New York: W.W. Norton, 1996), 123.

102. *Labor Age*, July 1923, 21.

103. Stories about the Irish patriot, Eamon De Valera, making appeals for assistance (The Irish Freedom Fund Drive) to Irish miners in Butte, Montana (as well as to other audiences across America) told of events in the Irish Civil War. His speeches were reported throughout the country by various media. *AOH Bulletin*, March 1922; The *Catholic Tablet*, 26 March 1922, 1; *Butte Bulletin*, 29 March 1922; and *The New York World*, 24 March 1922.

104. *Labor Age,* July 1923.

105. *Labor Age*, October 1922.

106. *Labor Age*, September 1927.

107. *Labor Age*, January 1930.

108. *Labor Age*, March 1922.

109. *Labor Age*, March 1922, 24.

110. Used here, "Americanism" is looked upon "not patriotically, as a personal attachment, but rather as a highly attenuated, conceptualized, platonic, impersonal attraction toward a system of ideas, a solemn assent to a handful of final notions—democracy, liberty, opportunity, to all of which the American adheres rationalistically because it does him good, because it gives him work, because, so he thinks, it guarantees his happiness." Leon Samson, "Americanism and Surrogate Socialism," in *Failure of a Dream? Essays in the History of American Socialism*, ed. John Laslett and Seymour Martin Lipset (New York: Anchor Books, 1974.), 426.

111. "Halt at Once the Vicious Red Program of World Enslavement," *Polish-American Journal (Republica-Gornik)*, May 1923.

112. Throughout 1923 (at the height of the *Republica-Gornik* campaign) no issue reports on ethnic struggles or discusses the concept of ethnicity. See *Labor Age* issues from January through December of 1923.

113. Samson, "Americanism and Surrogate Socialism," 426.

114. Samson, "Americanism and Surrogate Socialism," 426.

115. Tindall and Shi, *America*, 154.

116. Floyd Dell, *Intellectual Vagabondage* (New York: Ivan R. Dee) 1991.

117. Robert K. Murray, "Centralia: An Unfinished American Tragedy," *Northwest Review* (Spring 1963): 7-22.

118. *Labor Age*, "The Northwest Reports Success," August 1920, 8–10; "Happiness through Group Action," December 1923, 22; "The Month," July 1924, 22-25 and "American Labor at Portland," October 1923.

6
Tainted Sources: Government/Media Misrepresentations in the Case of the International Workers Order

Thomas J. Edward Walker

With the end of World War II, the United States achieved its early twentieth-century desire to become the world's most economically vital and militarily powerful nation. To maintain this hegemony the American government crafted a foreign and domestic policy agenda that served notice to both friend and foe alike that what was good for the United States was also necessary for the maintenance of world order. A major component of America's new domestic agenda was the reorganization of its official culture. Solidifying the parameters of this new cultural identity were the nation's three most politically powerful institutions: government, media, and business. This new political coalition set guidelines which all but dictated an official cultural behavior for American citizens. Unnoticed, for the most part, in this political phenomenon was the effect all of this would have on American democracy. This was a heady time for America; it was "an age of cultural anxiety." Claiming to be the target of sinister forces, pertinent federal and state governmental bodies organized investigations of individuals and groups who were, in their opinion, "un-American." Assisting government in this crusade were the mainstream mass communications industry (the media), which created sensationalistic and banner headlines reflecting official notions of "justice," and "democracy," and corporate America, which compiled "blacklists" of those who did not conform to the new American cultural norm. The political power of this coalition was compounded by the actions of the Soviet Union as it rose to challenge American hegemony in international affairs. The Soviets had their own ideas for world domination. They were not about to sit back and let the United States take the prize. What followed became known as the Cold War: the competition between the United States and the Soviet Union for global supremacy. As the Soviet Union was officially perceived by Americans to be a Communist state it was not such a stretch for the new cultural coalition to link its cause to anti-Communism. In the aftermath, it became not only necessary to contain the Communist menace abroad but to prevent it, as well, from coming to America's shores. This fear of Communism was not new to the American landscape. It had been a national "taboo" for much of the twentieth century. But with the evolution of the Cold War and an expansion of official government to fight it, American anti-Communism reached new heights of institutional intensity. It was in such a volatile atmosphere that, on December 5, 1947, United States Attorney General Tom Clark published an official list of 90 supposedly subversive organizations operating within the United States.[1] The list, according to sociologist Patricia Cayo Sexton:

> assembled without advance hearings or protection of the innocent, widely used in loyalty and congressional hearings, became an effective blacklist. The funds and membership of groups on the list declined, meeting places were denied, and charters were revoked in some cases. Later, members of the listed groups were made ineligible for public housing, and veterans were denied benefits for enrollment in listed schools; on local and state levels, various penalties were imposed, including refusal of admission to the bar of lawyers belonging to listed groups. The list grew rapidly, . . . to 197 in 1950, and later to over 300. Since nobody knew which group would be listed next, public fear of participation in any group, political or otherwise, grew.[2]

The International Workers Order (IWO) was prominent among the groups assembled for official sanction. Clark's list, as well as his commentary about the organizations named to it, was printed in mainstream newspapers across the nation almost verbatim. Leading the media onslaught warning of an official communist conspiracy was the December 5, 1947 front page banner headline of the *New York Times*, "*90 GROUPS, SCHOOLS NAMED ON U.S. LIST AS BEING DISLOYAL.*"[3]

For a federal official to publicly label the IWO (or any organization for that matter) subversive, without due process, was an extraordinary step. Clark chose to ignore the acceptable legal boundaries for official sanction which the Constitution outlines. His action both challenged the framework for American democracy and shocked tens of thousands of IWO Americans who learned that, at least in the eyes of the Attorney General of the United States, their mutual benefit society was backed by a group whose intention was to overthrow the Federal government. Most members of the IWO believed that they belonged to a fraternal insurance society that provided life insurance, hospital and disability coverage, and dental insurance to individuals who would ordinarily have not qualified for such benefits. Traditional insurance carriers were reluctant to offer these coverage opportunities to immigrants and low-salaried workers, two characteristics which defined most IWO members. Nevertheless, while the organization was unlike other commercial insurance companies or traditional fraternal societies (the Order sold its policies within a secular fraternal framework), the IWO was still a company legally sanctioned to sell insurance. It had been doing business since the State of New York granted it a charter on June 19, 1930, and, by late 1947, had insured over 1,000,000 members. But the IWO was other things as well. It was a cultural organization, which gave security to those who were unfamiliar with their new surroundings as they attempted to integrate into their new American environment. The Order satisfied individual needs for familiar surroundings by providing companionship through the association of people gathered together in the same language. By recreating the cultural patterns of the member's previous homeland, the IWO helped to alleviate situations of loneliness as well as afford members a wealth of information to assist them in avoiding the mistakes of those who came before them. The IWO was also an educational organization that supplemented traditional American educational processes with additional knowledge necessary to gain respectable and financially rewarding employment and to assist the member to become a fully integrated citizen. Finally, it was a political organization as well, tied to the Communist Party of the United States—a legal organization—advocating an electoral politics in support of the American worker.

As it was constituted then, the IWO fused a political message supporting a worker's struggle against capitalism with insurance, mutual aid benefits, and fraternal assistance. In its "*General Declaration of Principles,*" the IWO declared:

> The International Workers Order is a fraternal benefit society. Its principles are based on the experiences and progressive traditions of American fraternalism. The Order provides sick, disability and death benefits. . . . The IWO is founded on the principles of democratic fraternalism. Its doors are open to all regardless of sex, nationality, race, color, creed or political affiliations. . . . The cultural heritage of every one of the many national and racial groupings which make up the American people has contributed to and enriched the life and the traditions of our country. . . . The fraternal service of the IWO aims primarily to help the toiling people. . . . In the spirit of these principles, the IWO pledges to activize [sic] its members to support labor's economic and social efforts.[4]

The self-interests and goals of the organization, however, found little acceptance in the Cold War political atmosphere, defined in the United States by a growing intolerance toward Communism and a continual search for "loyalty."

Specifically, during the late 1940s, Republican critics began suggesting that the Truman administration was "soft" on Communism. While the Attorney General's motives for creating a list of "subversives" were no doubt complex, the accusations leveled at the presidential cabinet provided a strong catalyst. Clark's warnings about the existence of a Communist conspiracy served to highlight the government's anti-Communist stance. To justify his list, Clark claimed that communists were everywhere, "in factories, offices, butcher shops, on street corners, in private businesses, and each carries with them the germs of death for society."[5] Such inflammatory rhetoric became so persuasive and extensive during the Cold

War that it influenced mainstream political activities to such an extent, that even political partisans began to "borrow" from each other in their denunciations of domestic Communism and the Soviet Union. A case in point is Clark's successor, J. Howard McGrath, who warned in 1949 that:

> Communists . . . are everywhere—in factories, offices, butcher shops, in private businesses. . . . At this very moment [they are] busy at work—undermining your government, plotting to destroy the liberties of every citizen, and feverishly trying in whatever way they can, to aid *the Soviet Union*.[6]

Because many Americans were tuned into such rhetoric and openly supportive of the Attorney General's listing of subversive organizations, citizens began to be on the lookout for Communist conspirators. Specifically, in key areas of government and the defense industry, the list, along with Administrative Executive Order 9835, establishing the Federal Employee Loyalty Program, served as a litmus test for individuals and groups to prove their patriotism. This was the jumping-off point from which the government launched extensive "loyalty" probes aimed at removing "disloyal Americans" from their politically sensitive jobs. These administrative initiatives, however, did not stem the rising tide of legislative actions aimed at thwarting the "red peril." In an attempt to steal President Harry S. Truman's thunder, Congressional Republicans, fresh from taking control of the House of Representatives in the 1946 November elections, unleashed a series of hegemonic initiatives. The House Un-American Activities Committee (HUAC) expanded upon its investigation of communists infiltrating the government, labor, and even the Democratic Party, by initiating one of the most spectacular public forums against communism during the Cold War.[7] By 1951 HUAC had extended its list of subversive organizations and individuals to 624.[8] Congress also passed, over Truman's veto, the Immigration and Nationality Act, which eliminated individuals labeled as subversives (including homosexuals) from citizenship or securing a visa to enter the country.[9] For its part, the media, in conjunction with government and industry, used the list to organize a press onslaught against a "monolithic communist conspiracy" that was attempting to co-opt the public mind. As the public came to accept the notion that such a conspiracy existed, its thirst for news about it grew. The media responded eagerly with elaborate headlines regarding the discovery of un-American activities. Readers angrily applauded government/media identifications of traitors even if such labeling severely challenged traditional notions of American freedom and liberty. In short, as legal historian Arthur Sabin states, it was a time of "great fear," where institutions of the American right and citizen frustrations competed for political power through a public recognition of their patriotic zeal.

> Encouraged by elements in the Catholic Church, right-wing groups, the American Legion, the U.S. Chamber of Commerce, the House Committee on un-American Activities, conservative intellectuals, sensation-seeking newspapers and magazines, all the post-war frustrations, Korean War frustrations seemed to focus on

the simple explanation of an internal enemy—domestic Communist . . . the atmosphere was one of fear—fear as to one's past associations, politics, or even family. Loyalty to America was no longer presumed, but had to be proven by anti-
Red acts or statements. Even what one read could make one suspect.[10]

Any organization or individuals associated with named subversive organizations
were deemed to be disloyal to the country. The subject of official harassment, an-
onymous accusations and public humiliation, they became the victims of an institutional attempt to save American democracy from the "red peril."

Many organizations folded and those that survived saw their financial capacity to fight allegations against them diminish. Furthermore, those who remained in
the surviving groups ran the additional risk of incurring social isolation. For many
members, the imposition of having un-American labels applied to their person
created social discomfort as well as financial uncertainty. While many Americans
were enjoying new lifestyles in the postwar era, those who belonged to stigmatized groups did not share in the new American prosperity. Once they were identified,
their friends and neighbors disappeared, oftentimes their children were ridiculed
at school, and all career aspirations were put on hold, if not lost altogether. As the
scope of the government/media witch-hunt intensified, those associated with front
groups, or who were fellow travelers, or were simply those who were suspected of
having leftist leanings found it difficult to withstand the pressure. Some dropped
from sight. Some took up new residences and found new identities. Some had
political epiphanies. Some even went to jail.

> Prosecutions of US Communist Party members under the Smith Act, state sedi-
> tion trials, and contempt proceedings gave the United States a growing number of
> political prisoners. By 1952, 110 persons had been indicted or imprisoned under
> the Smith Act, about half of them trade unionists.[11]

As the dragnet of official prosecution was extended even to those of the mainstream political left of center variety, many Americans began to feel the harsh
reality of the new loyalty demands. Labor union leaders calling for the emergence
of a working class consciousness, democrats who wanted to extend the promises
of the New Deal to those who as yet had not realized them became pariahs in
American communities.

Un-Americanism had expanded to such profound political proportions that by
the end of the decade the left's voice in mainstream politics had been effectively
muted in a series of official actions which, encouraged by public support, denied
many people the right of freedom of expression. The number of people affected
grew in conjunction with the growth of the governmental/media hit list. The greatest number of victims, however, came from the American labor movement. According to Professor Cayo Sexton:

> Some 13.5 million people, or about one in five people in the labor force, were
> affected by loyalty-security programs as a condition of employment. Some 10,000
> were fired from their jobs—about 3,900 federal, 5,400 private, and 1,000 state

and local employees. Besides those fired, over 20,000 were formally charged between 1947 and 1953 with disloyalty under the federal program alone, most charges
involving an association with a suspect person, often a family member. At a federal cost of some $350 million during that period not a single spy was uncovered
by the loyalty-security programs.[12]

Initially, organized labor defended the rights of workers accused of disloyalty,
but as American trade unions moved more and more to the political right during
the Cold War, they relinquished this role. By 1950, loyalty probes of employees
had become the norm. Over five million government employees, for instance, had
been subjected to them by this time. Any political or social nonconformity became
grounds for being fired. Interracial relationships, homosexual inclinations or acquaintances, even support for the advancement of civil rights for disenfranchised
Americans could cost someone their government job. A thousand government employees resigned their jobs in protest over government loyalty tests while hundreds more were dismissed because of their association with organizations named
on Clark's list.[13] In the end, these loyalty probes set the cause of civil rights back
significantly. Operating under the institutional conjecture that in order to save democracy, the nation had to subvert its democratic freedoms, many Americans suffered undue hardships in the face of a new political ethic. The contradictions for
democracy that surfaced during this time of national hysteria finally became apparent in 1955 when, for the most part, official loyalty determinations were ended;
too late, perhaps, for those who suffered the emotional pain and ostracizing affects
of official persecution.

In the case of the IWO, their inclusion on the Attorney General's list was the
first in a series of official government actions that eventually led to the Order's
demise. Within ten days of its publication, the State of New York's Superintendent
of Insurance, Alfred J. Bohlinger, ordered an official examination of the Order's
affairs, including an investigation of the Order's fraternal activities. Official inquiries into the Order's activities had previously focused only on the organization's
financial conditions. This time, however, the investigation was extended to the
Order's political, educational and cultural activities.[14] As the temper of the times
demanded that more and more Americans demonstrate their loyalty, the IWO's
fraternal activities fell into question. For many Americans, patriotism was reflected
by membership in organizations like the John Birch Society, the Elks Club, and the
American Legion. The government/media campaign against the IWO clearly suggested that the Order did not fit into this category. Therefore, any sensationalistic
headline placing the Order in an unpatriotic image was not received as a challenge
to American cherished ideals or freedoms. To the contrary, such media creations
were viewed by most as a reflection of what was necessary to continue the pursuit
of American liberty. In such a climate it is not hard to see why, after the insurance
examiner's report surfaced thirteen months later, most of the cries deploring the
government action taken against the IWO came from those who were on the receiving end of similar governmental campaigns. In any event, Bohlinger's Deputy

James B. Haley's report went against the Order. In it he concluded that the "IWO was a Communist Party dominated organization . . . that the Order had abrogated its responsibilities to live up to its stated purpose . . . and had violated the meaning of the New York State Insurance Law." In the opinion of Superintendent Haley, the IWO should be liquidated. The U. S. Attorney General signed on as a co-advocate.[15]

The IWO appealed Haley's conclusion to the New York State Insurance Commission's appeal board. This move was of little help to the Order. On December 14, 1950, Deputy Superintendent of Insurance, Manuel Robbins, reaffirmed the examiner's report:

> . . . the Order, in conducting such fraternal activities (as outlined in the Report and elaborated on at the Hearing), has willfully violated its charter, and . . . its further continuance in business is such a hazard as to warrant its liquidation as herein recommended.[16]

With Robbins' decision in hand Superintendent Bohlinger filed a motion with the New York State Supreme Court for a permanent injunction to prevent the Order from conducting its business. Such immediate action was necessary, according to Bohlinger, because of the IWO's relationship with the CP, in that it caused a hazard to national security.[17] During the petition hearing an agent of the Federal Bureau of Investigation (FBI) appeared and advised the court of the agency's cooperation in the IWO investigation. The IWO had thus experienced the full weight of government power; both federal and state authority. The court granted the injunction on December 18, 1950.[18] On that date the Insurance Department seized all IWO property and assets and proceeded to conduct the Order's business from that point forward. The IWO was legally prevented from recruiting new members, underwriting its own insurance, dispensing funds, and engaging in fraternal and cultural activities. "It was the beginning of the end for the IWO."[19] After a series of legal appeals, culminating in the United States Supreme Court's refusal to hear the case, the IWO was officially liquidated on August 30, 1954. This was done in spite of the fact that no technical or fraudulent claims had ever been levied against the IWO in its insurance operation.

Historical arguments about the demise of the IWO have generally followed two courses. During a period of national hysteria, through actions which were questionable within the American democratic framework, official government sanction aided and abetted by the mass communications media, influenced a large segment of the population to support government oppression toward the IWO. The second premise surrounds the notion that the IWO had within it the seeds for its own destruction. By supporting an ideological program that prevented it from varying its policies, the Order actually assisted the government in its attempt to destroy the organization. Both of these explanations have validity. In the aftermath of World War II, the U.S. Government coalesced with corporate America and the mainstream mass communications industry in a xenophobic witch-hunt against domestic Communism which mirrored the threat of Communist expansion, real and perceived, from abroad. The resultant political actions cost many American citizens their livelihoods, their homes, and their friends and acquaintances. It mattered not whether the accused were actually Party members, or if they just held liberal views; public indictment was assured. The government/media case against the IWO was mounted in a political environment based on the fear and fantasy of the existence of a Communist conspiracy. In the end, while nothing was ever proven to invalidate the insurance operation of the Order, the IWO was, nevertheless, liquidated due to its "relationship" with the CP.

This is not to say that the IWO was falsely linked to the Communist Party, but that it was unjustly linked by a government/media partnership to an ominous ideological spectre that countless people feared but few could accurately characterize. From its very beginning, the IWO enthusiastically mirrored the party's calls of support for Soviet expansionism and totalitarianism. Indeed, IWO membership never challenged the organization's leaders when they called for continuing support of the USSR in the face of American protests over Soviet suppression of democracy in Eastern Europe. Such posturing hardly coincided with American principles of democracy and justice and exacerbated the already negative view of the Order produced as a result of official actions against it. The question arose as to how IWO members, as good Americans, could stand by as Stalin ruthlessly suppressed his own citizens in pogrom after pogrom.

It is not surprising that in this environment of fear and doubt the departure of members from the organization began to increase. In an attempt to steady the exodus of members the IWO shifted political gears by suggesting that the government had no right to interfere in the activities of a private business enterprise. This salute to free enterprise from a supposedly working-class organization was a bit too disingenuous for much of the American public to accept. Paradoxically then, the more the IWO answered the charges against it, the more the organization became recognized as a vanguard for Communist dictatorship around the world. Against such a backdrop, official actions against the Order became justified in the public mind.

Nevertheless, civil liberties and freedoms are powerful American values. It is conceivable to think that even in times of fear and fantasy that Americans who believe in the integrity of their democratic principles would come to the Order's defense. The case against the IWO was not so strong that the only resolve was to liquidate it. It was not within the realm of the impossible that the government and the IWO could have worked out a solution that would have allowed the Order to continue. After all, the fraternal organization was well positioned to take a leading role in carrying out the tenets of the New Deal and promoting social reform in America. Even though the organization was established and operated under the watchful eye of the Communist Party, it also served as a mutual benefit society for over one million people, primarily immigrants and first-generation Americans. To this extent, the IWO reflected the history of America, the new integrating into the established whole, in pursuit of the American dream. So, why did Americans, who believe in such a tradition, not come to the aid of those who were being denied the blessings of American liberty?

The IWO's political agenda provides an understanding of why Americans rarely offered a helping hand during the organization's time of troubles. From the start the Order attempted to become an effective spokesperson for the politically disadvantaged. A major focus of this activity was the labor movement. IWO lodges played a key role in the formation of the Congress of Industrial Organizations (CIO) during the 1930s, especially in the drive to organize the steel industry. The Order's contribution to the creation of the Steel Workers Organizing Committee (SWOC) in Pennsylvania, Ohio, and West Virginia was significant. Like the steel industry itself, the IWO had a large constituency of eastern and southern European individuals and families. The Order's appeal to steel workers was obvious, a cultural affinity with reciprocal results. But rallying the membership in the cause of trade unionism, while successful in many instances, quickly brought the Order to the attention of what became the government/corporate alliance against organized labor. Remembering the part the Order played in organizing the steel, auto, and rubber industries during the 1930s, corporate America in the late 1940s stood clearly in support of the official actions mounted against the IWO by the government/media coalition at that time. The corporate reaction to the plight of the IWO in postwar America was as contemptible as it was resolute. Corporate America stood firmly behind the government/media coalition as it mounted a fierce and successful legislative attack on American labor.

Fresh from their support of such antilabor legislation as the 1947 Taft-Hartley Act, corporate America positioned itself squarely behind the anti-Communist momentum generated by its Cold War allies, the government/media coalition. American corporations spent substantial sums of money on political candidacies, media advertising and the financing of private loyalty probes which aided the official witch-hunt against Communism. Opening their treasuries in support of political candidates who advocated being tough on Communism, American business was able to bring influence upon the creation of a public mind that extended Communism to "socialists, liberals, and labor activists."[20] This was made easy due to the centralization of business interests brought about by the changing dynamics of American capitalism following the war.

> the successful effort to make all challenges to the anti-communist business creed look treasonous deserves some of the credit for the strange disappearance of the issues of fair distribution and concentration of corporate power during most of the postwar period. It was not easy during this period to admit the existence of a class conflict without running the risk of being labeled a crypto or creeping subversive. Business groups devoted considerable resources to blunderbuss attacks on leftists and radicals who raised such issues . . . business a prime mover in forging a patriotic consensus in which the legitimacy of its own rapidly expanding power was seldom questioned . . . The effect has been to eliminate serious economic and social criticism of the basic institutions of American life . . . and to make the business creed the official standard for defining the national interest.[21]

Confronted by laws such as Taft-Hartley, unions and those who advocated a work-ing-class solidarity were forced into a position that labeled them un-American if they stood up against the passage of right-to-work laws, plant shut-downs, or even government/media efforts against fraternal organizations advocating the emergence of a working-class consciousness.

The media propaganda campaign against the IWO during the late 1940s and early 1950s had an element of working-class orientation although not in any tradi-tional sense. Building on the notion that trade unionism oriented in a leftist genre was foreign to American ideals, media headlines were able to fashion union orga-nizing activities into a foreign conspiracy directed by America's enemies. There was no greater enemy at this time than the Soviet Union. Banner headlines baited the public into viewing some union leaders, particularly those in the CIO, as being Communists. This headline sensationalism campaign encouraged the purge of much of the leadership in the CIO. The media campaign against the Order was just as intense. In tying the IWO to the CP the media was able to package the Order's trade union efforts as both foreign and conspiratorial. Projecting the image of the IWO as a front for the party eliminated it from being considered an American worker's organization. Consequently, the more the IWO attempted to speak for workers, the more such efforts worked against the organization. Speaking such rhetoric was not only disloyal but un-American as well. Newspaper headlines were quick to comment on the appeals made to labor by the IWO. The front page of the April 26, 1949 *New York Times* heralded such sentiment: "*Fraternal Organiza-tions Called Fifth Column: Slav Congress and IWO,*" easily transformed the IWO from an American fraternal insurance society to one whose insurance activities and labor sympathies were tied to a foreign and enemy constituency.[22] Such head-lines continued unabated throughout the IWO's appeal of its liquidation order. Painting the organization as being honeycombed with spies seeking to infiltrate and undermine American institutions, the media alerted unions, public education, and ethnic fraternities to the "IWO conspiracy." Again, the *New York Times* led the way with its cryptic and sensationalistic headline, " *Loyalty Listings Upheld by Appeals Court: IWO Penal Action Forbidden,*" in identifying un-American and treasonous conspiratorial activity.[23] Increasingly, IWO members became fright-ened and confused by such headlines. More and more members began to react with panic and despair, abandoning a commitment to that which had previously been viewed as necessary and secure. Official government figures show that be-tween 1949 and 1951 IWO membership decreased by one third.[24]

This shaking of the membership tree led to the IWO's demise, a demise that can be directly linked to the actions of a government/media hegemony, compli-cated by a post–World War II public hunger for both accusation and absolution.

Most citizens in the United States do not have the time or the opportunity to attend to the maintenance of democracy. Outside of electoral politics, Americans are positioned far from the policy-making processes of the nation. Even in the realm of electoral politics, once elected, representatives feel little compulsion to carry out any promises made during their campaigns. For the most part, elected officials are usually unaware (outside of polling) of the policy preferences of their constituents. As a result, many of them subscribe to the notion that elections do not supply mandates for particular policy initiatives. In the rare cases where those elected representatives may feel bound by their campaign promises, they often lack the means to effect them. Furthermore, while political parties can help to position candidates toward a particular political agenda, they cannot force them to abide by the party's platform. In addition, the legislative process is so complex that political opposition to any given policy initiative can emerge to filibuster or even block the legislation entirely, reducing further the victorious party's platform goals. Lastly, the electoral process includes only a small representation of citizens who have the power to make political decisions. The enactment and implementation of policy is heavily influenced by interest group politics with the corporate community being the largest group represented. Businessmen and corporate executives do not stand for election, nor do key bureaucratic civil servants, whose job is to implement policies enacted in the legislative process. In the end, the electoral process is mainly a symbolic device to reassure citizens that democratic theory in America is in place.[25] Accordingly, citizens have become dependent upon key institutions to represent their political views. The press is such an institution.

In the post–World War II period the press saw itself as the bully pulpit of American democracy, the mediating voice standing guard over the democratic process. But despite the role the press had assigned itself, it is clear that it did not perform it in an unobstructed manner. Much as the case is today, the press in postwar America was a business, and as such, cared not to offend its financial interests, in particular, those who advertised on its airwaves or in its newspapers. As Michael Parenti notes:

> The notion that the media are manipulated by big moneyed interests is dismissed by some as a "conspiracy theory." But there is nothing conspiratorial about it. Because they pay the bills, advertisers regard their influence over media content as something of a "right." And media executives seem to agree. As erstwhile CBS president Frank Stanton said: "Since we are advertiser-supported we must take into account the general objective and desires of advertisers as a whole."[26]

Along with being influenced by corporate advertisers the media also is under the watchful eye of government. As reporters rely on government sources for their information, media objectivity becomes highly suspect. When changes in official policy take place the media is organized so as to reflect the changes in its coverage of the event or in its editorializing of the impact of the event. In the end the manipulation of the media by government takes place because the media reports what the government is doing based on the information supplied to it by its government sources. While the relationship between the two institutions at times may be a convoluted one, the outcome is the same; the notion of a free press is obstructed. Again, in the words of Michael Parenti:

In sum, those who see the news as being the outcome of objective reportage, by
professionally trained, independent journalists are missing much of the picture.
What passes for the "news" is a product of many forces, involving the dominant
political culture and powerful economic and government institutions—all dedicated to maintaining an ideological monopoly, controlling the flow of information and opinions in ways that best advance their interests. That so many journalists fail to see this is evidence of how thoroughly they themselves are part of the
news-manufacturing process.[27]

During the Cold War, the media, in alliance with official government and the corporate community, created an anatomy of power that conditioned the public to
accept the legitimacy of certain prevailing political attitudes. Challenging such a
power structure was difficult for it meant establishing a group-based politics whose
aim was the dispersal of decision-making power in such a manner as to supply
American citizens with control over the political decisions that affected their lives.
In theory as well as in practice this represented the creation of a nonconformist
political movement at a time when conformity was the expectation for human
nature. Citizens choosing this path directed their political energies toward ways
that seemed (at least according to the existing power structure) inappropriate to
American design; a reliance by "nontraditional Americans" on "unconventional
interest groups" to make their voices heard. Such political interest group activities
were not new to America. Many of the prominent post–World War II interest groups
had been active in American politics throughout the twentieth century. Trade unions,
sounding their call on behalf of American industrial workers; progressive groups,
lifting their voice to demand political change; and protest groups that spoke out
against segregation, poverty, poor educational opportunities, and the exploitation
of citizens by unscrupulous capitalists were all politically active.

These unconventional groups (the IWO included) often competed against each
other and sometimes even coalesced as they attempted to gain access to the decision-making center. But they also competed with traditional alliances of power.
During the initial stages of the Cold War, this political landscape created considerable conflict and tension among the American polity. Mediating this, at least in
theory, were the nation's two key political servants: the Constitution and the press.
The Constitution, and the U.S. Department of Justice that serves it, having set the
standards for the enactment of law and the protection of individual liberty throughout
American history, have traditionally stood guard over the nation's political integrity. But with the publication of Attorney General Tom Clark's list, the legal mediator for the substance and reality of political agendas was eclipsed. Constitutional mediation became personal mediation. It was now Mr. Clark who deemed what
was "politically correct." Previous Constitutional notions insinuating that the American legal system was an impartial observer were rendered moot by his action.

With few exceptions, the media, rather than cry out against such a usurpation
of power, relinquished its role as an ideological mediator and fell into line behind
the Attorney General's irresponsible pronouncements. This may not, however, be

too difficult to understand. America's corporate media had for some time been waging a war against job rights for its workers. The political left had organized many efforts in support of the media worker's trade unionizing activities. That a worker's group could be officially attached to the communist movement spelled political respectability for editorial executives. While the media is the only private enterprise recognized by the Constitution to stand watch over the nation's political process, such political responsibility may become blurred when a "call to arms" comes from other official quarters. It is not too surprising then to find the mainstream press at times in concert with the Attorney General. Working together during the initial stages of the Cold War, these two servants of democracy expressed an official ideology that challenged the broad and flexible standards of citizen loyalty encouraged by the Constitution. For its part, the press was no longer free of undue influence. By propagating the official message the press, in 1947, officially rejected its political charge which Michael Parenti defines as having, "no established ideology, no racial, gender, or class bias . . . Supposedly committed to no persuasion. . . ."[28] As the Cold War intensified, the scope of legal protection for individual rights diminished, as did the idea of a free and independent press. As a result, the interpretation of law often favored the protection of the state at the expense of individual rights and the media acted as a cheerleader for this enterprise. While many in the government/media coalition truly believed America was being duped by a communist conspiracy, the policies pursued in the name of this belief were often at odds with a free press's Constitutional responsibilities. But in the environment of the Cold War, images that the country was infested with communists made it perfectly acceptable to subvert democracy in order to save it.

By creating images of loyalty, patriotism, and other standards for citizen identity during the Cold War, the media propagated an oversimplification of what it was to be an "American." Standing at the forefront of the media vanguard was the print news gathering industry (unlike today, where television news has taken the lead as the "centennial of democracy"). Positioning itself as a halfway house between government and the people, the media offered critical discussions mounted in headlines, newspaper editorials, and syndicated columns for all to read. Reporting the news from a position of presumed neutrality, the mainstream print media claimed to challenge powerful political opinions and bias in their coverage of events. On balance, however, during the Cold War, there was little that resembled a neutral midpoint between the government and the American citizen. In many instances the mainstream media in the late 1940s and early 1950s reported verbatim the Truman Administration's read on foreign policy. Headlines and editorial support of official policies more often than not complimented the "Truman Doctrine" and its official application to confront Soviet expansionism including the infiltration by Communists into American life. In the war against Communism the press reflected a clear and unyielding support of government action. Headlines of Communist conspiracies and Soviet designs on America were standard fare. Press anti-Communism soon extended to anti–New Deal, antilabor, and anti-opposition to any group that challenged official Cold War policies, including those opposed to American military industrial expansion. A free press with its objective, informative, and balanced delivery of information had become an eager ally of compliance with the introduction of the "red menace."

In the aftermath of the publication of the Attorney General's list, headlines regarding the IWO mirrored warnings against Soviet aggrandizement and internal subversion by Communist spies. They represented an urgency of a threat to American democracy that prodded the average citizen to paint the IWO as un-American. As the headlines tolerated no criticism of themselves, they were removed from normative political challenge. In a sense they created their own political reality. They represented what James Fallows sees as an urgency that has little to do with the news, but rather that which is aimed at framing the goals and interests of a nation, based on what is attention-getting that day.[29] Headline assumptions about the IWO, as a Communist front group, became a major obstacle in keeping the investigation of the Order in perspective. The reporting of trial and hearing events were translated into public indictments against the Order and its members. Ironically, these printed indictments found their way into the official investigation of the IWO. FBI documents about the investigation of the fraternal organization, obtained under the Freedom of Information Act, substantiate this point.[30] The ongoing duplicitous relationship between government and media not only placed the IWO within an un-American context, but also in the unenviable position of being hard-pressed to counter the official accusations. As the investigation continued the official use of media headlines became more commonplace (see figures 1–9).[31]

That the official investigation provoked additional government and media harassment against the IWO and its members can be seen in any number of cases. In California, a Sacramento dentist, Dr. Krishna Chandra, was arrested for deportation as an alien because of his past membership in the IWO. Chandra had lived in California since 1910, but could not formally apply for citizenship because, as an immigrant native to India, he was unable to do so under American immigration laws. When

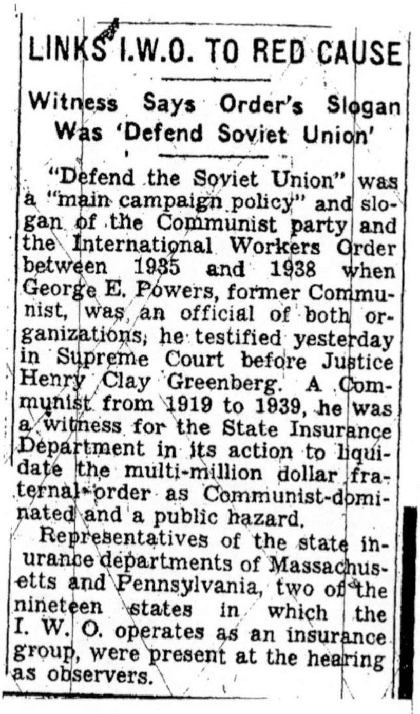

LINKS I.W.O. TO RED CAUSE

Witness Says Order's Slogan Was 'Defend Soviet Union'

"Defend the Soviet Union" was a "main campaign policy" and slogan of the Communist party and the International Workers Order between 1935 and 1938 when George E. Powers, former Communist, was an official of both organizations; he testified yesterday in Supreme Court before Justice Henry Clay Greenberg. A Communist from 1919 to 1939, he was a witness for the State Insurance Department in its action to liquidate the multi-million dollar fraternal order as Communist-dominated and a public hazard.

Representatives of the state insurance departments of Massachusetts and Pennsylvania, two of the nineteen states in which the I. W. O. operates as an insurance group, were present at the hearing as observers.

Figure 6.1
New York Times 1 February 1951

LINKS I.W.O. TO RED CAUSE

Witness Says Order's Slogan Was 'Defend Soviet Union'

"Defend the Soviet Union" was a "main campaign policy" and slogan of the Communist party and the International Workers Order between 1935 and 1938 when George E. Powers, former Communist, was an official of both organizations, he testified yesterday in Supreme Court before Justice Henry Clay Greenberg. A Communist from 1919 to 1939, he was a witness for the State Insurance Department in its action to liquidate the multi-million dollar fraternal order as Communist-dominated and a public hazard.

Representatives of the state insurance departments of Massachusetts and Pennsylvania, two of the nineteen states in which the I. W. O. operates as an insurance group, were present at the hearing as observers.

f.l.

file 61-7341

INDEXED - 71

NOT RECORDED

63

TITLE

CLASS Internal Security

From NY

DATED FEB 1 1951

Figure 6.2
FBI copy filed June 28 1951

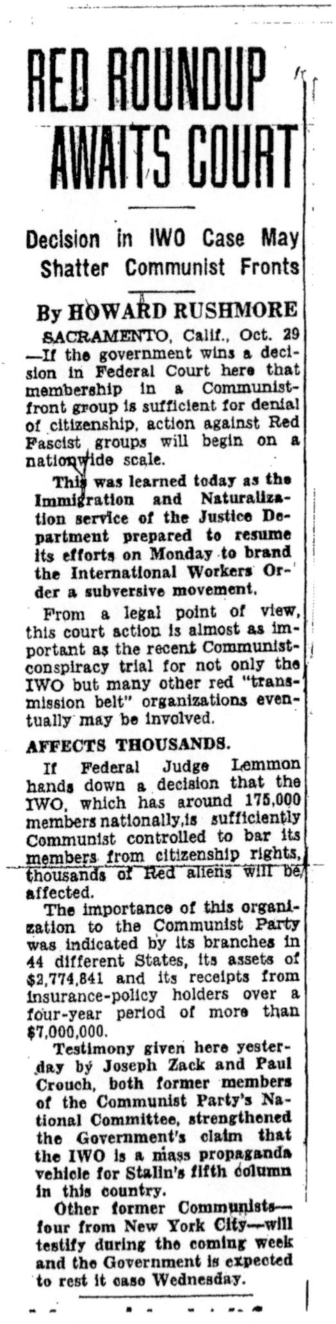

RED ROUNDUP AWAITS COURT

Decision in IWO Case May Shatter Communist Fronts

By HOWARD RUSHMORE

SACRAMENTO, Calif., Oct. 29 —If the government wins a decision in Federal Court here that membership in a Communist-front group is sufficient for denial of citizenship, action against Red Fascist groups will begin on a nationwide scale.

This was learned today as the Immigration and Naturalization service of the Justice Department prepared to resume its efforts on Monday to brand the International Workers Order a subversive movement.

From a legal point of view, this court action is almost as important as the recent Communist-conspiracy trial for not only the IWO but many other red "transmission belt" organizations eventually may be involved.

AFFECTS THOUSANDS.

If Federal Judge Lemmon hands down a decision that the IWO, which has around 175,000 members nationally, is sufficiently Communist controlled to bar its members from citizenship rights, thousands of Red aliens will be affected.

The importance of this organization to the Communist Party was indicated by its branches in 44 different States, its assets of $2,774,841 and its receipts from insurance-policy holders over a four-year period of more than $7,000,000.

Testimony given here yesterday by Joseph Zack and Paul Crouch, both former members of the Communist Party's National Committee, strengthened the Government's claim that the IWO is a mass propaganda vehicle for Stalin's fifth column in this country.

Other former Communists— four from New York City—will testify during the coming week and the Government is expected to rest its case Wednesday.

Figure 6.3
New York Journal American
Oct 30 1949

the official ban against Indian immigration was lifted after World War II, Dr. Chandra applied for his American citizenship. His application was denied by the U.S. Immigration and Naturalization Service (INS), however, even though the INS inspector could find nothing in his past that was anti-American beyond his lapsed membership in the IWO.[32]

Media indictments of other IWO members found their way into official investigations of them as well. The cases of Andrew Dmytryshyn and Samuel Milgrom are cases in point. Dmytryshyn, vice president of the Order's Ukranian section, and Milgrom, national secretary of the IWO, were arrested for deportation on the grounds of being members of an organization that circulated material advocating the overthrow by force of the government of the United States and violation of citizenship regulations. News headlines regarding the arrests sensationalized their activities beyond the official charges. The *New York Times* headlined the Dmytryshyn affair as "*SUSPECTED RED HELD FOR OUSTER: Organizer for Worker's Unit Accused of Backing Plot to Overthrow U.S*" (see figure 10).[33] In Milgrom's case it was much the same: "*Sam Milgrom Called a Spy: Labeled As One of the Top Espionage Agents by FBI Man*" (See figure 11).[34] An INS Board of Appeals dismissed the charges on the basis that the IWO did not display or write any printed matter which advocated the overthrow of the U.S. government by force. Simply being a member of the IWO evidently did not merit the deportation of registered aliens, and therefore, the two men were exonerated. This did not bother the *New York Times*, however, which re-interpreted the INS position in a headline that read, "*TEST IS ON TO LINK COMMUNISTS-I.W.O: U.S. Contends at Deportation Hearing That Membership in Two*

Mr. Tolson
Mr. Ladd
Mr. Clegg
Mr. Glavin
Mr. Nichols
Mr. Rosen
Mr. Tracy
Mr. Harbo
Mr. Mohr
Tele. Room
Mr. Nease
Miss Gandy

RED ROUNDUP AWAITS COURT

Decision in IWO Case May Shatter Communist Fronts

By HOWARD RUSHMORE

SACRAMENTO, Calif., Oct. 29—If the government wins a decision in Federal Court here that membership in a Communist-front group is sufficient for denial of citizenship, action against Red Fascist groups will begin on a nationwide scale.

This was learned today as the Immigration and Naturalization service of the Justice Department prepared to resume its efforts on Monday to brand the International Workers Order a subversive movement.

From a legal point of view, this court action is almost as important as the recent Communist-conspiracy trial for not only the IWO but many other red "transmission belt" organizations eventually may be involved.

AFFECTS THOUSANDS.

If Federal Judge Lemmon hands down a decision that the IWO, which has around 175,000 members nationally, is sufficiently Communist controlled to bar its members from citizenship rights, thousands of Red aliens will be affected.

The importance of this organization to the Communist Party was indicated by its branches in 44 different States, its assets of $2,774,841 and its receipts from insurance-policy holders over a four-year period of more than $7,000,000.

Testimony given here yesterday by Joseph Zack and Paul Crouch, both former members of the Communist Party's National Committee, strengthened the Government's claim that the IWO is a mass propaganda vehicle for Stalin's fifth column in this country.

Other former Communists—four from New York City—will testify during the coming week and the Government is expected to rest it case Wednesday.

G. I. R. -7

File

INDEXED - 60

80 DEC 12 1949

60 DEC 19 1949

Journal American
OCT 3 0 1949

Figure 6.4
FBI copy filed 19 December 1949

TWO ARRESTS SPUR CHECK OF I.W.O. STATUS

State Insurance Unit Says License Renewal Is In Question

Sam Milgrom called one of top espionage agents in country.................Page 5

Steps to learn whether the International Workers Order, Inc., two officers of which were arrested last week in New York in deportation proceedings, is a bona fide fraternal association were initiated yesterday by the Maryland State Insurance Department.

Claude A. Hanley, insurance commissioner, sent a letter to the I.W.O. in New York informing the organization its insurance license would not be renewed July 1 unless it forwarded information on its organization and membership in Maryland.

In its present classification as a "fraternal," premiums paid the I.W.O. are exempt from the two per cent State tax.

Mr. Hanley acted after receiving reports of the arrest of Andrew Dmytryshyn, alias Andrew Dolin, I.W.O. vice president, and Samson Milgrom, executive secretary, from Robert E. Dineen, superintendent of insurance in New York.

Released In Bail

Dmytryshyn was charged with being a member of an organization that advocates forcible overthrow of the United States Government.

Milgrom, who has several aliases, was arrested on a warrant stating he re-entered this country after being deported on charges he was a member of a group which advocated the violent overthrow of the Government.

Both were released in $5,000 bail. The cases have been interpreted as a move by the Justice Department to set up test cases showing the I.W.O. is operated by the Communist party. The I.W.O. is licensed to sell insurance in eighteen states and the District of Columbia.

"The I.W.O. is purportedly a fraternal organization but is in

(Continued on Page 26, Column 4)

ARRESTS SPUR I.W.O. PROBE

State Insurance License May Not Be Renewed

(Continued from Page 38)

fact part and parcel of the Communist party," Edward J. Shaughnessy, district director of the Immigration and Naturalization Service, said in New York the day Dmytryshyn was arrested.

Called "Fruitful Source"

He said the I.W.O. offered "a fruitful source of revenue to the Communist party."

Mr. Dineen, who sent Mr. Hanley photostatic copies of newspaper accounts of the arrests "for your information" and without comment, said in his accompanying letter:

"You will recall that in our report on examination of the International Workers Order, Inc., dated January 25, 1949, there was reference to the fact that the fraternal aspects of the order's activities would be the object of further study. This report has been in preparation over the past several months and now is nearing completion."

Writing to the I.W.O., Mr. Hanley said:

"We have received some information here at the State Insurance Department of Maryland that the International Workers Order, Inc., is not a bona fide fraternal and cannot meet the requirements of a fraternal society under the existing law.

"You are, therefore, requested at your earliest convenience to furnish this department with a list of the lodges in the State of Maryland, the name and location of each lodge and a list of the officers and members in each of the various lodges within the State of Maryland.

"Failure on your part to conform with the above request will result in the refusal on the part of the State Insurance Department of Maryland to renew your license for the year beginning July 1, 1950."

The I.W.O. was listed as a subversive organization in 1947 by former Attorney General Tom C. Clark. Top officers are Rockwell Kent, the artist, president; John E. Middleton, vice president; Dave Greene, recording secretary, and Peter Shipka, secretary-treasurer.

Mr. Hanley said that if Dmytryshyn and Milgrom were "convicted or deported" he would suspend the I.W.O.'s Maryland license "until they get responsible people to head up the organization."

He said, in connection with his letter to the I.W.O., that he had authority only to stop future business, not to cancel existing policies.

According to the 1949 annual report of the I.W.O. to the State Insurance Department, twelve of the organization's 1,767 lodges are in Maryland.

Figure 6.5

Figure 6.6

Baltimore Morning Sun 18 May 1950

TWO ARRESTS SPUR CHECK OF I.W.O. STATUS

State Insurance Unit Says License Renewal Is In Question

Sam Milgrom called one of top espionage agents in country....................*Page 5*

Steps to learn whether the International Workers Order, Inc., two officers of which were arrested last week in New York in deportation proceedings, is a bona fide fraternal association were initiated yesterday by the Maryland State Insurance Department.

Claude A. Hanley, insurance commissioner, sent a letter to the I.W.O. in New York informing the organization its insurance license would not be renewed July 1 unless it forwarded information on its organization and membership in Maryland.

In its present classification as a "fraternal," premiums paid the I.W.O. are exempt from the two per cent State tax.

Mr. Hanley acted after receiving reports of the arrest of Andrew Dmytryshyn, alias Andrew Dolin, I.W.O. vice president, and Samson Milgrom, executive secretary, from Robert E. Dineen, superintendent of insurance in New York.

Released In Bail

Dmytryshyn was charged with being a member of an organization that advocates forcible overthrow of the United States Government.

Milgrom, who has several aliases, was arrested on a warrant stating he re-entered this country after being deported on charges he was a member of a group which advocated the violent overthrow of the Government.

Both were released in $5,000 bail.

The cases have been interpreted as a move by the Justice Department to set up test cases showing the I.W.O. is operated by the Communist party. The I.W.O. is licensed to sell insurance in eighteen states and the District of Columbia.

The I.W.O. is purportedly a fraternal organization but is (Continued on Page 26, Column 4)

The Morning Sun
Baltimore, Md.
May 18, 1950

ARRESTS SPUR I.W.O. PROBE

State Insurance License May Not Be Renewed

(Continued from Page 38)

fact part and parcel of the Communist party," Edward J. Shaughnessy, district director of the Immigration and Naturalization Service, said in New York the day Dmytryshyn was arrested.

Called "Fruitful Source"

He said the I.W.O. offered "a fruitful source of revenue to the Communist party."

Mr. Dineen, who sent Mr. Hanley photostatic copies of newspaper accounts of the arrests "for your information" and without comment, said in his accompanying letter:

"You will recall that in our report on examination of the International Workers Order, Inc., dated January 25, 1949, there was reference to the fact that the fraternal aspects of the order's activities would be the object of further study. This report has been in preparation over the past several months and now is nearing completion."

Writing to the I.W.O., Mr. Hanley said:

"We have received some information here at the State Insurance Department of Maryland that the International Workers Order, Inc., is not a bona fide fraternal and cannot meet the requirements of a fraternal society under the existing law.

"You are, therefore, requested at your earliest convenience to furnish this department with a list of the lodges in the State of Maryland, the name and location of each lodge and a list of the officers and members in each of the various lodges within the State of Maryland.

"Failure on your part to conform with the above request will result in the refusal on the part of the State Insurance Department of Maryland to renew your license for the year beginning July 1, 1950."

The I.W.O. was listed as a subversive organization in 1947 by former Attorney General Tom C. Clark. Top officers are Rockwell Kent, the artist, president; John E. Middleton, vice president; Dave Greene, recording secretary, and Peter Shipka, secretary-treasurer.

Mr. Hanley said that if Dmytryshyn and Milgrom were "convicted or deported" he would suspend the I.W.O.'s Maryland license "until they get responsible people to head up the organization."

He said, in connection with his letter to the I.W.O., that he had authority only to stop future business, not to cancel existing policies.

According to the 1949 annual report of the I.W.O. to the State Insurance Department, twelve of the organization's 1,767 lodges are in Maryland.

Figure 6.7
FBI copy filed July 14 1950

INSURANCE SET-UPS CALLED RED DISGUISE

Charles Baxter of Cleveland, a former Communist party functionary, testified yesterday that he had been taught, while a student at the Moscow International Lenin Institute, that American Communists should enter the fraternal insurance field to supply the party with a "permanent basis" for its work.

Mr. Baxter, who said he left the party in 1945, appeared at a deportation hearing against Andrew Dmytryshyn, a vice president and organizer of the Ukrainian-American Fraternal Branch of the International Workers' Order. Mr. Dmytryshyn is charged with being an alien member of a group affiliated with the Communist party. The proceeding was held at the Immigration and Naturalization Service District Headquarters, 70 Columbus Avenue.

The witness, a former seaman, is now employed as an analyst for the Immigration Service in Cleveland. He told the hearing that he had attended the Moscow school in 1929 and 1930, and had been taught Marxist principles, methods of conducting civil warfare, use of firearms, trade unionism and other studies. Activities in the fraternal insurance field in this country were to serve as "a logical development of all the language group work in the United States," he said.

Later in 1930, when he was in San Francisco, Mr. Baxter said, the party's central committee issued a directive that the I. W. O was to be organized. He said he attended sessions of the organization in California and Ohio. He added that his duty at the meetings was to obtain signatures for party election petitions and financial aid.

Figure 6.8
New York Times
1 February 1951

is Identical" (See figures 12 and 13).[35] The *New York Journal American* took even greater liberties with the facts established in the hearing and the Appeal Board's subsequent decision. In an article headlined, "*Says Red Official Was IWO Boss*," the *Journal American* reporter covering the case, Howard Rushmore, himself a former member of the CP who had testified as a government witness against Dmytryshyn and Milgrom, linked them to other IWO members who were portrayed as communists in his story.[36] A copy of Rushmore's article made it into FBI files and was used in the agency's investigation against the IWO (See figure 14). Throughout the government's case against the Order Rushmore continued to bear witness for them even as he covered the legal proceedings.

Press and official sanctions against the IWO continued throughout the Insurance Department's investigation against it. In New York City, the Board of Education attempted to prevent the Order from using its classrooms after school hours. The IWO had long been permitted to have access to after school facilities for its cultural educational programs.[37] Despite this, the urgency of the times demanded that the Order no longer be permitted to hold such classes. Publicly attacking the order as an agency for the "communist conspiracy," the press accentuated official calls to end the Board's practice. Banner headlines that "Reds" were teaching New York City school children appeared in many New York newspapers before any formal hearings on the matter took place. The *New York World Telegram* led the way in late November 1948 with its headline, "*Charges*

INDEXED - 9!

INSURANCE SET-UPS CALLED RED DISGUISE

Charles Baxter of Cleveland, a former Communist party functionary, testified yesterday that he had been taught, while a student at the Moscow International Lenin Institute, that American Communists should enter the fraternal insurance field to supply the party with a "permanent basis" for its work.

Mr. Baxter, who said he left the party in 1945, appeared at a deportation hearing against Andrew Dmytryshyn, a vice president and organizer of the Ukrainian-American Fraternal Branch of the International Workers Order. Mr. Dmytryshyn is charged with being an alien member of a group affiliated with the Communist party. The proceeding was held at the Immigration and Naturalization Service District Headquarters, 70 Columbus Avenue.

The witness, a former seaman, is now employed as an analyst for the Immigration Service in Cleveland. He told the hearing that he had attended the Moscow school in 1929 and 1930, and had been taught Marxist principles, methods of conducting civil warfare, use of firearms, trade unionism and other studies. Activities in the fraternal insurance field in this country were to serve as "a logical development of all the language group work in the United States," he said.

Later in 1930, when he was in San Francisco, Mr. Baxter said, the party's central committee issued a directive that the I. W. O. was to be organized. He said he attended sessions of the organization in California and Ohio. He added that his duty at the meetings was to obtain signatures for party election petitions and financial aid.

INDEXED - 9

NOT RECORDED
42 SEP 19 1950

Times
AUG 1 0 1950

Figure 6.9
FBI copy filed 19 September 1950

SUSPECTED·RED HELD FOR OUSTER

Organizer for Workers Unit Accused of Backing Plot to Overthrow U. S.

Andrew Dolin, Ukrainian-American branch organizer of the International Workers Order, was arrested yesterday in deportation proceedings. He was charged with being a member of an organization that advocates forcible overthrow of the United States Government.

"The I. W. O. is purportedly a fraternal organization but is in fact part and parcel of the Communist party," said Edward J. Shaughnessy, district director of the Immigration and Naturalization Service.

Mr. Shaughnessy said the organization had been "a fruitful source of revenue to the Communist party." He said the I. W. O. claims to have 164,809 members, $6,126,-000 in assets, and $110,950,482 insurance in force.

Dolin, who also goes by the name of Dmytryshyn, according to Mr. Shaughnessy, was arrested at his home, 208 East Thirteenth Street. He is 58 years old, was born in Austria, and came here in 1915. He is a vice president of the I. W. O.

After being taken to Ellis Island, Dolin was released on $5,000 bail put up by Abner Green of the American Committee for the Protection of Foreign Born. A hearing date will be fixed later.

The I. W. O. was listed by former Attorney General Tom C. Clark in 1947 as a subversive organization. Rockwell Kent, the artist, as president; Representative Vito Marcantonio, as vice president, and others at that time issued a statement that the organization would "fight back with every means at its disposal to protect its integrity and security."

Mr. Kent and Peter Shipka, secretary-treasurer, issued a denial yesterday that the I. W. O. "prints and distributes literature which advocates the overthrow of the Government by force and violence."

They charged the arrest was "merely another facet of the savage persecution by the present Federal Administration of the foreign-born and all progressives to impose thought-control in order to suppress opposition against the developing war hysteria."

Figure 6.10
New York Times 10 May 1950

Reds Instruct Kids in City Schools."[38] The subsequent hearings on the matter extended even beyond the IWO when protesters demanded to know who was responsible for opening the public schools to the organization in the first place. By the time of the January 20, 1949 Board of Education meeting, press headlines had stirred up such a public furor that the Board voted unanimously to bar the Order from using its schools. Media sensationalism about the Order's use of schools, however, soon extended to other constituencies, creating an inquisition against anything politically left-of-center in the city's educational pedagogy. Headlines, in the *New York Sun* and other city newspapers, for instance, followed up the Board's revocation of the Order's right to use school classrooms by insinuating that there

SAM MILGROM CALLED A SPY

Labeled As One Of Top Espionage Agents By FBI Man

Hartford, Conn., May 17 (AP)—An FBI undercover agent testified today at the Draper-Adler libel trial that Sam Milgrom was "one of the top espionage agents in the country."

The witness, Matthew Cvetic, called Milgrom the "boss" of Gerhart Eisler, Communist leader who fled the United States last year.

Cvetic identified Milgrom only as an official of the International Workers Order (I.W.O.), a social and insurance fraternity cited many times as a Communist organization.

Milgrom was arrested a week ago for deportation as an alien Communist. He is charged with re-entering the country illegally after a previous deportation.

Met Eisler In Chicago

The witness said he met Eisler in Chicago last year before the latter jumped bail and stowed away on a ship leaving the United States. Added Cvetic:

"I was introduced to Eisler by Sam Milgrom, whom I knew as one of the top espionage agents in the country who is an official of the I.W.O. and Eisler's boss."

Cvetic said he joined the Communist party as an FBI undercover agent and was assigned by the Government to look into Communist activities in the Pittsburgh industrial area.

He testified that Harmonica Player Larry Adler and Dancer Paul Draper were regarded by Communist party members in that area as "Communist entertainers."

Testifies In Her Defense

The two entertainers are suing a Greenwich (Conn.) housewife, Mrs. Hester McCullough, for $200,000 in damages.

They charge she falsely called them pro-Communists and thereby caused them to lose thousands of dollars in entertainment bookings. Cvetic testified in Mrs. McCullough's defense.

He was asked about Draper's reputation among Communists in the Pittsburgh area and replied:

"His general reputation was that of a Communist entertainer who was available for entertainment of Communist-front organizations."

Doesn't Know Them

Of Adler, the short, stocky Cvetic testified:

"He, also, had the reputation for being available for entertainment by Communist-front organizations."

Cvetic said he did not know either entertainer personally.

During the war, the witness said, western Pennsylvania had about 1,500 Communists. But membership since has "dribbled down" to about 550, he added.

On crossexamination, it was pointed out to him that Henry A. Wallace, Progressive party leader, got more than 4,000 presidential votes in the Pittsburgh area in 1948. He was asked:

"It must follow then that there are some people who are not Communists who voted for Wallace, isn't that right?"

"Yes, the figures speak for themselves," replied Cvetic.

Cassini Backs Defense

The defense put into the record during the day a deposition from Igor Cassini, society editor of the New York Journal-American. He alleged that Draper and Adler made remarks from the stage of the Roxy Theater in New York two years ago concerning Wallace's candidacy for President.

Both Draper and Adler have denied speaking in favor of Wallace from the Roxy stage.

Late in the day, Defense Attorney MacDonald Dewitt sought to convince the jury that Draper and Adler brought on themselves much of the adverse publicity they claim caused them to lose bookings.

He said such publicity followed their action in attaching Mrs. McCullough's property after they filed the libel suit. Such a pretrial attachment is permitted under Connecticut law. The entertainers later withdrew the attachment.

Figure 6.11
Baltimore Sun 18 May 1950

were other red fronts who also were involved in educating New York's children. All of these articles ended up in the files of the FBI as well. (See figures 15–20)

As the press propagated anticommunist hysteria during the Cold War, official responses to this became more commonplace, which in turn, were applauded by the media. The politics of the news media encouraged the enactment of a series of legislative acts aimed at containing Communist activity, such as the McCarren Act of 1950, which called for the registration of all Communist and Communist-front groups. The Act also authorized the building of internment camps to hold, without trial, anyone suspected of subversive activity during times of nationally declared emergencies. In such a political atmosphere, no politician who held aspirations of holding or being re-elected to office wanted to be labeled in the press as being "soft on Communism." As the Insurance Department's examination of the Order evolved, New York State Governor Thomas Dewey showed his patriotic mettle by jumping on the anti-IWO bandwagon. Reacting to what he said he had read in the *New York Times* about the Insurance Department's examination, he authorized a legal investigation of the Order in general. In an interview conducted by historian Howard Brown in 1976, Paul Williams, Special Assistant Attorney General for the State of New York substantiates this point:

> Brown: What I was wondering was—you were a Special Assistant Attorney General for the State of New York?
> Williams: I was appointed that for the purpose of conducting this investigation. I also was appointed Special Deputy Superintendent of Insurance, I think—or Counsel to the Insurance Department—because first, you recall, there was a hearing in the Insurance

TEST IS ON TO LINK COMMUNISTS-I. W. O.

U. S. Contends at Deportation Hearing That Membership in Two Is Identical

The Immigration and Naturalization Service began a test yesterday of the proposition that membership in the International Workers Order is equivalent to membership in the Communist party.

This argument was presented at a hearing in district headquarters of the service, 70 Columbus Avenue, in deportation proceedings against Andrew Dmytryshyn. The respondent is a vice president and organizer of the Ukrainian-American Fraternal Branch of the I. W. O. The organization, which has insurance benefits, claims more than 160,000, against an estimated 55,000 Communist party members.

Isidore Englander, counsel for Mr. Dmytryshyn, denounced the proceedings as unfair, and made a long but unsuccessful plea for an adjournment so that he could apply to the Federal Court for an injunction to halt them. He said he would ignore the hearing today and apply for the injunction.

Mr. Englander charged that the hearing officer, William J. Wyrsch, because of his long association with the Naturalization Service was not a suitable person to conduct the hearing. Mr. Wyrsch remarked that he was not biased and pointed out that he would not decide the case but would submit it to the Commissioner of Immigration and Naturalization for a ruling.

At Mr. Wyrsch's decision to open the taking of testimony, Mr. Englander offered a stipulation. He said his client was born in Dolyna, the Ukraine, Dec. 2, 1891, entered the United States at Detroit on Nov. 15, 1915, and had been a member of the Communist party since 1919 and was now a member, though he had been out of the party from 1939 to 1948.

Mario T. Noto, examining officer for the Naturalization Service, declined to accept any stipulation except one admitting the Government's charge that as an I. W. O. member Mr. Dmytryshyn was committed to overthrow of the Government by force and violence.

The principal witness called yesterday was George Edward Powers, an organizer of the Communist party in 1919 who left the organization in 1939 because of Stalin's pact with Adolf Hitler.

Mr. Powers testified that the Communist position was that capitalism must be destroyed entirely and that this could be done only by violent revolution. He told of having served the I. W. O. as part of his duties as a "good, obedient, disciplined Communist" and was still on the stand when the hearing

Figure 6.12
New York Times 12 July 1950

TEST IS ON TO LINK COMMUNISTS-I. W. O.

U. S. Contends at Deportation Hearing That Membership in Two Is Identical

The Immigration and Naturalization Service began a test yesterday of the proposition that membership in the International Workers Order is equivalent to membership in the Communist party.

This argument was presented at a hearing in district headquarters of the service, 70 Columbus Avenue, in deportation proceedings against Andrew Dmytryshyn. The respondent is a vice president and organizer of the Ukrainian-American Fraternal Branch of the I. W. O. The organization, which has insurance benefits, claims more than 160,000, against an estimated 55,000 Communist party members.

Isidore Englander, counsel for Mr. Dmytryshyn, denounced the proceedings as unfair, and made a long but unsuccessful plea for an adjournment so that he could apply to the Federal Court for an injunction to halt them. He said he would ignore the hearing today and apply for the injunction.

Mr. Englander charged that the hearing officer, William J. Wyrsch, because of his long association with the Naturalization Service, was not a suitable person to conduct the hearing. Mr. Wyrsch remarked that he was not biased and pointed out that he would not decide the case but would submit it to the Commissioner of Immigration and Naturalization for a ruling.

TITLE

CLASS Internal Security

From NY Times

JUL 1 2 1950

Figure 6.13
FBI copy filed 15 September 1950

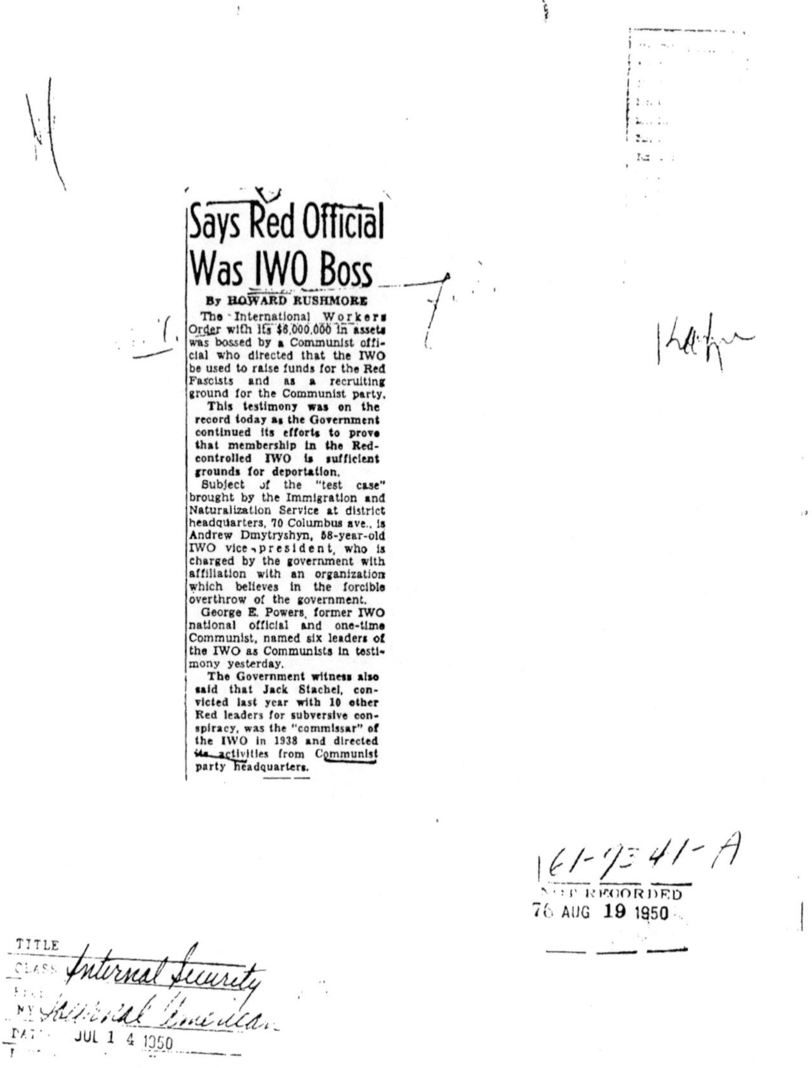

Says Red Official Was IWO Boss

By HOWARD RUSHMORE

The International Workers Order with its $8,000,000 in assets was bossed by a Communist official who directed that the IWO be used to raise funds for the Red Fascists and as a recruiting ground for the Communist party.

This testimony was on the record today as the Government continued its efforts to prove that membership in the Red-controlled IWO is sufficient grounds for deportation.

Subject of the "test case" brought by the Immigration and Naturalization Service at district headquarters, 70 Columbus ave., is Andrew Dmytryshyn, 58-year-old IWO vice-president, who is charged by the government with affiliation with an organization which believes in the forcible overthrow of the government.

George E. Powers, former IWO national official and one-time Communist, named six leaders of the IWO as Communists in testimony yesterday.

The Government witness also said that Jack Stachel, convicted last year with 10 other Red leaders for subversive conspiracy, was the "commissar" of the IWO in 1938 and directed its activities from Communist party headquarters.

161-9341-A
NOT RECORDED
76 AUG 19 1950

TITLE
CLASS Internal Security
NY Journal American
DATE JUL 1 4 1950

Figure 6.14
FBI copy filed 19 August 1950

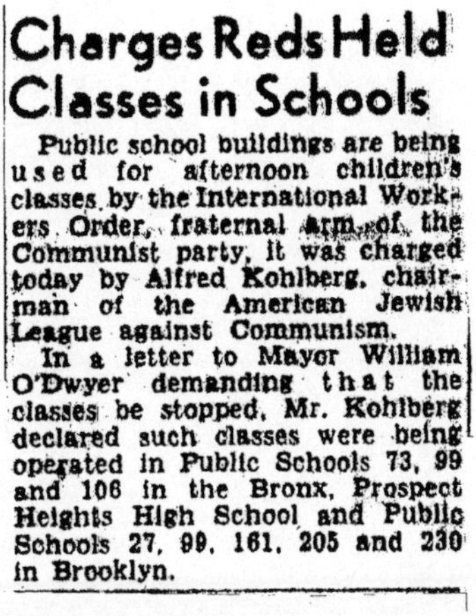

Charges Reds Held Classes in Schools

Public school buildings are being used for afternoon children's classes by the International Workers Order, fraternal arm of the Communist party, it was charged today by Alfred Kohlberg, chairman of the American Jewish League against Communism.

In a letter to Mayor William O'Dwyer demanding that the classes be stopped, Mr. Kohlberg declared such classes were being operated in Public Schools 73, 99 and 106 in the Bronx, Prospect Heights High School and Public Schools 27, 99, 161, 205 and 230 in Brooklyn.

Figure 6.15
New York World Telegram 23 November 1948

Department, and there was a Hearing Officer and the case was presented to him. In private the case was presented to him. Then he would make a ruling and on the basis of that ruling authorize us to go ahead with a proper proceeding before the Supreme Court.

Brown: Had you worked with the Insurance Department before?

Williams: No, I never worked with them before. I think the way the matter came up is that for many years I'd been a friend of Governor Dewey. Governor Dewey called me one day from Albany and asked me if I would care to be the Hearing Officer for the Insurance Department in connection with their claims that the IWO was a communist organization, or communist dominated. I told the Governor then that I would not care to be the Hearing Officer. I would prefer to be the Special Attorney General. The way I became acquainted with Governor Dewey is that both he and I served as Assistant United States Attorneys back in 1931, 32, and 33 under George who was United States Attorney here for the Southern district of New York. Governor Dewey at the time was the Chief Assistant U.S. Attorney. So he knew of me and my work. I was of course later asked by him to become one of his three top Assistants when he became Special District Attorney.

Brown: In New York City?

Williams: In New York City. But I was already in this office of the predecessor firm as a partner. So, I didn't choose to go with him, but he did know of me, and anyhow he got in touch with me.

Brown: When was that? Do you remember exactly?

Williams: Well he called me, I think it was late 1949 or early 1950.

Brown: That was probably after . . . I read the report of the Insurance Examiner, James Haley, who requested in 1948—(I am just trying to set this up chronologically in my mind)—this prior to the actual Insurance Department hearing as you set up?

Williams:That's right. And I remember that Governor Dewey said the thing that had caused him to wonder about the IWO was an article which appeared in the New York Times which charged the IWO with being a communist organization. And he said, I don't know whether it is true or not, but I can't afford as the Governor of this state to let the challenge go unanswered. So will you find out for me? At first he asked me to be a Hearing Examiner, and then later saying if you prefer to be the prosecutor, and in fact it is not the prosecutor but the Special Assistant Attorney General, I will appoint you for that.

Brown: I was always curious . . . had you ever heard of the IWO before the case?

Williams: Never.

Brown: I'd be interested in finding out someday . . . exactly how . . . to talk to some of these people (members) to see what their reaction was . . . to get a different perspective. Especially if they did not know anything about any communist connection at all. So we know how the group actually got going. So when you say that Governor Dewey spoke to you about . . . it seems that he actually discovered, much to his surprise, the presence of this group.

Williams: No, not that. He didn't discover it. He read the New York Times and the New York Times was a very responsible paper. When it published this account . . . he was sufficiently . . . I'd say that he had to do something about it. If you're the Governor of the state, you just can't sit by and have charges made against one of your insurance companies.[39]

By creating a temper that encouraged official action against the IWO, the media pursued a course irresponsible to its Constitutional charge and void of public neutrality. What passed as news not only mirrored government information, but also instigated further official inquiries into the Order's activities; indeed, Governor Dewey's belief that the IWO was a subversive organization was based upon a headline he read in the *New York Times*. Given the direction of that paper's headlines concerning the Order since the Attorney General's list had been published, it would have been difficult for any elected official not to take action, let alone the Governor of the State of New York. In retrospect it seems clear that by the beginning of 1950, in the case against the IWO, the official bond between government action and mainstream media headlines could not be denied.[40]

Devastating press reports about the IWO during the insurance examination continued after Deputy Superintendent Haley's 145-page recommendation that the IWO be liquidated on the grounds that the organization was a front for the Communist Party, and as such, was in violation of the New York State Insurance Code. Reporting this and subsequent events, the *New York Times* headlined government's legal actions thusly: *"Insurance Lodge Sued As Red-Ruled: State Plea to Wind Up Workers Order Charges Party Uses It for Subversive Purposes."*[41] By framing the government's objective in such a manner the media extended the reader's perception to the point where it corresponded to the government's position. A public mind created by powerful socializing agencies does not necessarily

Mr. Tolson
Mr. Clegg
Mr. Glavin

Charges Reds Instruct Kids in City Schools

Charges that the International Workers Order, fraternal arm of the Communist party, was using public school buildings for afternoon children's classes were made today by Alfred Kohlberg, chairman of the American Jewish League Against Communism.

In a letter to Mayor William O'Dwyer, Mr. Kohlberg declared that the classes were being conducted in Public Schools 73, 99 and 106 in the Bronx, and Prospect Heights High School and Public Schools 27, 99, 161, 205 and 230 in Brooklyn.

'Action Necessary.

"We consider," Mr. Kohlberg said, "immediate ection necessary—first, to stop the opening of any further schools to Communist groups;—second, to revoke the permission already granted; and third, to discover who is to blame for the opening of the schools to the IWO."

Mr. Kohlberg, pointing out that the IWO was listed by Attorney General Tom Clark as subversive, quoted an IWO pamphlet which declared it to be the aim of the group to "bring to the children and its schools the true meaning and aims of the capitalist armies and navies."

'Essentially Non-Jewish.

Mr. Kohlberg said the several of the classes were being sponsored by the IWO's affiliated Jewish Peoples Fraternal Order. He said that they are "essentially non-Jewish since they are anti-religious, following the atheistic Communist party line."

Mr. Kohlberg assured the mayor that neither he nor the Board of Education were being criticized but that "the City of New York, through its own schools, should not be a party to the corruption of American children."

G.I.R. 2

DEC 29 1948

N. Y. World Telegram

NOV 23 1948

DEC 31 1948

Figure 6.16
FBI copy filed 31 December 1948

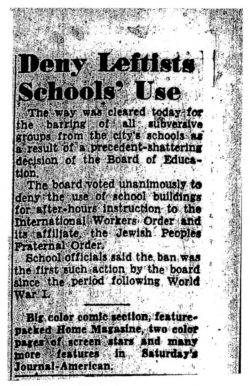

Figure 6.17
New York Journal American 21 January 1949

reexamine itself at the courtroom door. Legal arbiters do not operate in a vacuum.
Each is a product of individual and group identities which challenge the neutrality
of jurisprudence. Individual political perspectives, self-perceptions, fears, frustrations, hopes and desires help to enforce, reflect, and organize political constituencies which bear influence upon legal decision-making. It was within such an environment that the IWO appealed the decision for its liquidation.

On January 29, 1950, the appeal process got underway in the New York State
Supreme Court. During the three-month hearing that followed, no less than 46
witnesses testified (mostly refuting the testimony of IWO members). One hundred
and thirteen affidavits were introduced in evidence as were 350 documents (in-
cluding inflamatory news headlines the FBI had in its possession about the Order).
All of this amounted to approximately 5200 pages of testimony.[42] In the end, New
York State Supreme Court Justice Henry Clay Greenberg decided for the State of
New York and against the IWO in late June of that same year:

> The testimony of the respondent, as a whole, failed to meet and refute the charges
> made by the Superintendent of Insurance. Its evidence established that the IWO
> did carry on an insurance function and that there was much fraternal, social and

Mr. Tolson
Mr. Clegg
Mr. Glavin
Mr. Ladd
Mr. Nichols
Mr. [illegible]
Mr. [illegible]
Mr. [illegible]
Mr. [illegible]
Mr. [illegible]
Mr. [illegible]
Mr. [illegible]
Mr. Quinn Tamm
Mr. Nease
Miss Gandy

Use of Schools Denied Leftists

The way was cleared today for the barring of all subversive groups from the city's schools as a result of a precedent-shattering decision of the Board of Education.

The board voted unanimously to deny the use of school buildings for after-hours instruction to the International Workers Order and its affiliate, the Jewish Peoples Fraternal Order.

School officials said the ban was the first such action by the board since the period following World War I.

'TOOLS OF COMMUNISTS.'

Representatives of the IWO, which has been named by U. S. Attorney General Clark as a subversive organization, have repeatedly refused to answer the board's questions as to whether the teachers of their "cultural" classes were Communists.

The board acted after George Timone, member from Manhattan, declared that if the IWO continued to use school buildings:

"We would in effect become willing tools of the Communist Party. We would be assisting and subsidizing them in the entrapment of our public school children into receiving Communist indoctrination."

Lee Pressman, leftist former CIO counsel, leaped to his feet and demanded to be heard after the vote was taken, but board members walked out.

A detail of 15 police cleared the board hall at 110 Livingston st., Brooklyn, of 200 booing and hissing spectators.

Earlier, Pressman had refused to answer when asked whether the IWO teachers were Reds.

The board's action resulted from charges of the American Jewish League Against Communism that the IWO has been teaching Communist doctrines in the classes sponsored by its affiliate.

161-7[illegible]-A
NOT RECORDED
98 MAR 11 1949

INDEXED - 58
EX-6

Journal American
JAN 21 1949

Figure 6.18
FBI copy filed 11 March 1949

Schools Ban I. W. O. Classes

Act Without Dissent After Hearing Charges That Group Is Subversive.

Classes conducted in school buildings in late afternoons and evenings by the International Workers Order henceforth will be barred. Without a dissenting vote, with three of its nine members absent, the Board of Education yesterday imposed the ban on the organization, including the Jewish Peoples Fraternal Order, a subsidiary of the I. W. O.

The ban followed a three-hour public hearing last Thursday, at which the American Jewish League A g a i n s t Communism charged the J. P. F. O. with being Communist-dominated and subversive. Spokesmen for the order vehemently denied the charge, but their protestations went unheeded by the school board members.

Commissioner George A. Timone, who said the group conducts classes in nine public school buildings, cited a list of official agencies which have branded the I. W. O. as subversive. He said that "this board and the people of that "this board and the people of American Jewish League Against Communism for first bringing to our attention this flagrant misuse of school buildings."

Sees Communist Line.

Lee Pressman and other officials of the order had argued that the I. W. O. conducted classes in Jewish history, literature and culture, as well as in American history and the Hebrew language. However, Timone said that the classes were in fact used to indoctrinate children in the ways of revolution. The drive to indoctrinate children is the new Communist line to offset losses in the trade labor movement, Timone said.

Timone also cited statements by I. W. O. officials themselves, some of them published in the Daily Worker, official Communist publication, as evidence of what the I. W. O. classes seek to accomplish.

"In the light of the record now before us," Timone said, "if we failed to revoke immediately the permits of the I. W. O. to use our classrooms, we would, in effect, become willing tools of the Communist party. We would be assisting and subsidizing them in the entrapment of our public school children into receiving Communist indoctrination."

Moss States Position.

Commissioner Maximilian Moss said he voted to oust the J. P. F. O. because its classes are not conducted by teachers licensed by the Board of Examiners. All classes taught by teachers who have not been specifically licensed by the examiners should be kept from the public schools, he declared.

Clauson explained after the meeting that he voted to oust the classes because "continuance of classes by the I. W. O. in the public schools is decidedly of a controversial nature and a cause for dissension among the citizens who support our public schools." These are the grounds cited by the State Education Department as warranting a school board in denying the use of public school buildings to organizations which apply for them.

Other board members who voted for the I. W. O. ban, which will become effective on February 28, were Commissioners Anthony Campagna, Harold C. Dean and Vito F. Lanza. Absentees were Commissioners Charles J. Bensley, John M. Coleman and James Marshall.

When the vote was taken and the meeting declared adjourned, Pressman and most of the 200 others present jumped to their feet in protest. Many of them hurled imprecations at the board members, but police cleared the meeting room. The police also dispersed J. P. F. O. supporters who sought to hold a street meeting outside the school board building at 110 Livingston street, Brooklyn.

Figure 6.19
New York Sun
21 January 1949

Schools Ban I. W. O. Classes

Act Without Dissent After Hearing Charges That Group Is Subversive.

Classes conducted in school buildings in late afternoons and evenings by the International Workers Order henceforth will be barred. Without a dissenting vote, with three of its nine members absent, the Board of Education yesterday imposed the ban on the organization, including the Jewish Peoples Fraternal Order, a subsidiary of the I. W. O.

The ban followed a three-hour public hearing last Thursday, at which the American Jewish League Against Communism charged the J. P. F. O. with being Communist-dominated and subversive. Spokesmen for the order vehemently denied the charge, but their protestations went unheeded by the school board members.

Commissioner George A. Timone, who said the group conducts classes in nine public school buildings, cited a list of official agencies which have branded the I. W. O. as subversive. He said that "this board and the people of" that "this board and the people of American Jewish League Against Communism for first bringing to our attention this flagrant misuse of school buildings."

Sees Communist Line.

Lee Pressman and other officials of the order had argued that the I. W. O. conducted classes in Jewish history, literature and culture, as well as in American history and the Hebrew language. However, Timone said that the classes were in fact used to indoctrinate children in the ways of revolution. The drive to indoctrinate children is the new Communist line to offset losses in the trade labor movement, Timone said.

Timone also cited statements by I. W. O. officials themselves, some of them published in the Daily Worker, official Communist publication, as evidence of what the I. W. O. classes seek to accomplish.

"In the light of the record now before us," Timone said, "if we failed to revoke immediately the permits of the I. W. O. to use our classrooms, we would, in effect, become willing tools of the Communist party. We would be assisting and subsidizing them in the entrapment of our public school children into receiving Communist indoctrination."

Moss States Position.

Commissioner Maximilian Moss said he voted to oust the J. P. F. O. because its classes are not conducted by teachers licensed by the Board of Examiners. All classes taught by teachers who have not been specifically licensed by the examiners should be kept from the public schools, he declared.

Clauson explained after the meeting that he voted to oust the classes because "continuance of classes by the I. W. O. in the public schools is decidedly of a controversial nature and a cause for dissension among the citizens who support our public schools." These are the grounds cited by the State Education Department as warranting a school board in denying the use of public school buildings to organizations which apply for them.

Other board members who voted for the I. W. O. ban, which will become effective on February 28, were Commissioners Anthony Campagna, Harold C. Dean and Vito F. Lanza. Absentees were Commissioners Charles J. Bensley, John M. Coleman and James Marshall.

When the vote was taken and the meeting declared adjourned, Pressman and most of the 200 others present jumped to their feet in protest. Many of them hurled imprecations at the board members, but police cleared the meeting room. The police also dispersed J. P. F. O. supporters who sought to hold a street meeting outside the school board building at 110 Livingston street, Brooklyn.

Figure 6.20
FBI copy filed 13 February 1949

WITNESS SAYS REDS SHARED I. W. O. FUNDS

A former Communist party national committeeman testified yesterday that 20 per cent of the proceeds of affairs given by the International Workers Order in Buffalo in the early Nineteen Thirties were turned over to the Communist party.

Manning Johnson, a Government analyst employed by the Immigration and Naturalization Service here, gave his testimony in the State Insurance Department's case against the I. W. O. The department is seeking to take it over on the grounds it is dominated by the Communist party and is a public hazard under the insurance laws.

Mr. Johnson, who previously gave evidence in the Gerhart Eisler and Harry Bridges cases, listed several Communist fund-raising campaigns in which he said the I. W. O. had a quota substantially larger than any other Communist-dominated organization. He left the party shortly after the Nazi-Soviet pact in 1939.

Testifying about a number of Communist national committee and political bureau meetings in the Nineteen Thirties, Mr. Johnson identified Max Bedacht, former I. W. O. general secretary, and William Weiner, former president, as having attended them. Decisions on I. W. O. policies were made at these meetings, he declared.

The proceedings, held before Justice Henry Clay Greenberg in Supreme Court, will be resumed at 10 A. M. today.

Figure 6.21
New York Times 2 February 1951

WITNESS SAYS REDS SHARED I. W. O. FUNDS

A former Communist party national committeeman testified yesterday that 20 per cent of the proceeds of affairs given by the International Workers Order in Buffalo in the early Nineteen Thirties were turned over to the Communist party.

Manning Johnson, a Government analyst employed by the Immigration and Naturalization Service here, gave his testimony in the State Insurance Department's case against the I. W. O. The department is seeking to take it over on the grounds it is dominated by the Communist party and is a public hazard under the insurance laws.

Mr. Johnson, who previously gave evidence in the Gerhart Eisler and Harry Bridges cases, listed several Communist fund-raising campaigns in which he said the I. W. O. had a quota substantially larger than any other Communist-dominated organization. He left the party shortly after the Nazi-Soviet pact in 1939.

Testifying about a number of Communist national committee and political bureau meetings in the Nineteen Thirties, Mr. Johnson identified Max Bedacht, former I. W. O. general secretary, and William Weiner, former president, as having attended them. Decisions on I. W. O. policies were made at these meetings, he declared.

The proceedings, held before Justice Henry Clay Greenberg in Supreme Court, will be resumed at 10 A. M. today.

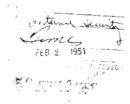

INDEXED - 7

RECORDED

Figure 6.22
FBI copy filed 28 June 1951

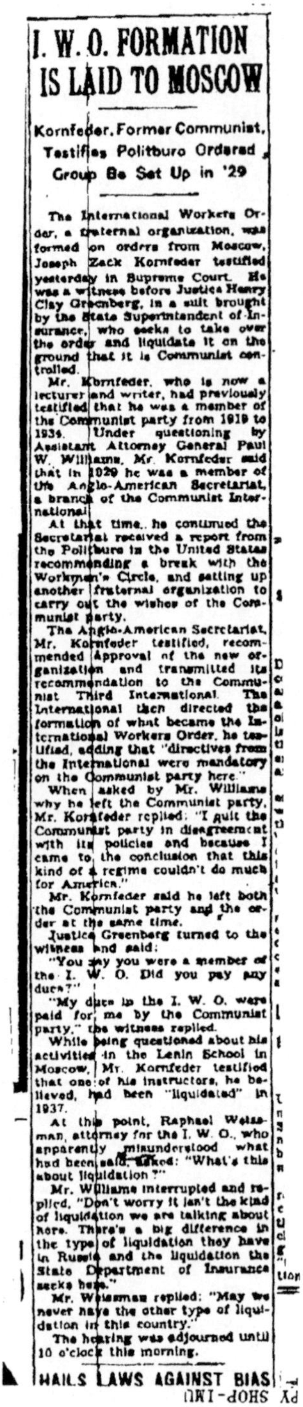

I. W. O. FORMATION IS LAID TO MOSCOW

Kornfeder, Former Communist, Testifies Politburo Ordered Group Be Set Up in '29

The International Workers Order, a fraternal organization, was formed on orders from Moscow, Joseph Zack Kornfeder testified yesterday in Supreme Court. He was a witness before Justice Henry Clay Greenberg, in a suit brought by the State Superintendent of Insurance, who seeks to take over the order and liquidate it on the ground that it is Communist controlled.

Mr. Kornfeder, who is now a lecturer and writer, had previously testified that he was a member of the Communist party from 1919 to 1934. Under questioning by Assistant Attorney General Paul W. Williams, Mr. Kornfeder said that in 1929 he was a member of the Anglo-American Secretariat, a branch of the Communist International.

At that time, he continued the Secretariat received a report from the Politburo in the United States recommending a break with the Workmen's Circle, and setting up another fraternal organization to carry out the wishes of the Communist party.

The Anglo-American Secretariat, Mr. Kornfeder testified, recommended approval of the new organization and transmitted its recommendation to the Communist Third International. The International then directed the formation of what became the International Workers Order, he testified, adding that "directives from the International were mandatory on the Communist party here."

When asked by Mr. Williams why he left the Communist party, Mr. Kornfeder replied: "I quit the Communist party in disagreement with its policies and because I came to the conclusion that this kind of a regime couldn't do much for America."

Mr. Kornfeder said he left both the Communist party and the order at the same time.

Justice Greenberg turned to the witness and said:

"You say you were a member of the I. W. O. Did you pay any dues?"

"My dues in the I. W. O. were paid for me by the Communist party," the witness replied.

While being questioned about his activities in the Lenin School in Moscow, Mr. Kornfeder testified that one of his instructors, he believed, had been "liquidated" in 1937.

At this point, Raphael Weissman, attorney for the I. W. O., who apparently misunderstood what had been said, asked: "What's this about liquidation?"

Mr. Williams interrupted and replied, "Don't worry it isn't the kind of liquidation we are talking about here. There's a big difference in the type of liquidation they have in Russia and the liquidation the State Department of Insurance seeks here."

Mr. Weissman replied: "May we never have the other type of liquidation in this country."

The hearing was adjourned until 10 o'clock this morning.

HAILS LAWS AGAINST BIAS

charitable activity engaged in by the IWO and its subordinate lodges. In addition, work which it did in behalf of civil rights and labor organizations, while political in nature, had commendable immediate objectives if, of course, the purpose and intent were proper. Furthermore, there is nor doubt from the evidence that many members of the IWO lodges came in solely because of the insurance benefits or social and fraternal participation and were not Communists or even clearly aware of the ties between the IWO and the Communist Party. However, this evidence does not overcome or even equal the evidence of the Superintendent of Insurance establishing the fact that the leadership and direction of the IWO was Communist, and that the immediate objectives of insurance and fraternalism were means toward developing a wide organization of workers, under Communist guidance, could be developed from their political views into adherents of the Communist program. Even if many of the members may have been unaware of any of the objectives for which they joined, the organization took its character and meaning not from these innocent members but from the leaders and the program they carried out, making use of the innocent as well as the more politically astute members. It is difficult to escape the conclusion, based on the overwhelming evidence in this case, that the insurance and social reform activities of the IWO were with calculated design contrived to lure into the Order the great mass of workers and thus expose them to Communist teaching and doctrines and bring them within the sphere of the Communist Party.[43]

Having established a linkage between the IWO and the CP, Judge Greenberg next proceeded to address the legal consequences of the legally sanctioned relationship. Two questions were central to the issue: 1) was the IWO/CP connection hazardous to the policyholders of the Order; and 2) due to its connection with the CP was the IWO then in default of its charter, and, as such, abrogating the insurance laws of the State of New

Figure 6.23
New York Times 2 February 1951

Mr. Tolson
Mr. Ladd
Mr. Clegg
Mr. Glavin
Mr. Nichols
Mr. Rosen
Mr. Tracy
Mr. Harbo
Mr. Belmont
Mr. Mohr
Tele. Room
Mr. Nease
Miss Gandy

I. W. O. FORMATION IS LAID TO MOSCOW

Kornfeder, Former Communist, Testifies Politburo Ordered Group Be Set Up in '29

The International Workers Order, a fraternal organization, was formed on orders from Moscow, Joseph Zack Kornfeder testified yesterday in Supreme Court. He was a witness before Justice Henry Clay Greenberg, in a suit brought by the State Superintendent of Insurance, who seeks to take over the order and liquidate it on the ground that it is Communist controlled.

Mr. Kornfeder, who is now a lecturer and writer, had previously testified that he was a member of the Communist party from 1919 to 1934. Under questioning by Assistant Attorney General Paul W. Williams, Mr. Kornfeder said that in 1929 he was a member of the Anglo-American Secretariat, a branch of the Communist International.

At that time, he continued the Secretariat received a report from the Politburo in the United States recommending a break with the Workmen's Circle, and setting up another fraternal organization to carry out the wishes of the Communist party.

The Anglo-American Secretariat, Mr. Kornfeder testified, recommended approval of the new organization and transmitted its recommendation to the Communist Third International. The International then directed the formation of what became the International Workers Order, he testified, adding that "directives from the International were mandatory on the Communist party here."

When asked by Mr. Williams why he left the Communist party, Mr. Kornfeder replied: "I quit the Communist party in disagreement with its policies and because I came to the conclusion that this kind of a regime couldn't do much for America."

Hoagland

61-7341
~~HQ~~ 5958

TITLE Internal Security
Times FEB 6 1951
INDEXED - 56

161-7341-A
NOT RECORDED
MAY 22 1951

60 MAY 24 1951

Figure 6.24
FBI copy filed 24 May 1951

York? Greenberg concluded that in both instances the answer was yes. As the IWO was forever linked to the CP and the intention of the party was politically motivated, then the IWO policyholder was substantially at risk and as such the insurance law had been broken:

> Where the competitive or superseding objective is a political faith linked with a party whose leaders have been convicted of advocating the overthrow of government by force and violence, and is ideologically attuned to a foreign power now engaged with controversy with this nation, the fortunes of insurance functions are indeed hazardous. There is an obvious risk that when the ultimate political purposes so require, the insurance functions will be deliberately sacrificed in whole or in part, or will otherwise suffer from changes of political fortune.[44]

The IWO appealed Greenberg's decision to the State Court of Appeals. On April 23, 1953, the Appeals Court unanimously affirmed the decision to liquidate the Order. The Order's last hope was the U.S. Supreme Court, but on October 19, 1953, the Court refused to hear the IWO's petition to rehear the case. The IWO had run out of legal options. It was forced to liquidate.

Between Superintendent Bohlinger's determination to disband the IWO and the U.S. Supreme Court's failure to rehear the case, the government/media relationship continued unabated. Newspaper headlines were framed in such a manner that for most readers, too rushed to read the entire story about the Order's raison d'être, their view of the IWO reflected that of the government. Such methods of misrepresentation at once allowed the media to fully complement the official position, while at the same time encouraged the press to selectively and deliberately set the course for eventual legal determinations about the IWO. Following Bohlinger's suit, the *New York Times* politically motivated its readers with conclusions about the goals and interests of the IWO before the Order's legal appeal process was concluded. Organizing the limits for public discourse were such *Times* headlines as: "*Witness Says Reds Shared I.W.O. Funds*," and "*I.W.O. Formation Is Laid To Moscow.*"[45] In the process, the media fused its reporting of events with that of the official case against the IWO (See figures 21–24).[46] As the appeal evolved, the media continued to press the government's case, expanding its own political agenda well beyond the legal boundaries set in the hearings. Such reportage was not, however, without negative effects for the government. Bold and politically motivated headlines encouraged many IWO members to question the financial guarantees of their insurance policies. While media headlines supported the government's case against the IWO, they also, perhaps subliminally, instilled a desire for many to cancel their insurance policies. Alarmed by the economic consequences of a mass exodus of IWO policyholders, Superintendent Bohlinger sent a letter to all members of the Order telling them that their insurance was secure. He went on to say that his office was seeking a reinsurer to guarantee their policies, "as near to the same terms as possible."[47]

While media headlines during the appeal did little to complicate the reinsuring process, they continued to frame the need for the Order's liquidation. Never calling into question the political motives of those testifying for the government, press headlines hammered away at the IWO's adherence to the party line. Issues of insurance security and stability were absent from newspaper accounts and renderings of trial proceedings. A steady litany of accusations by former party members against the IWO produced media headlines such as: "*6 OFFICERS IN I.W.O. IDENTIFIED AS REDS*," "*IWOers Gave 10G to Red 11*," and "*Some Capitalistic Communists*."[48] For individuals who just skimmed the news, the dominant impression about the Order was slanted by the headlines. There was no need to read the content of the stories below them. There was no need to address the consequences of such propaganda for the IWO, or for that matter, the free expression of ideas. The reduction of testimonial vocabulary to that which packaged the perception that the Order was a Communist-controlled organization served also to enhance the negative image of the IWO for the public. In the end, the valiant and patriotic prosecutorial defenders of democracy and their media allies could do no wrong in their war against the treasonous, if not foreign, conspirator. They also did not prevent the Continental Assurance Company from assuming "all policies in force on the date of liquidation under substantially the same terms that were in effect theretofore."[49] Corporate America was satisfied as well.

During the Order's lifetime over one million members passed through its rolls, the overwhelming number of whom were not Communists. The IWO gained most of its members from the immigrant communities which stood mainly outside the mainstream of life. Not many American organizations during the economic and socially tumultuous years of the Great Depression and world war aided immigrant workers in their attempt to obtain life insurance and medical protection or to assist them in their efforts to integrate into the American community-at-large. The IWO was unique in its championing of unpopular causes that set it apart from other fraternally segregated organizations. During much of its lifetime it received praise for its efforts from a wide group of diverse political interests. Local government, organized labor, and the medical health community all praised the IWO's efforts in providing the immigrant industrial workers a secure place in their new American setting.[50] These activities and official kudos about the IWO, however, received little media attention within the hysterical atmosphere of the Cold War. In the late 1940s and early 1950s the twists and turns of the Cold War produced a public demand to hold the "red menace" at bay. Official repression of dissent and media rhetoric joined in a determined alliance in attacking everything politically left of center and "alien" to the American way of life. Obtaining most of its news from official sources, the media quickly became manipulated by these sources. As the media embellished the information received beyond normal literary and professional boundaries they influenced the creation of a public mind whose political opinions deviated little from official policy.

While it would be hypocritical to plead the IWO's case apart from the Communist Party, it is also difficult to see the government's actions against the Order as reflecting a strict compliance to Constitutional guidelines. During the Cold War the scope of legal protection for those who did not conform to the status quo was quite limited. Such was the case of the IWO. The rights of the Order to serve as a forum for its members to speak freely and publicize their ideas was taken away by the court. In this time of antiradical hysteria the legitimacy of the IWO as an insurer was challenged by a repressive government, as a propagandized and victimized public stood by and watched not only the American legal system but government agencies such as the INS and the FBI manipulate Constitutional guarantees. Mirroring the government assaults on American freedoms, the media created a public bias against the IWO. Boldly printed headlines, surfacing in the insecure genre of the Cold War, favoring event over content and sensationalism over objectivity inspired a lockstep with the corporate march against working-class organizations. More to the point, it is demonstrably obvious to anyone who has their head screwed on correctly that the part played by corporate America in the official case against the IWO was that of a politically interested party. Its anti-red, antilabor ferocity was a pretext for something that clearly extended beyond the boundaries of free enterprise. Corporate America's aim was to maintain its control over the decision-making process of government to insure that the economic benefits that would flow from the industrial armaments perpetrated by the Cold War, would continue to flow in its direction. To this extent, corporate America was able to generate enough media-inspired anti-Communist hysteria to serve not only its profit seeking appetite, but to compromise the country's commitment to the guarantee of freedom of expression and civil rights for all Americans, not just an elite few.

The effects of this Cold War government-media-corporate alliance not only challenged existing American ideals but stifled once and for all any notion of the emergence of a working-class consciousness in postwar America. American workers during the Cold War viewed themselves first as patriots then as workers. Assisting in this denial of a working-class reality were editors and news reporters who patriotically switched their "exposés" from worker's rights to communist influence in the union movement, from health and safety issues on the job to security clearances for workers, from working place tenure to the affiliations and beliefs of workers off the job. Headlines demanded that workers and worker's organizations pass a loyalty litmus test. Those who did not were stigmatized in the press as subversive, devious, and treasonous and were formally disassociated from the labor movement:

> Time and again the Red Peril theme propagated by the governmental-industrial-media complex played an effective part in (1) setting back or limiting the struggles and gains of labor; (2) distracting popular attention from the recessions and crises of capitalism by directing grievances toward interior or alien foes; and (3) marshalling public support for huge military budgets, cold war policies and . . . Third World interventions to make the world safe for corporate investment and politics.[51]

For the IWO such a juggernaut was demonstrably costly. For the solidarity of workers the cost of this experience is still being calculated.

Notes

1. U.S. Government, *Subversive Activities Control Board* (Washington, D.C.: U.S. Government Printing Office, December 1947).

2. Patricia Cayo Sexton, *The War on Labor and the Left: Understanding America's Unique Conservatism* (Boulder, Colo.: Westview Press, 1991), 151.

3. *New York Times*, 5 December 1947, 1.

4. "IWO Constitution and By Laws," CPA Collection, Michigan State University, East Lansing, Mich., 3–4.

5. Michael Schaller, Virginia Scharff, and Robert Schulzinger, *Present Tense: The United States Since 1945* (Boston, Mass.: Houghton Mifflin, 1996), 75.

6. John Mack Faragher, et al., *Out of Many: A History of the American People* (Englewood Cliffs, N.J.: Prentice Hall, 1994), 842.

7. HUAC was officially created by the U.S. House of Representatives in 1938. Chaired by the staunch anti-Communist Martin Dies of Texas, it expanded official anti-Communist activity into the investigation of prominent New Deal programs and those who headed them. See George Brown Tindall and David E. Shi, *America: A Narrative History* (New York: W. W. Norton, 1996), 1192.

8. Robert J. Goldstein, *Political Repression in Modern America* (Cambridge, Mass.: Schenkman, 1978), 200.

9. Faragher, et al., *Out of Many*, 839.

10. Arthur J. Sabin, *Red Scare in Court: New York versus the International Workers Order* (Philadelphia: University of Pennsylvania Press, 1993), 83–4.

11. Michael Parenti, *Inventing Reality: The Politics of News Media* (New York: St. Martin's, 1993), 118.

12. Cayo Sexton, *The War on Labor and the Left*, 152.

13. Cayo Sexton, *The War on Labor and the Left*, 75.

14. William M. Goldsmith, "The Theory and the Practice of the Communist Front" (Ph.D. diss., University of Michigan, 1979), 625.

15. Department of Insurance of the State of New York, *In the Matter of the Hearings on the Report of the International Workers Order, Opinion and Findings by the Deputy Superintendent* (December 1948).

16. Department of Insurance of the State of New York, *Report on Examination of International Workers Order; Opinion and Findings by the Deputy Superintendent, 15 December 1950*. See Goldsmith, "The Theory and the Practice," 627.

17. Federal Bureau of Investigation File on the International Workers Order. Photocopy of *New York Times*, 16 December 1951, 6.

18. Goldsmith, *"The Theory and the Practice,"* 628.

19. Goldsmith, *"The Theory and the Practice,"* 628.

20. Cayo Sexton, *The War on Labor and the Left*, 154.

21. Cayo Sexton, *The War on Labor and the Left*, 154..

22. *New York Times*, 26 April 1949, 1.

23. *New York Times*, 25 March 1950, 1.

24. Department of Insurance of the State of New York. *Third and Final Report on the IWO* (31 August 1954): 6.

25. Charles E. Lindblom and Edward J. Woodhouse, *The Policy-Making Process* (Englewood Cliffs, N.J.: Prentice Hall, 1993), 90-103.

26. Parenti, *Inventing Reality*, 35.

27. Parenti, *Inventing Reality*, 69.

28. Parenti, *Inventing Reality*, 5.

29. James Fallows, *Breaking the News: How the Media Undermine Democracy* (New York: Vintage, 1997), 131.

30. *New York Times*, 4 February 1948; *FBI copy*, 5 February 1948.

31. *New York Times*, 1 February 1951, L5; *FBI copy* 28 June 1951; *New York Journal American*, 30 October 1949; *FBI copy*, 19 December 1949; *Baltimore Morning Sun*, 18 May 1950; *FBI copy*, 14 July 1950; and *New York Times*, 10 August 1950, 12; *FBI copy*, 19 September 1950.

32. Goldsmith, *"The Theory and the Practice,"* 626.

33. *New York Times*, 10 May 1950.

34. *Baltimore Sun*, 18 May 1950, 5.

35. *New York Times*, 12 July 1959, 10.

36. *New York Journal American*, 14 July 1950, 2.

37. Thomas J. Edward Walker, *Pluralistic Fraternity: The History of the International Workers Order* (New York: Garland, 1991), 62.

38. *New York World Telegram*, 23 November 1948, 1.

39. "Interview of Paul Williams, Special Attorney General for the State of New York, 1940–1950 by Howard Brown," Oral History Collection, Tamiment Institute Library, New York University, New York.

40. As the Attorney General's list went up through the courts, the reportage of the matter was a reoccurring event. *New York Times* headlines spelled out the future fate of the IWO (20 April 1949—*"SUBVERSIVE LIST UPHELD: Court Refuses to Order Clark to Strike Off Workers Order"*; 26 April 1949—*"Fraternal Organizations Called Fifth Column: Slav Congress and I.W.O"*; and 25 March 1950—"Loyalty Oustings By U.S. Upheld By Appeals Court: I.W.O. Penal Action Forbidden," to name a few).

41. *New York Times*, 16 December 1950, 6.

42. Goldsmith, "The Theory and the Practice," 631.

43. Goldsmith, "The Theory and the Practice," 632.

44. Goldsmith, "The Theory and the Practice," 634.

45. *New York Times*, 1 and 2 February 1951.

46. *New York Times*, 2 February 1951, 9; *New York Times*, 6 February 1951; *FBI copies*, 28 June 1951 and 24 May 1951.

47. "Alfred J. Bohlinger to All Members of the IWO," 24 January 1951, Tamiment Institute Library, New York University, New York.

48. *New York Times*, 31 January 1951, 1; *New York Daily News*, 30 March 1951; *Chicago Daily Tribune*, 11 February 1951, 18.

49. Department of Insurance of the State of New York, *Third and Final Report*, 2.

50. Walker, *Pluralistic Fraternity*, 109-115.

51. Parenti, *Inventing Reality*, 122-123.

A Final Thought

These chapters demonstrate that popular culture in the West during the twentieth century has produced an alteration of previous class interpretations surrounding the notion of work. By fusing culture within advertising copy, media presentations, entertainment productions, and other self-mediated forces of popular culture to a single official world, traditionally shared narratives about the nature of work have been transformed. As the forces of popular culture more and more influenced the ordering of the conjunction of civic life, economic enterprise, and social reality, past identities gave way to newly empowered and nonnegotiable descriptions of worker discourse and behavior. Previous class paradigms were replaced by a new cultural order, which created and crystallized new universalities within a continuous circuitry of image-based representations. Common-sense assumptions about everyday life were stereotyped in such a manner as to define and represent true identities of British, German, Italian, and American workers. Illustrated by visual images, these new identities reflected a briefer and much more condensed creation of an individual's place in modern society. In the hands of such a powerful cultural force, such identities were easily integrated into the new fluid identity of modern culture. More to the point, the modern worker saw it as being necessary for the maintenance of a successful life. Aspiring to the lowest common denominator, British workers at the turn of the twentieth century were encouraged to consume their cocoa in order to shape a new middle-class identity for themselves. With the rise to power of Adolf Hitler, German laborers eagerly rejected past paradigms of worker identification and rallied around symbols of national identity that forged new boundaries of race and work. After World War II, Italian workers transcended their previous urban and rural working-class status to that of Cold War warrior at the behest of their radio priest, Don Camillo, who fashioned them as soldiers, not workers, in the army of god and freedom. And finally, during the "American century," workers in the United States were encouraged by a mass-mediated cultural process to equate their daily labors with a new socially constituted upwardly mobile identity, leaving their working-class roots behind to fulfill a new proprietorship within the "American Dream." In the end, these new forces of cultural hegemony in the West overcame traditional working-class identities, painstakingly molded together over time by diverse yet common experiences, generating and reproducing new working-class equivalencies within a popular parlance.

But while the history of the twentieth century has shown powerful cultural forces at work creating a fantasy life, such a cultural phenomenon should not be overestimated. The circuitous representations of such a cultural force may never fully realize its potential, if only because of the difficulty of reproducing a continuous popular parlance in an ever-changing world. The difficulties arising from the diffusion of power within the hegemonic compulsion to bring influence upon behavior, and from the ambiguities surfacing from the application of illusion to practice, are inherent weaknesses within such a cultural paradigm. Furthermore, the constant push for new technologies to replace existing mediums of measurement, the evolution of linguistic dichotomies caused by the idiosyncracies of the newly defined arrangements, and the social displacements that occur because of the newly created aspirations, may reject not only the stated goals of the enterprise but the capacity to maintain the existing structures of mass-mediation as well. All of these difficulties produce mistaken assumptions about the power of image over reality; assumptions that challenge the capacity for socially powerful cultural frameworks to effectively mediate the discord brought on by the creation and maintenance of new social identities. In other words, no existing cultural paradigm lives up to its exacting requirements, and, therefore, no existing cultural identification can become truly manifest. Nonetheless, it behooves us all to have a proper understanding of the phenomenon of cultural hegemony.

Thomas J. Edward Walker
Williamsport, Pennsylvania
December 21, 2000

Bibliography

Agocs, Sandor. *The Troubled Origins of the Italian Catholic Labor Movement: 1878–1914.* Detroit: Wayne State University Press, 1988.

Angeli, Michele. *Aronte Lunese.* Pisa, Italy: Prosperi, 1835.

Angus, Ian and Sut Jhally, eds. *Cultural Politics in Contemporary America.* New York: Routledge, 1989.

Aronowitz, Stanley. *False Promises.* New York: McGraw-Hill, 1973.

Bader, Michael J. "Bruce Springsteen, Tom Joad, and the Politics of Meaning." *Tikkun* 11, no. 2: 32–33.

Baer, G. W. *The Coming of the Italian-Ethiopian War.* Cambridge, Mass.: Harvard University Press, 1976.

Barrett, James Wyman. *Joseph Pulitzer and His World.* New York: Vanguard Press, 1941.

Barthes, Roland. *Mythologies.* New York: Hill and Wang, 1987.

Battaglia, Roberto. *La Prima Guerra d'Africa.* Turin, Italy: Einaudi, 1958.

Beales, Derek. *The Risorgimento and the Unification of Italy.* London: Longman, 1981.

Bell, David H. "Worker Culture and Worker Politics: The Experience of an Italian Town." *Social History* iii (March 1978): 1–21.

Bell, Donald H. *Sesto San Giovanni: Workers, Culture, and Politics in an Italian Town: 1880–1922.* New Brunswick, N.J.: Rutgers University Press, 1986.

Bell, Rudolph. *Fate and Honor: Family and Village: Demographic and Cultural Change in Rural Italy since 1800.* Chicago: University of Chicago Press, 1979.

Berger, John. *Ways of Seeing.* New York: Viking Press, 1972.

Bernhardt, Debra and Rachel Bernstein. *Ordinary People, Extraordinary Lives.* New York: New York University Press, 2000.

Bernieri, Antonio. *Carrara*. Genoa, Italy: Sagep, 1985.

———. *Cento anni di storia sociale a Carrara: 1815–1921*. Milan, Italy: Feltrinelli, 1961.

———. *Il Porto di Carrara: storia e attualita*. Genoa, Italy: Sagep, 1983.

———. *Storia di Carrara Moderna: 1915–1935*. Pisa, Italy: Pacini, 1983.

Bernstein, Irving. *A History of the American Worker: The Lean Years*. Boston, Mass.: Houghton-Mifflin Company, 1960.

Bertozzi, Massimo. *Massa*. Genoa, Italy: Sagep, 1985.

Bessel Richard. *Fascist Italy and Nazi Germany: Comparisons and Contrasts*. Cambridge: Cambridge University Press, 1996.

Bessel, Richard, ed. *Fascist Italy and Nazi Germany: Comparisons and Contrasts*. Cambridge, U.K.: Cambridge University Press, 1996.

Biagioli, Giuliana. "La diffusione della mezzadria nell' Italia centrale: Un modello di sviluppo demografico ed economico."*Bolletino di demografia storica* 3 (March 1986): 219–35.

Bigi, Ernesto and Alessandro Guidoni. *Massa nella Storia*. Massa, Italy: Tipografia Sociale Apuana, 1961.

Bloom, Jon. *The Voice of Labor Educators*. Katonah, N.Y.: Brookwood Labor College, 1997.

Bondanella, Peter. *Italian Cinema: From Neorealism to the Present*. New York: Ungar, 1988.

Borghese, G. A. "Mussolini the Revolutionary: The Intellectual Flux." In *Italy from the Risorgimento to Fascism: An Inquiry into the Origins of the Totalitarian State*, edited by A. William Salomone. London: David and Charles Publishers, 1971.

Branscomb, H. Eric. "Literacy and a Popular Medium: The Lyrics of Bruce Springsteen." *Journal of Popular Culture* 27 (1993): 29–42.

Briggs, Asa. *Social Thought and Social Action: A Study of the Work of Seebohm Rowntree, 1871–1954*. London: Longman, 1961.

Bromell, Nicholas. "Both Sides of Bob Dylan: Public Memory, the Sixties, and the Politics of Meaning." *Tikkun* 10, no. 4 1996.

Bruner, Jerome. "Myth and Identity." In *Myth and Mythmaking*, ed. Henry A. Murray. Boston, Mass.: Beacon Press, 1969.

Buhle, Paul. *Taking Care of Business*. New York: Monthly Review Press, 1999.

Burleigh, Michael and Wolfgang Wippermann. *The Racial State: Germany 1933–1945*. Cambridge, U.K.: Cambridge University Press, 1991.

Butler, M. B. "Stand Up, You Humble Slaves." *The Industrial Worker* (10 September 1910).

Cabona, Ferrando, Isabella Crusi and Elizabetta Crusi. *Storia dell' Insediamento in Lunigiana, Alta Valle Aullela*. Genoa, Italy: Sagep, 1982.

———. *Storia dell'Insediamento in Lunigiana, Valle del Rosario*. Genoa, Italy: Sagep, 1982.

Cammett, John M. *Antonio Gramsci and the Origins of Italian Communism*. Stanford, Calif.: Stanford University Press, 1967.

Campbell, Joan. *Joy in Work, German Work. The National Debate, 1500–1945*. Princeton, N.J.: Princeton University Press, 1989.

Campbell, Joseph. *Myths to Live By*. New York: Viking, 1972.

Campolonghi, Luigi. *Pontremoli: Una Cittadina Italiana fra L'80 e il '900*. Venice, Italy: Marsilio, 1988.

Cardoza, Anthony. *Agrarian Elites and Italian Fascism: The Province of Bologna: 1901–1926*. Princeton, N.J.: Princeton University Press, 1982.

Carrillo, Elisa A. *Alcide de Gasperi: The Long Apprenticeship*. Notre Dame, Ind.: University of Notre Dame Press, 1965.

Carsten, F. L. *The German Workers and the Nazis*. Aldershot, U.K.: Scolar Press, 1995.

Cassels, Alan. *Fascist Italy*. Arlington Heights, Ill.: Harlan Davidson, 1985.

Cayo Sexton, Patricia. *The War on Labor and the Left: Understanding America's Unique Conservatism*. Boulder, Colo.: Westview Press, 1991.

Chabod, Federico. *A History of Italian Fascism*. London: Weidenfeld and Nicolson, 1963.

Cinel, Dino. *The National Integration of Italian Return Migration: 1870–1929*. Cambridge, U.K.: Cambridge University Press, 1991.

Clark, Martin. *Antonio Gramsci and the Revolution that Failed*. New Haven, CT: Yale University Press, 1977.

———. *Modern Italy: 1871–1982*. New York: Longman, 1984.

Clough, Shepard B. *The Economic History of Modern Italy*. New York: Columbia University Press, 1964.

Collier, Richard. *Duce: A Biography of Benito Mussolini*. New York: Viking Press, 1971.

Collison, Robert. *The Story of Street Literature: Forerunner of the Popular Press*. London: Longman, 1973.

Coppa, Frank J. *Planning, Protectionism, and Politics in Liberal Italy: Economics and Politics in the Giolittian Age*. Washington D.C.: Catholic University of America Press, 1971.

Corner, Paul. *Fascism in Ferrara: 1915–1925*. London: Oxford University Press, 1975.

CPA Collection. Michigan State University. East Lansing, Mich.

Crew, David, ed. *Nazism and German Society, 1933–1945*. New York: Routledge, 1994.

Crossick, Geoffrey. *The Lower Middle Class in Britain, 1870–1914*. New York: Croon Helm Ltd., 1977.

Davis, James C. *Rise from Want: A Peasant Family in the Machine Age*. Philadelphia: University of Pennsylvania Press, 1986.

Davis, John A. 'The Age of the Risorgimento." In *Oxford History of Italy*, edited by George Holmes. Oxford, U.K.: Oxford University Press, 1997.

Dawidoff, Nicholas. "The Pop Populist." *New York Times Magazine* (26 January 1997): 27–33+.

De Grand, Alexander. *Italian Fascism: Its Origins and Development*. Lincoln: University of Nebraska Press, 1982.

De Grazia, Victoria. *Consenso e Cultura di Massa nell'Italia Fascista: L' Organizzazione del Dopolavoro*. Bari, Italy: Editori Laterza, 1981.

Deakin, P. W. *The Brutal Friendship: Mussolini, Hitler and the Fall of Italian Fascism*. New York: Harper and Row Publishers, 1962.

Dell, Floyd. *Intellectual Vagabondage*. New York: Ivan R. Dee, 1991.

Denisoff, R. Serge. *Sing a Song of Social Significance*. Bowling Green, Ohio: Bowling Green State University Press, 1983.

Der Derian, James and Michael Shapiro. *International/Intertextual Relations*. New York: Lexington, 1989.

Dubofsky, Melvyn. *Labor in America: A History*. Wheeling, IL: Harlan Davidson, 1999.

Ebert, Teresa L. "Postmodernism's Infinite Variety." In *The Women's Review of Books* 8 no. 4. January 1991.

Elliot, Blanche B. *A History of English Advertising*. London: Business Publications Limited, 1962.

Ellul, Jacques. *Propaganda: The Formation of Men's Attitudes*. New York: Vintage, 1965; England: Blackwell, 1993.

England, George Allan. "Our Hopeless Highbrows." *The Call* (30 January 1911).

Fallows, James. *Breaking the News: How the Media Undermine Democracy*. New York: Vintage, 1997.

Fara, Amelio. *La Spezia*. Bari, Italy: Laterza, 1983.

Faragher, John Mack, et al. *Out of Many: A History of the American People*. Englewood Cliffs, N.J.: Prentice Hall, 1994.

Filippelli, Ronald R. *American Labor and Postwar Italy, 1943–1953*. Stanford, Calif.: Stanford University Press, 1989.

Fink, Leon. *In Search of the Working Class*. Urbana: University of Illinois Press, 1994.

Fiske, John and John Hartley. *Reading Television*. London: Methuen, 1978.

Flax, Jane. "Postmodernism and Gender Relations in Feminist Theory." In *Feminism/Postmodernism,* edited by Linda B. Nicholson. New York and London: Routledge, 1990: 39–62.

Forland, Egil. "Bringing It All Back Home *or* Another Side of Bob Dylan: Midwestern Isolationist." *Journal of American Studies* 26 (1992): 337–55.

Frei, Norbert. *National Socialist Rule in Germany: The Fuehrer State, 1933–1945*. Oxford,

Gallo, Max. *Mussolini's Italy: Twenty Years of the Fascist Era*. New York: Macmillan Publishing Company, 1974.

Gary, Dorothy. "Another Glimpse of the South." *Labor Age* (November 1927).

———. "Concluding Sketches of a Submerged South," *Labor Age* (January 1928).

Gilbert, Mark. *The Italian Revolution: The End of Politics Italian Style?*. Boulder, CO: Westview Press, 1995.

Gili, Jean. *Arrivano i mostri: i volti della commedia italiana*. Bologna, Italy: Cappelli, 1980.

Ginsborg, Paul. *A History of Contemporary Italy: Society and Politics, 1943–1988*. London: Penguin Group, 1990.

Gnocchi, Alessandro. *Giovannino Guareschi: una storia italiana*. Milan, Italy: Rizzoli, 1998.

Goffman, Erving. *Gender Advertisements*. Cambridge, Mass.: Harvard University Press, 1979.

Goldsmith, William M. "The Theory and the Practice of the Communist Front." Ph.D. diss. University of Michigan, 1979.

Goldstein, Robert J. *Political Repression in Modern America*. Cambridge, Mass.: Schenkman, 1978.

Gombrich, E. H. *Art and Illusion*. New York: Pantheon Books, 1961.

Gramsci, Antonio. *Selections from Political Writings 1910–1920*. New York: International Publishers, 1977.

Grew, Raymond. *A Sterner Plan for Italian Unity: The Italian National Society in the Risorgimento*. Princeton, N.J.: Princeton University Press, 1963.

Grunberger, Richard. *A Social History of the Third Reich*. London: Penguin Books, 1971.

Guareschi, Giovanni. "Don Camillo's Dilemma." In *Light on the Mountain*, ed. by John Kennedy, trans Frances Frenaye. Garden City, N.J.: Catholic Family Books Club, 1957.

———. *Comrade Don Camillo*, trans Frances Frenaye. New York: Farrar, Straus and Giroux, 1964.

———. *Don Camillo and His Flock*, trans Frances Frenaye. New York: Grosset and Dunlap, 1952.

———. *Don Camillo and the Devil*, trans Frances Frenaye. London: Gollancz, 1957.

———. *Don Camillo and the Prodigal Son*, trans Frances Frenaye. London: Gollancz, 1952.

———. *Don Camillo Meets the Flower Children*, trans Frances Frenaye. New York: Farrar, Straus and Giroux, 1969.

———. *Don Camillo prende il diavolo per la coda*, trans Frances Frenaye. Milan, Italy: Rizzoli, 1956.

———. *Don Camillo's Dilemma*, trans Frances Frenaye. New York: Farrar, Straus and Young, 1954.

———. *Don Camillo's Dilemma*, trans Frances Frenaye. New York: Grosset and Dunlap, 1954.

———. *Don Camillo's Dilemma*, trans Frances Frenaye. New York: Pocket Books, 1966.

———. *Mondo piccolo: Don Camillo e i giovanni d'oggi*, trans Frances Frenaye. Milan, Italy: Rizzoli, 1969.

———. *Mondo piccolo: Don Camillo*, trans Frances Frenaye. Milan, Italy: Rizzoli, 1948.

———. *Mondo piccolo: Il compagno Don Camillo*, trans Frances Frenaye. Milan, Italy: Rizzoli, 1963.

———. *Il Dilemma di Don Camillo*, trans Frances Frenaye. Milan, Italy: Rizzoli, 1953.

———. *Don Camillo Meets the Hell's Angels*, trans Frances Frenaye. London: Gollancz, 1970.

———. *Don Camillo Takes the Devil by the Tail*, trans Frances Frenaye. New York: Farrar, Straus and Cudahy, 1957.

———. *Mondo piccolo: Don Camillo e il suo gregge*, trans Frances Frenaye. Milan, Italy: Rizzoli, 1953.

———. *The House that Nino Built*, trans Frances Frenaye. New York: Farrar, Staus & Young, 1953.

———. *The Little World of Don Camillo*, trans Frances Frenaye. New York: Farrar, Straus and Giroux, 1950.

Gurevitch, Michael, Tony Bennet, James Curran and Janet Woollacott, eds. *Culture, Society and the Media*. London: Routledge, 1982.

Gutman, Herbert. *Labor Age*. New York: Greenwood Reprints, 1968.

Hall, Stuart. "Notes on Deconstructing the Popular." In *People's History and Social Theory*, edited by Raphael Samuel. Boston: Routledge and Kegan Paul, 1981.

Hattenhauer, Darryl. "Bob Dylan as Hero: Rhetoric, History, Structuralism and Psychoanalysis in Folklore as a Communicative Process." *Southern Folklore Quarterly* 45, 1981: 69–88.

Hearder, Harry. *Italy: A Short History*. Cambridge, U.K.: Cambridge University Press, 1997.

Herd, Harold. *The Making of Modern Journalism*. London: G. Allen and Unwin, Ltd., 1927.

Hobsbawm, Eric. *Workers: Worlds of Labor*. New York: Pantheon Books, 1984.

Hollis, Patricia. *The Pauper Press*. London: Oxford University Press, 1970.

Holmes, George, ed. *The Oxford History of Italy*. Oxford, U.K.: Oxford University Press, 1997.

Holmes, Madelyn. *Forgotten Migrants: Foreign Workers in Switzerland before World War I*. Cranbury, N.J.: Associated University Presses, 1988.

Holsworth, Robert D. "Workingclass hero." *Christianity and Crisis* (28 October 1985): 430–31.

Horn, Max. *The Intercollegiate Socialist Society, 1905–1921: Origins of the Modern American Student Movement*. Boulder, Colo.: Westview Press, 1979.

Horowitz, D. L. *The Italian Labor Movement*. Cambridge, Mass.: Harvard University Press, 1963.

Hostetter, Richard. *The Italian Socialist Movement: Origins: 1860–1882*. Princeton, N.J.: D. Van Nostrand Company, 1958.

Intercollegiate Socialist Society. Papers. Tamiment Institute Library, New York University, New York.

International Workers Order Papers. Tamiment Institute Library, New York University, New York.

Jacini, Stefano. *I Risultati della Inchiesta Agraria*. Turin, Italy: Piccola Biblioteca Einaudi, 1976.

Jacoby, Daniel. *Laboring for Freedom*. Armonk, N.Y.: ME Sharpe, 1998.

Jacques, Martin and Francis Mulhern, eds. *The Forward March of Labor Halted?* London: NLB, 1981.

Joll, James. *The Anarchists*. London: Longman, 1964.

Jones, Gareth Stedman. *Languages of Class: Studies in English Working Class History, 1832–1982*. New York: Cambridge University Press, 1983.

Josephson, Susan G. *From Idolatry to Advertising: Visual Art and Contemporary Culture*. Armonk, N.Y.: M.E. Sharpe, 1986.

Joyce, Patrick. *Visions of the People: Industrial England and the Question of Class 1848–1914*. Cambridge, U.K.: Cambridge University Press, 1991.

Kelikian, Alice A. *Town and Country under Fascism: The Transformation of Brescia, 1915–1926*. Oxford, U.K.: Claredon Press, 1986.

Kershaw, Ian. *The "Hitler Myth": Image and Reality in the Third Reich*. Oxford, U.K.: Oxford University Press, 1987.

Kertzer, David I. *Family Life in Central Italy, 1880–1910: Sharecropping, Wage Labor and Coresidence*. New Brunswick, N.J.: Rutgers University Press, 1984.

———. and Richard P. Sailer, eds. *The Family in Italy: From Antiquity to the Present*. New Haven, Conn.: Yale University Press, 1991.

Kipnis. Ira. *The American Socialist Movement*. New York: Monthly Review Press, 1971.

Klaufe, Karl. "Symbolism in Advertising." *The Poster* (January 1899).

Kluger, Richard. *The Paper: The Life and Death of the New York Herald Tribune*. New York: Alfred A. Knopf, 1986.

Knox, Macgregor. *Mussolini Unleashed, 1939–1941: Politics and Strategy in Fascist Italy's Last War*. Cambridge, U.K.: Cambridge University Press, 1982.

Koon, Tracy H. *Believe, Obey, Fight: Political Socialization of Youth in Fascist Italy, 1922–1943*. Chapel Hill: University of North Carolina Press, 1985.

Kraditor, Eileen. *The Radical Persuasion*. Baton Rouge: Louisiana State University Press, 1981.

Langholz Leymore, Varda. *Hidden Myth*. New York: Heinemann, 1975.

LaPalombara, Joseph. *Democracy Italian Style*. New Haven, Conn.: Yale University Press, 1987.

Laslett, John and Seymour Martin Lipset, eds. *Failure of a Dream? Essays in the History of American Socialism*. New York: Anchor Books, 1974.

Lazzoni, Carlo. *Carrara e le sue villele: Guida storico, artistico, industriale seguita da brevi cenni su Luni e sue rovine*. Carrara, Italy: Drovandi, 1880.

League for Industrial Democracy. Papers. Tamiment Institute Library. New York University, New York.

Lee, Alan J. *The Origins of the Popular Press, 1855–1914*. Totowa, N.J.: Rowman & Littlefield, 1978.

Lindblom, Charles E. and Edward J. Woodhouse. *The Policy-Making Process*. Englewood Cliffs, N.J.: Prentice Hall, 1993.

Longhi, Jim. *Woody, Cisco and Me: Seamen Three in the Merchant Marine*. Chicago: University of Chicago Press, 1997.

Lorenzini, Pietro. "Tyranny of Stone: Economic Modernization and Political Radicalization in the Marble Industry of Massa-Carrara (1859–1914)." Ph.D. diss., Loyola University of Chicago, 1994.

LoRomer, David G. *Merchants and Reform in Livorno: 1814–1868*. Berkeley: University of California Press, 1987.

Lyons, Julie and George H. Lewis. "The Price You Pay: The Life and Lyrics of Bruce Springsteen." *Popular Music and Society* 9, no. 1 (1983): 13–24.

Lyttelton, Adrian, ed. *Italian Fascism from Pareto to Gentile*. London: Cape, 1973.

———. "Politics and Society 1870–1915." In *The Oxford History of Italy*, edited by George Holmes. Oxford, U.K.: Oxford University Press, 1997.

———. *The Seizure of Power: Fascism in Italy, 1919–1929*. London, England: Weidenfeld and Nicolson, 1973.

Mack Smith, Denis. *Cavour*. New York: Alfred A. Knopf, 1985.

———. *Italy and Its Monarchy*. New Haven, Conn.: Yale University Press, 1989.

———. *Italy*. Ann Arbor: University of Michigan Press, 1959.

———, ed. *The Making of Italy: 1796–1870*. New York: Harper and Row Publishers, 1968.

———. *Mussolini's Roman Empire*. New York: Viking Press, 1976.

Maior, Charles S. *Recasting Bourgeois Europe: Stabilization in France, Germany and Italy in the Decade after World War I*. Princeton, N.J.: Princeton University Press, 1975.

Mammarella, Giuseppe. *Italy after Fascism: A Political History. 1943–1963*. Montreal, Canada: Mario Casalini Press, 1964.

Manacorda, Giovanni. *Il Socialismo nella storia d' Italia*. Bari, Italy: Laterza, 1966.

Manoff, Robert Karl and Michael Schudson, eds. *Reading the News*. New York: Pantheon, 1986.

Mason, Tim. *Social Policy in the Third Reich: The Working Class and the "National Community."* Providence, RI: Berg Publishers, 1993

McLean, Iain. *Keir Hardie*. New York: St. Martin's Press, 1975.

Miller, James Edward. *The United States and Italy: 1940–1950*. Chapel Hill: University of North Carolina Press, 1986.

Mitchell, Otis C., ed. *Nazism and the Common Man: Essays in German History (1929–1939)*. Minneapolis, Minn.: Burgess Publishing Co., 1972.

Montgomery, David. *The Fall of the House of Labor*. New York: Cambridge University Press, 1987.

Mori, Giorgio. *Il capitalismo industriale in Italia: Processo d'industrializzazione e storia d'Italia*. Rome, Italy: Riuniti, 1977.

———, ed. *Storia D'Italia Le Regioni Dall' Unita a Oggi: La Toscana*. Turin, Italy: Giulio Einaudi, 1986.

Mori, Renato. *La Lotta Sociale in Lunigiana: 1895–1904*. Massa, Italy: Le Monnier, 1958.

Morris, James O. *Conflict Within the AFL: A Study of Craft Versus Industrial Unionism, 1901–1938*. Ithaca, N.Y.: Cornell University Press, 1958.

Morton, Marcia and Frederic Morton. *Chocolate: An Illustrated History*. New York: Crown Publishers, Inc., 1986.

Murray, Robert K. "Centrailia: An Unfinished American Tragedy." *Northwest Review* (Spring 1963): 7–22.

Nelson, Daniel. *Shifting Fortunes: The Rise and Decline of American Labor*. Chicago: Ivan R. Dee, 1997.

New York State Department of Insurance. *Third and Final Report on the IWO*. Albany: State of New York, 1950.

Noakes, J. and G. Pridham, eds. *Nazism 1919–1945: A History in Documents and Eyewitness Accounts*. Vol. I. New York: Schocken Books, 1983.

Oddy, Derek J. and Derek S. Miller, eds. *The Making of the Modern British Diet*. Totowa, N.J.: Rowman Littlefield, 1976.

Oral History Collection. Tamiment Institute Library, New York University, New York.

Orleck, Annielise. *Common Sense and a Little Fire*. Chapel Hill: University of North Carolina Press, 1995.

Pagani, Aldo. *I braccianti della valle padana*. Rome, Italy: N.p., 1932.

Palla, Emilio. *Massa e la sua gente*. Massa, Italy: Uliveti, 1984.

Parenti, Michael. *Inventing Reality: The Politics of News Media*. New York: St. Martin's, 1993.

Pascal, Richard. "Walt Whitman and Woody Guthrie: American Prophet-Singers and their People." *Journal of American Studies* 29 (1990): 41–59.

Peukert, Detlev. *Inside Nazi Germany: Conformity, Opposition, and Racism in Everyday Life*. New Haven, Conn.: Yale University Press, 1987.

Poulantzas, Nicos. *Fascism and Dictatorship: The Third International and the Problem of Fascism*. London: Verso, 1979.

Presbrey, Frank. *The History and Development of Advertising*. Garden City, N.Y.: Doubleday, 1929.

Procacci, Giuliano. *History of the Italian People*. Translated by Anthony Paul. New York: Harper and Row Publishers, 1968.

Pugliese, Orazio, Caterina Repetti, and Giulivio Ricci, eds. *Movimento Socialista in Lunigiana tra la fine dell' Ottocento e il Novecento*. Pontremoli, Italy: Artigianelli, 1990.

Raffaelli, Raffaello. *Monografla storica ed agraria del Circondario di Massa Carrara compilato fino al 1881*. Lucca, Italy: Rossi, 1882.

Rauch, Alan. "Bruce Springsteen and the Democratic Monologue." *American Studies* 29, no.1, 1988: 29–49.

Reid, Fred. *Keir Hardie: The Making of a Socialist*. London: Croon Helm, 1978.

Ricci, Giulivio. *Aulla e il suo Territorio Attraverso i Secoli*. Pontremoli, Italy: Artigianelli, 1990.

Richards, Thomas. *The Commodity Culture of Victorian England: Advertising and Spectacle, 1851–1914*. Stanford, Calif: Stanford University Press, 1980.

Roberts, David D. *The Syndicalist Tradition and Italian Fascism*. Chapel Hill: University of North Carolina Press, 1979.

Rodnitzky, Jerome. "Also Born in the USA: Bob Dylan's Outlaw Heroes and the Real Bob Dylan. *Popular Music and Society* 12, no. 2 (1988): 37–43.

Root, Waverly. *Food*. New York: Simon and Schuster, 1980.

Ross, Alex. "The Wanderer." *New Yorker* (10 May 1999): 56–67.

Rossi, Mario G. *Le Origini del Partito Cattolico: Movimento cattolico e lotta di classe nell' Italia liberale*. Rome, Italy: Editore Riuniti, 1977.

Rowntree, B. Seebohm. *Poverty: A Study of Town Life*. London: Thomas Nelson & Sons, 1913.

Sabin, Arthur J. *Red Scare in Court: New York versus the International Workers Order*. Philadelphia: University of Pennsylvania Press, 1993.

Sacchetti, Giorgio. *Sovversivi in Toscana*. Todi, Italy: Altre Edizioni, 1983.

Said, Edward. "Opponents, Audiences, Constituencies and Community." In *Postmodern Culture*, edited by Hal Foster. Port Townsend, Wash.: Bay Press, 1983.

Salomone, A. William. "The Risorgimento and the Political Myth of the Revolution that Failed." In *Italy from the Risorgimento to Fascism: An Inquiry into the Origins of the Totalitarian State*, edited by A. William Salomone. London: David and Charles Publishers, 1971.

———. *Italy in the Giolittian Era: Italian Democracy in the Making: 1900–1914*. Philadelphia: University of Pennsylvania Press, 1945.

Salvemini, Gaetano. *The Fascist Dictatorship in Italy*. New York: Howard Fertig, 1967.

Sampson, Henry. *A History of Advertising from the Earliest of Times*. London: Chatto and Windus, 1874.

Santarelli, Enzo. "The Economic and Imperial Background of Fascist Imperialism." In *The Axe Within: Italian Fascism in Action*, edited by Roland Sarti. New York: New Viewpoints, 1974.

Sarti, Roland. *Long Live the Strong: A History of Rural Society in the Apennine Mountains*. Amherst: University of Massachesetts Press, 1985.

Sassoon, Donald. *Contemporary Italy: Politics, Economy and Society since 1945*. London: Longman, 1986.

Sautter, William. "The American Workman." *The Industrial Worker* (12 February 1910).

Schaller, Michael, Virginia Scharff, and Robert Schulzinger. *Present Tense: The United States Since 1945.* Boston, Mass.: Houghton Mifflin, 1996.

Schoenbaum, David. *Hitler's Social Revolution: Class and Status in Nazi Germany 1933–1939.* New York: W.W. Norton & Co., 1980.

Schroth, Raymond. *The Eagle and Brooklyn.* Westport, Conn.: Greenwood, 1971.

Seiter, Ellen. "Semiotics, Structuralism and Television." In *Channels of Discourse, Reassembled,* edited by Robert C. Allen. London: Routledge, 1992.

Seton-Watson, Christopher. *Italy from Liberalism to Fascism: 1970–1925.* London: Methuen and Company, 1967.

Shi, David E. "Advertising and the Literary Imagination During the Jazz Age." *Journal of American Culture* 2, no. 2 (Summer 1979): 167–175.

Siegel, Tilla and Thomas von Freyberg. *Industrielle Rationaliserung uster dem Nationalsozialismus.* Frankfurt/Main, 1991

Spielvogel, Jackson. *Hitler and Nazi Germany: A History.* Englewood Cliffs, N.J.: Prentice Hall, 1988.

Spotts, Frederic and Theodor Wieser. *Italy: A Difficult Democracy: A Survey of Italian Politics.* London: Cambridge University Press, 1986.

Spriano, Paolo. *L'Occupazione delle fabbriche.* Turin, Italy: Giulio Einaudi Editore, 1975.

Sterns, Peter N. "Efforts at Continuity in Working-Class Culture." *Journal of Modern History* 52 (December 1980): 626–55.

Stevens, John D. *Sensationalism and the New York Press.* New York: Columbia University Press, 1991.

Sullivan, Brian R. "A Thirst for Glory: Mussolini, the Italian Military and the Fascist Regime: 1922–1940." Ph.D. diss., Columbia University, 1981.

Tagg, John. *The Burden of Representation.* Minneapolis: University of Minnesota Press, 1993.

Tallack, Douglas. *Twentieth Century America: Intellectual and Cultural Context.* New York: Longman, 1991.

Tannenbaum, Edward R. *The Fascist Experience: Italian Society and Culture, 1922–1945.* New York: Basic Books, 1972.

Tasca, Angelo. *Nascita e avvento del fascismo.* Florence, Italy: La Nuova Italia Editrice, 1950.

Thayer, Roscoe. *The Life and Times of Cavour.* Boston: Houghton Mifffin Company, 1911.

Thomas, Norman. *What is Industrial Democracy?* New York: LID Press, 1925.

Thomas, Norman and Harry Laidler. *The LID: Twenty Five Years of Social Pioneering.* New York: LID Press, 1926.

———. *The LID: Thirty Five Years of Educational Pioneering.* New York: LID Press, 1941.

Thompson, E. P. *The Making of the English Working Class.* New York: Pantheon Books, 1963.

Tindall, George Brown and David E. Shi. *America: A Narrative History.* New York : W.W. Norton, 1996.

Togliatti, Palmiro. *Lectures on Fascism.* New York: International Publishers, 1976.

Toniolo, Gianni. *An Economic History of Liberal Italy: 1850–1918.* London: Routledge, 1990.

Trevelyan, Macaulay. *Garibaldi and the Thousand*. London: Longman, Green and Company, 1912.

U.S. Government. *Subversive Activities Control Board*. Washington, D.C.: U.S. Government Printing Office, December, 1947.

Vernon, Anne. *A Quaker Business Man: The Life of Joseph Rowntree, 1836–1925*. London: Allen & Unwin, 1958.

Vincent, David. *Literacy and Popular Culture: England 1870–1914*. New York: Cambridge University Press, 1989.

Voss, Kim. *American Exceptionalism: The Knights of Labor and Class Formation in the Nineteenth Century*. Ithaca, N.Y.: Cornell University Press, 1993.

Walker, Mack, ed. *Plombieres: Secret Diplomacy and the Rebirth of Italy*. London: Oxford University Press, 1968.

Walker, Thomas J. Edward. *Pluralistic Fraternity: The History of the International Worker's Order*. New York: Garland, 1991.

Weber, Eugen. *Peasants into Frenchmen*. Stanford, Calif.: Stanford University Press, 1976.

Weeden, Chris. *Feminist Practice and Poststructuralist Theory*. New York: Basil Blackwell, 1987.

Wideman, John Edgar. *Philadelphia Fire*. New York: Henry Holt and Co., 1990.

Wiener, Joel, ed. *Papers for the Millions: The New Journalism in Britain, 1850s to 1914*. New York: Greenwood Press, 1988.

———. The War of the Unstamped: The Movement to Repeal the British Newspaper Tax. Ithaca, N.Y.: Cornell University Press, 1969.

Wightman Fox, Richard and T. J. Jackson Lears, eds. *The Culture of Consumption: Critical Essays in American History, 1880-1980*. New York: Pantheon Books, 1983.

Williams, Iolo A. *The Firm of Cadbury*. London: Constable and Co. Ltd., 1931.

Williams, Raymond. *Culture and Society*. New York: Harper and Row, 1958.

———. *Problems in Materialism and Culture*. London: NLB, 1980.

Williamson, Judith. *Decoding Advertisements*. London: Boyars, 1978.

Wiskermann, Elizabeth. *Fascism in Italy: Its Development and Influence*. London: Macmillan, 1970.

Woolf, Stuart J. *Fascism in Europe*. New York, Methuen, 1968.

About the Contributors

Daniel J. Doyle is Professor of History at the College of Technology of Penn State University. He holds a Ph.D. in Philosophy from St. John's University and is the author of numerous articles on propaganda, technology, and society.

Douglas A. Lea is Professor of History and Director of the European Union Program at Kutztown University of Pennsylvania. He holds graduate degrees in German History from the London School of Economics and the Pennsylvania State University.

Pietro Lorenzini is Professor of History and Political Science at Elgin Community College in Elgin, Illinois. He holds a Ph.D. in Italian History from Loyola University of Chicago and a J.D. from the University of Illinois.

David S. Sims is Associate Professor of English and Poetry at the College of Technology of Penn State University, and author of *Intrusions and Lassitude,* a collage of poems. Professor Sims holds an M.F.A. from the University of Alaska.

Thomas J. Edward Walker is Professor of History, Philosophy, and Politics at the College of Technology of Penn State University and author of *Pluralistic Fraternity: The History of the International Workers Order.* He holds a Ph.D. in American History from the University of Chicago.

Cynthia Gwynne Yaudes is a Ph.D. candidate in American Studies and History at Indiana University in Bloomington. When she is not writing her dissertation, she teaches, edits the *Indiana University American Studies Newsletter,* and organizes for Indiana's Graduate Employees Union.